"THE HIGHER CHRISTIAN LIFE"

SOURCES FOR THE STUDY OF THE HOLINESS, PENTECOSTAL, AND KESWICK MOVEMENTS

A forty-eight-volume facsimile series reprinting extremely rare documents for the study of nineteenth-century religious and social history, the rise of feminism, and the history of the Pentecostal and Charismatic movements

Edited by

Donald W. Dayton
Northern Baptist Theological Seminary

Advisory Editors

D. William Faupel, *Asbury Theological Seminary*
Cecil M. Robeck, Jr., *Fuller Theological Seminary*
Gerald T. Sheppard, *Union Theological Seminary*

A GARLAND SERIES

OBERLIN:
THE COLONY AND THE COLLEGE
1833–1883

James H. Fairchild

Garland Publishing, Inc.
New York & London
1984

For a complete list of the titles in this series
see the final pages of this volume.

Library of Congress Cataloging in Publication Data

Fairchild, James H.
OBERLIN : THE COLONY AND THE COLLEGE.

("The Higher Christian life")
Reprint. Originally published: Oberlin, O. :
E.J. Goodrich, 1883.
Includes index.
1. Oberlin College—History. 2. Oberlin (Ohio)—
History. I. Title. II. Series.
LD4168.3.F35 1984   378.771'23   84-18849
ISBN 0-8240-6416-X (alk. paper)

The volumes in this series are printed on
acid-free, 250-year-life paper.

Printed in the United States of America

John Keep

OBERLIN:

The Colony and the College.

1833-1883.

By JAMES H. FAIRCHILD,

President of Oberlin College.

OBERLIN, O.

E. J. GOODRICH.

—

1883.

To the few that still survive of those who aided in laying the foundations at Oberlin, and to the memory of those who are gone; to the many who helped to rear the walls, " even in troublous times ;" to all who by word, or deed, or prayer, or gift, during the FIFTY YEARS, have shared in the work, this Record is faithfully inscribed.

PREFACE.

———

Fifty years have passed since a community and a college were planted together in the woods of Northern Ohio. An invitation has gone forth to all who, during the fifty years, have been numbered with the Community or the College, to return to the family heritage for a brief reunion. As a help toward rendering the occasion a season of interest and profit, this brief record has been prepared. No one can feel more sensibly than the author the inadequacy of the presentation. The struggles and triumphs of the fifty years cannot be written. There are many single lives that have been wrought into the work, any one of which could only be inadequately presented in a volume like this. The record as given is necessarily limited to the outward and visible changes and movements which have marked the years, while the inward and spiritual history must be left unrecorded.

And even much that is visible and tangible must be passed over without notice; probably facts more important that some presented in these pages have been thus omitted. The author has had no personal interests to serve, no feelings to gratify, no theories to sustain. If important omissions or other errors shall appear, they must be attributed to imperfections of apprehension or of recollection. In general, facts are stated with little exhibition of authorities. Where such facts have been matters of record the proper records have been consulted; but to a great extent they depend upon personal observation and memory, and can have no other endorsement. The reader will make due allowance for all the liabilities involved.

J. H. F.

OBERLIN, May, 1883.

CONTENTS.

CHAPTER VIII.

CHAPTER IX.

CHAPTER X.

CHAPTER XI.

OBERLIN.

CHAPTER I.

THE ORIGIN OF THE ENTERPRISE.—ITS FOUNDERS.

OBERLIN is known in the world as an institution
of learning and a community, the two having a common origin and a common history. As seen to-day,
it is a pleasant village of thirty-five hundred inhabitants, surrounded by a prosperous farming community, in the midst of which stands a college with its
various departments, theological, collegiate, preparatory, and musical, and an average yearly attendance
of twelve to fifteen hundred students.

The foundations of the college and the town were
laid together, in the spring of 1833, in what was then
an unbroken forest, in the south part of the township of Russia, county of Lorain, and state of Ohio.
The tract of land secured for the purpose was three
miles square, with a very level surface and a somewhat stiff clay soil, entirely covered with the heavy
timber of Northern Ohio, beech and maple predomi-
nating, with a plentiful intermingling of oak, white-
wood, elm, ash, and hickory, and other varieties
usually found in such forests.

The people who took possession of this tract were

a number of Christian families, gathered from the different New England states, with a few from New York and Northern Ohio, who came to establish a colony and an institution of Christian education, with the added object of making desirable homes for themselves and their children.

Such a movement, of course, could not spring up of itself. The projectors and prime movers in the enterprise were Rev. John J. Shipherd, pastor of the Presbyterian Church in Elyria, in the same county, and his associate and friend Philo P. Stewart, extensively known in the country as the inventor of the Stewart Stoves.

John J. Shipherd was the son of Hon. Zebulon R. and Elizabeth B. Shipherd, and was born in West Granville, Washington Co., N. Y., March 28, 1802. He was carefully and religiously educated, and while at school at Pawlet, Vt., in preparation for college, his conscious religious life opened in a conversion which began in intense conviction and conflict, and resulted in great peace and joy. From this time to the end of his days his character and life were marked with profound earnestness and restless activity.

He had prepared to enter the college at Middlebury, Vt.; and while spending a few days at home, before leaving for college, under a slight indisposition, proposing to take a remedy, he swallowed, by mistake, a poison. By vigorous measures his life was saved; but to the end of his days he was afflicted with persistent irritation of the coats of the stomach, and with greatly impaired eyesight. After repeated endeavors to resume his studies he reluctantly accepted the necessity, and turned his attention to such business as opened to him.

In 1824 he married Miss Esther Raymond, of Ballston, N. Y., and removed to Vergennes, Vt., to engage in the marble business. He had assumed that his poor eyesight, which prevented his reading more than a few minutes continuously without intense pain, utterly precluded the idea of his preparing for the gospel ministry. All his prepossessions and convictions were on the side of a full education as a requisite for the work, and he resisted decidedly every intimation that such a duty could be his. But after a long conflict in his own mind, and many marked providences, he entered the study of Rev. Josiah Hopkins, of New Haven, Vt., where he spent a year and a half, in company with other young men, in theological study. He had already acquired a system of short-hand writing, and his associates in study helped him with their eyes. He adopted the practice of arranging the heads and subdivisions of his discourse upon a card, in stenographic characters, because his eyesight would not permit him to write in full; and this practice he maintained throughout his life. His first year in the ministry was with the church in Shelburne, Vt. The next two years he was engaged in the general Sunday-school work in the state, making Middlebury his headquarters, editing a Sunday-school paper, and travelling throughout the state in the work of organizing schools. Then, under a strong conviction that the " Valley of the Mississippi"—as the whole country west of the mountains was then called—was to be the field of his life-work, he took a commission from the American Home Missionary Society, and "went out, not knowing whither he went." At Cleveland he fell in with Rev. D. W. Lathrop, who had just closed his labors as pastor of the church in Elyria, and upon his invitation he came to Elyria in October, 1830, and was installed pastor of the church the February following. During the two years of his pastoral work at Elyria, he was intensely occupied in revival labors in his own parish, and in the region round about; and under the same restless impulse to hasten the coming of God's kingdom, he tendered his resignation in October, 1832, and entered upon the work of laying the foundations at Oberlin, being now thirty years of age.

Philo Penfield Stewart was born in Sherman, Conn., July, 1798, hence was about four years older than Mr. Shipherd. When ten years of age, on account of his father's death, he was sent to live with his maternal grandfather in Pittsford, Vt., and at the age of fourteen he was apprenticed to his uncle in Pawlet, Vt., to learn saddle and harness making. In this apprenticeship he served seven years, with a term of three months each year in the Pawlet Academy, a privilege which he greatly prized and thoroughly improved. Young Stewart had a natural mechanical bent, and was famed as a whittler in his childhood; but the calling to which he devoted these seven years of his life did not afford scope for his genius, and had no special attractions for him. Under the influence of a Christian teacher in the academy, he had devoted his life to the Master's service; and after completing his apprenticeship he experienced a sort of second conversion, in a conflict with his love of money, which seemed a natural tendency in his character. Thus he was prepared, at the age of twenty-three, to accept an appointment from the American Board to a mission among the Choctaws in the state of Mississippi. The journey of almost two thousand miles to his field of labor he made on horseback, a pair of saddle-bags containing his whole outfit. The officers of the Board had furnished him seventy dollars for his travelling expenses. But from the time of starting he entered upon his missionary work, and preached the Gospel in the families along the way, until he reached the Choctaw Nation, at an expense to the Board of only ten dollars for himself and his horse.

An important part of his work at the mission was the superintendence of its secular affairs, for which he was well fitted. In addition he taught the boys' school, and with the help of an interpreter held services on the Sabbath in the different Indian settlements. His health failing, he returned to Vermont to recruit, but returned again to the mission, in 1827, with a re-enforcement of one young man and three young women, whom he took over the long journey in a wagon, at an expense only slightly greater than that involved in his own journey six years before.

In 1828 Mr. Stewart, now thirty years of age, married Miss Eliza Capen, one of the young women whom he had taken out to the mission, the preceding year, from Pittsford, Vt.; and together they wrought in the mission two or three years more, when

Mrs. Stewart's broken health compelled them to return North and resign the mission work. Still on the outlook for a field of Christian labor, he corresponded with his old friend, Mr. Shipherd, the companion of his boyhood at Pawlet Academy; and as a result, leaving Mrs. Stewart behind, he joined him at Elyria in the spring of 1832, and became an inmate of his family. Thus the two founders of Oberlin were trained for their work, and finally brought together. They were one in consecration to the great cause, ready for any sacrifice which the work required; were alike in their general views of the wants of the world and the aim of Christian labor; were both born reformers, strongly impressed with the conviction that the Church as well as the world needed to be lifted up to a higher plane of life and action, and with an intense purpose to make their own lives contribute to this result.

In constitution and natural movement they were greatly unlike. Mr. Shipherd was ardent, hopeful, sanguine, disposed to underestimate difficulties and obstacles; while Mr. Stewart was slow and cautious, apprehensive of difficulties, and inclined to provide for them in advance. It is rare that two men unite in a common enterprise who are more unlike in natural temperament. They had entire confidence in each other, in respect to rectitude of heart and purpose; yet their co-operation doubtless involved some difficulty. A brief extract from a letter from Mr. Stewart to Mr. Shipherd, written soon after they had entered upon the Oberlin work, gives intimation that they sometimes felt the difficulty: " The letter was no less acceptable because it contained a complaint against your poor, erring brother. I thank you for opening your mind so freely—hope you will always do so. Then, when you have occasion to find fault with what I say or do, if I cannot give a justifiable reason for my conduct, I will confess. The difference in our views of things arises, no doubt, from the cause which you stated, and as long as we co-operate together we shall doubtless often feel like complaining of each other. But if these complaints are given and received in Christian love and kindness, no injury will be done. You acknowledge that you are constitutionally inclined to go *too fast*, and I acknowledge that I am disposed, from the same cause, to go *too slow*. If this be true, a word of admonition now and then from each other may be salutary. . . . But after all, I would not have you like me in your constitutional temperament, if I could. I think we may balance each other, and become mutual helps. If you should occasionally feel a little impatience at my *moderation*, and I at your *impetuosity*, it would not be strange ; but if we are always in the exercise of that charity which hopeth all things, it will be well at the last."

During the summer of 1832 these two men talked and prayed together over the wants of the world, and especially of the " Mississippi Valley," and gradually there grew up in their minds a scheme of a community and school where their ideas of Christian living and education could be realized. Mr. Shipherd was especially interested in the establishment of a community of Christian families, from which, to a great extent, worldly influences should be excluded, and where gospel principles should prevail in place of worldly views and fashions. At times he seemed to incline even to a community of property, as the surest means of overruling selfishness, and subordinating all interests to the common good. It was no part of his plan to concentrate the interests of the community upon itself. His thought was to establish a centre of religious influence and power for the generation of forces which should work mightily upon the surrounding country and the world—a sort of missionary institution for training laborers for the work abroad.

Mr. Stewart, on the other hand, was especially attracted by the idea of a school where study and labor should be combined, and the whole establishment conducted upon such principles of thrift and economy, that enterprising students could defray all their expenses by their labor, without any detriment to their progress in study. His mind reverted to the academy in Pawlet, Vt., where he had spent six hours a day in the schoolroom, and almost as many in his uncle's shop, and still made satisfactory progress in study. The same academy furnished an example of young men and young women pursuing study together, in the same school and the same classes, with increased interest and profit, as he thought, on both sides; and thus his ideal school must involve manual labor and co-education.

Mrs. Shipherd shared in their consultations and prayers, and in a brief record of those times she thus gives the scene in which the diverse views became consolidated into a common plan:

"In their deliberations they would exchange views; one would present one point of interest and another a different one. Mr. Stewart proposed a college, of which Mr. Shipherd could not at first see the necessity, as Hudson College was in its infancy, and poorly sustained; but Mr. Stewart suggested the manual-labor system, which Mr. Shipherd fully approved. Thus they labored and prayed, and while on their knees asking guidance, the whole plan developed itself to Mr. Shipherd's mind, and before rising to his feet he said, 'Come, let us arise and build.' He then told Mr. Stewart what had come into his mind—to procure a tract of land and collect a colony of Christian families that should pledge themselves to sustain the school and identify themselves with all its interests. They came down from the study, and Mr. Shipherd, with a glowing face, said, 'Well, my dear, the child is born, and what shall its name be?' He then related what had passed through his mind."

John Frederic Oberlin, a German pastor of Waldbach, in the Vosges Mountains, in Eastern France, had died a few years before, and an interesting account of his labors in elevating the people of his parish had been published in this country, as a Sunday-school book. This little volume had been recently read in Mr. Shipherd's family, and thus OBERLIN was adopted as the name of the establishment which was yet to be.

The earliest known presentation of the purpose

and plan is found in a letter from Mr. Shipherd to his father and mother, dated Elyria, August 6, 1832, as follows:

"I have been deeply impressed of late with the certainty that the world will never be converted till it receive from the Church *a better example, more gospel laborers, and more money.* We do not now keep pace with the increase of population in our own country. Something *must* be done, or a millennium will never cheer our benighted world. The Church must be restored to gospel simplicity and devotion. As a means which I hope God would bless to the accomplishment of some part of this work, I propose through his assistance to plant a colony somewhere in this region, whose chief aim shall be to glorify God, and do good to men, to the utmost extent of their ability. They are to simplify food, dress, etc., to be industrious and economical, and to give all over their current or annual expense for the spread of the Gospel. They are to hoard up nothing for old age, or for their children, but are mutually to covenant that they will provide for the widowed, orphan, and all the needy as for themselves and families. They are to establish schools of the first order, from the infant school up to an academic school, which shall afford a thorough education in English and the useful languages; and, if Providence favor it, at length instruction in theology—I mean *practical* theology. They are to connect workshops and a farm with the institution, and so simplify diet and dress that, by *four* hours' labor per day, young men will defray their entire expense, and young women working at the spinning-wheel and loom will defray much of their expense. And all will thus save money, and, what is more, promote muscular, mental, and moral vigor.

"In these schools all the children of the colony are to be well educated, whether destined to professional or manual labor; for those designing to be mechanics will learn their trades while in a course of study. These schools will also educate school-teachers for our desolate Valley, and many ministers for our dying world; also instruct the children and youth of the surrounding population. To do this we want some twenty-five or more *good* families, and two thousand dollars' outfit for the schools. Dear parents, shall I try? I do feel that such an establishment would not only do much itself, but exert a mighty influence upon other churches, and lead them along in the path of gospel self-denial.

"I have given you but a brief and imperfect sketch, but you will discern its bearings. In all this Brother Stewart, formerly assistant missionary to the Choctaws, is with me."

In a letter to his mother, dated a month later, he says:

"My confidence in the utility of our colonizing plan is strengthened by prayer, meditation, and conference with the intelligent and pious; yet I feel that it is a mighty work, difficult of accomplishment. But when any one goes about a great and good work Satan will roll mountains in his way. Believing that all he has rolled in our way can be surmounted through the grace of God, and that I can do more for His honor and the good of souls in this valley of dry bones by gathering such a colony and planting it, with its literary and religious institutions, in this region, I am inclined, Providence favoring, to *resign my charge,* and spend the winter at the East for the purpose."

The resignation followed, and was accepted by the church, October 29, 1832. These two men then addressed themselves without delay to the work of putting forward their favorite enterprise. In the selection of a location the general fact had already been determined in their minds that they were to build somewhere in Northern Ohio, and on the Western Reserve ; but the definite site remained to be selected. Judge Ely, of Elyria, proposed to Mr. Shipherd to give for the purpose the land which now forms the beautiful portion of the village known as "The Point," but which was then covered with a dense forest. Another site proposed was in Brownhelm, to be constituted of two or three farms lying on the beautiful North Ridge Road. But neither of these situations gave sufficient scope to Mr. Shipherd's ideal community. There must, in his view, be room, for a score or two of farms, for the public grounds of a large school, and for the village centre which such a community would naturally form. It was also essential to his idea, that this community should have opportunity to develop its own social life, and its social and religious institutions, apart from any community already constituted. Hence a considerable tract, remote from existing settlements, must be secured. To buy out any such

settlement with its improved lands seemed impossible.

The earliest immigrants to this region had naturally taken up the more accessible and more desirable
portions of the country—the shore of the lake, the
pleasant ridges running parallel to the shore, and
the banks of the larger streams. The level clay
land of the south part of Russia township remained
in its primitive state, and the proprietors had
offered, upon certain conditions, five hundred acres
of this land for educational purposes. The day following the season of prayer in which light seemed to
fall upon their project, Messrs. Shipherd and Stewart mounted their horses, and took their course
through the woods, about eight miles, to this undisturbed portion of the forest. The line of a road,
north and south, through the tract had been marked,
years before, by a party of surveyors, who felled the
trees for a breadth of about four rods ; and this roadway was now grown thickly over with bushes. At
a certain point on the west side of this roadway, our
friends dismounted, tied their horses to a tree, and
knelt under the boughs of another, in prayer for divine guidance. A hunter came up soon after, who
informed them that about ten minutes before they arrived, a black bear with her two cubs had come down
the tree to which they tied their horses. How our
friends interpreted this omen we are not told, but
they settled upon this ground for the Oberlin that
was to arise ; and an undisputed tradition, running
back to the earliest days of the settlement, designates
the beautiful elm near the south-east corner of the

college park as the tree under which they knelt to pray. That brush-covered road is now Main Street, in the village of Oberlin.

Messrs. Street & Hughes, the owners of this tract, resided in New Haven, Conn. Captain Redington, of South Amherst, about six miles north, was their agent for the sale of the land ; but in a transaction of such importance it seemed necessary to treat with the proprietors themselves. The colonists, too, who were to take possession of this portion of the wilderness, must come chiefly from the East. The desirable Christian families in the region had already passed through the experience of an emigration, and the work of making homes in the heavy-timbered country; and one such experience, however enjoyable, suffices in general for a lifetime. Hence those must be appealed to who could look with complacency upon such an enterprise. Such people lived in Vermont, New Hampshire, and Massachusetts, and Mr. Shipherd had a wide acquaintance among them. Hence a journey must be made to New England for the threefold purpose of securing the land, the money, and the men. In November, 1832, Mr. Shipherd undertook this journey.

The decision to launch out thus upon an untried experiment cost him a struggle. He was naturally hopeful and sanguine. His life-long habit had been, to depend upon Divine guidance, as indicated in some inward conviction or illumination. The evidence that he was to go forward was, to his mind, unquestionable. The plan of the enterprise he had accepted as divinely given, and through all his re-

HISTORIC ELM.

maining years he was accustomed to refer to it as the pattern shown him in the Mount. But thus far he had little human sympathy in his undertaking. As a devoted servant of God, and an earnest and effective preacher of the Gospel, he had, during the two years of his residence in Elyria, secured a wide influence. He possessed the confidence of the ministers and the churches of the region. But the scheme of a college and a colony, to be located in the wilderness, which he presented as the reason for his resignation of the pastorate, seemed too visionary to command the respect of reasonable and prudent men. His earnestness and devotion and intense conviction could scarcely save it from ridicule. Here and there a single person was brought into sympathy with his views. This was the situation when he set out on horseback for his eastern campaign. Mrs. Shipherd's record gives us some insight into the inward conflict :

" He had his horse saddled at nine o'clock in the morning, but was unable to proceed before three in the afternoon. The adversary assailed him and presented every possible thing to discourage him ; he prayed and agonized for light, but the temptation continued. He finally started, but had to return ; he had forgotten something, and we had to have a second parting. The third time he had to turn back, but I was not aware of it. He finally proceeded on his way a few miles until he came to a piece of woods, where he dismounted and fell upon his knees and acknowledged to the Lord that he had no desire for the work if it was not His will, and that he could not proceed until he had a 'Thus saith the Lord.' He arose from his knees with his heart full of praise, and remounted his horse with these words, 'With Jesus at home;' and this assurance followed him through all his years of travelling without a cloud crossing his mind.

" He accomplished the journey and arrived in New Haven in about two weeks, where he stopped with friends of ours. The day after his arrival he called on Messrs. Street & Hughes, and laid his plan before them, and asked the gift of five hundred acres for a Manual Labor School, proposing to gather a colony of families who should pay a dollar and a half an acre, for five thousand acres in addition, representing that this would bring their lands into market, and thus prove a mutual benefit. But they could not see the prospect. He called on them day after day unsuccessfully, until at length he came down from his room one morning, and remarked to the lady of the house, our friend, 'I shall succeed to-day;' and she told me afterwards that his face shone like the face of Moses. He accordingly went over to the office, and after the morning salutations one of the firm said, 'Well, Mr. Shipherd, we have concluded to accept your proposition.' They adjusted matters, and he was prepared to proceed with his work of collecting the colony."

The arrangement was to sell the five thousand acres, bought for one dollar and a half an acre, to colonists, at an advance of one dollar an acre, and thus secure a fund of five thousand dollars for laying the foundations of the college. But Mr. Shipherd engaged that from this fund a saw-mill and a grist-mill should be erected, to be owned by the college, as these were essential to the very existence of the colony, and there was no probability that the mills could be erected as a private enterprise.

It was to be a distinctively Christian colony, and this was to be secured by personal consultation, on the part of Mr. Shipherd, with families of farmers and mechanics in New England churches, who gave promise of usefulness in the enterprise, and who could be induced to join it. This feature of the plan had been criticised in advance by some as an undesirable arrangement, involving a waste of Christian influence. It was urged that Christians were scattered abroad in the community providentially, for the very purpose of contact with the world, and the good that results from it. Even Mr. Stewart, in letters addressed to Mr. Shipherd, while on his eastern tour, expresses his own doubts upon this point. But there was little ground for apprehension in the matter; sinners soon found their way to the colony without an invitation.

To secure colonists of the right stamp, and inspire them with the true idea of the enterprise, they were asked to subscribe to the following covenant, called

The Oberlin Covenant.

"Lamenting the degeneracy of the Church and the deplorable condition of our perishing world, and ardently desirous of bringing both under the entire influence of the blessed Gospel of peace; and viewing with peculiar interest the influence which the valley of the Mississippi must exert over our nation and the nations of the earth; and having, as we trust, in answer to devout supplications, been guided by the counsel of the Lord: the undersigned covenant together under the name of the Oberlin Colony, subject to the following regulations, which may be amended by a concurrence of two thirds of the colonists:

" 1. Providence permitting, we engage as soon as practicable to remove to the Oberlin Colony, in Russia, Lorain County, Ohio, and there to fix our residence, for the express purpose of glorifying God in doing good to men to the extent of our ability.

" 2. We will hold and manage our estates personally, but pledge as perfect a community of interest as though we held a community of property.

" 3. We will hold in possession no more property than we believe we can profitably manage for God, as His faithful stewards.

" 4. We will, by industry, economy, and Christian self-denial, obtain as much as we can, above our necessary personal or family expenses, and faithfully appropriate the same for the spread of the Gospel.

" 5. That we may have time and health for the Lord's service, we will eat only plain and wholesome food, renouncing all bad habits, and especially the smoking and chewing of tobacco, unless it is necessary as a medicine, and deny ourselves all strong and unnecessary drinks, even tea and coffee, as far as practicable, and everything expensive, that is simply calculated to gratify the palate.

"6. That we may add to our time and health money for the service of the Lord, we will renounce all the world's expensive and unwholesome fashions of dress, particularly tight dressing and ornamental attire.

"7. And yet more to increase our means of serving Him who bought us with His blood, we will observe plainness and durability in the construction of our houses, furniture, carriages, and all that appertains to us.

"8. We will strive continually to show that we, as the body of Christ, are members one of another; and will, while living, provide for the widows, orphans, and families of the sick and needy, as for ourselves.

"9. We will take special pains to educate all our children thoroughly, and to train them up, in body, intellect and heart, for the service of the Lord.

"10. We will feel that the interests of the Oberlin Institute are identified with ours, and do what we can to extend its influence to our fallen race.

"11. We will make special efforts to sustain the institutions of the Gospel at home and among our neighbors.

"12. We will strive to maintain deep-toned and elevated personal piety, to 'provoke each other to love and good works,' to live together in all things as brethren, and to glorify God in our bodies and spirits, which are His.

"In testimony of our fixed purpose thus to do, in reliance on Divine grace, we hereunto affix our names."

This was not a church covenant but a colonial covenant, and secured its end in presenting the purpose of the colony, and in turning away some that might have been drawn into the enterprise by considerations of these worldly advantages. In so far as it goes beyond a general expression of Christian consecration, it subsequently afforded occasion of earnest discussion, and sometimes, perhaps, of uncharitable judgment. It was at length found necessary to leave the determination of personal duty in practical affairs to the individual conscience; and thus, after a year or two, the covenant was no longer appealed to, in the settlement of differences of opinion upon these subjects. It doubtless had its part in giving form to the social and religious life of the place.

A prominent plan for raising funds, presented by Mr. Shipherd, was the establishment and sale of scholarships. Each donor of *one hundred and fifty dollars* was entitled perpetually to the privileges of the school for a single pupil. This scholarship did not provide for board or tuition or any other of the pupil's expenses, but merely secured to him a place in the school. The pupil must still meet all his expenses, as if he had no scholarship. The money paid for the scholarship was to be invested in lands, buildings, tools, and all the appliances of a manual-labor school, and the holder of the scholarship was to be entitled to the advantages which these afforded; and Mr. Shipherd hoped, and encouraged the donors to expect, that industrious and faithful students would be able to meet all necessary expenses, by their labor. The idea of the scholarship is thus expressed in his first published circular:

"The *one hundred and fifty dollars* is the proportion of the outfit money expended to furnish one individual with the privileges of the Oberlin Institute. It is therefore reasonable that those who enjoy these privileges should pay this cost, if able to do it. It is also right that indigent youth of promising talent and piety should become the beneficiaries of scholarships established by others who have the ability. It should be distinctly understood that students can be admitted to the boarding and manual-labor privileges of this seminary, only on scholarships established by themselves, their friends, or the benevolent in their behalf; and that these scholarships do not guarantee the student's support, nor any part of it, nor pay his tuition; but they are so expended as to furnish board, tuition, books, etc., at a very low rate, and give the beneficiary peculiar facilities for defraying the expense of these, by those services which are necessary, irrespective of support, to a finished Christian education."

The advantage possessed by the holder of the scholarship was, the guarantee of a place in the school. Others were received and enjoyed the same advantages, but they had no promise of a reception. During the earlier years, nearly half the applicants failed to obtain admittance for want of room. The scholarship system at length became the occasion of some complaint, when the facilities of the school were so extended that all applicants could be received; but the complaints were of the same nature as those of the laborers of the parable, who received every man the promised penny.

This eastern tour of Mr. Shipherd's to secure lands, funds, colonists, and students occupied him through the winter and spring and following summer, and in September, 1833, he returned to Elyria, and to Oberlin.

Meanwhile Mr. Stewart, joined by Mrs. Stewart in the fall of 1832, had remained at Elyria in the care of Mr. Shipherd's family, and especially occupied in the work of bringing to perfection a cooking-stove which he had invented, and which was known as the Oberlin stove. His original undertaking was to meet a necessity in Mrs. Shipherd's kitchen, by a stove made of sheet-iron; but the work proved so satisfactory that he extended the enterprise, in the expectation that his invention would not only prove useful to the community, but yield a profit which should contribute materially to the resources of the new enterprise. This was the beginning of the Stewart cooking-stove, which has become so well known throughout the country. It was his expectation that the success of his invention would warrant the trustees of the school in taking the pecuniary responsibility involved, and thus all the profits might go to the school; but the trustees never felt authorized to assume this responsibility.

While carrying forward the project of the cooking-stove, at Elyria, Mr. Stewart had the general supervision of the work of the new colony at Oberlin, meeting the colonists as they came forward from the East with information and counsel and encouragement, conducting such correspondence as the progress of the work called for, from this point, and holding frequent meetings with several gentlemen of the region who had consented to act as trustees of the enterprise. Thus the work at Oberlin was begun.

CHAPTER II.

THE WORK OF THE FIRST AND SECOND YEARS.

THE actual commencement of work upon the Oberlin tract was made by Mr. Peter P. Pease of Brownhelm, who, April 19, 1833, with his family, moved into a log house which he had erected, and which stood on the south-east corner of what is now the College Park, near the historical elm. Mr. Pease was therefore the first colonist. He was also a member of the "Board of Trust" already constituted, although the school was as yet without any corporate existence. The other members of this Board were Rev. J. J. Shipherd, Hon. Henry Brown of Brownhelm, Capt. E. Redington of Amherst, Rev. Joel Talcott of Wellington, Addison Tracy and P. P. Stewart of Elyria, J. L. Burrell of Sheffield, and Rev. John Keys of Dover; and these are the persons afterwards named as trustees in the charter secured from the State Legislature.

Mr. Pease at once entered upon the work necessary to prepare the way for the colony and the school, without reference to his personal interests as a colonist. He was to make such provision as was possible for the reception of the colonists as they should arrive, and superintend and hasten forward the work upon the building which was to receive the school. Mr. Shipherd in his ardor had encouraged the families coming on to expect that a steam saw-mill would be in operation in the early part of the summer of this year, and had assured the purchasers of scholarships that the school should be opened on the first of December. When it is remembered that the forest was not broken in upon until the middle of the spring months, that the tract was almost inaccessible for want of roads, that the entire country around was new, and that the simplest mechanical service could not be obtained at any point nearer than Elyria, eight miles distant, and that there were no funds to draw upon for the accomplishment of the work, it will be seen that the undertaking was formidable. But these men who constituted the Board of Trust were among the substantial men of the county, and the undertaking did not seem to them preposterous. Mr. Shipherd had somehow infused into them his own courage and faith. The colonists left their homes under the same inspiration, and all who came upon the ground caught the common enthusiasm. There was a single exception in the case of a young man, the first who came upon the ground from the East, who was very homesick when he reached Elyria, was not relieved on coming to Oberlin, and turned his face homeward in early summer, greatly disappointed. Such cases must of course occur, but they were rare.

The following extracts from a letter from the earliest colonists, addressed to Mr. Shipherd, still at the East, and dated "Oberlin Colony, Ohio, June 11, 1833," shows the spirit with which they accepted the situation:

"The few sheep that are collected at Oberlin rejoice at the opportunity of answering your letter directed to Bro. Pease, which we yesterday received with pleasure. The inquiries you make are very important. You ask, 'What are you doing spiritually to make a moral reform?' We answer, 'Very little; we have but just begun.' Through the good pleasure of our God we have been preserved and permitted to set our feet on the colonial ground; and it is *ground*, after all the reports we have heard about water and mud, although the season has been wet and cold. We assure you, brother, it is as good as was recommended to us. We fully believe it will sustain the settlement you propose. We are willing our brethren from the East should call and see for themselves, assuring them, if their motive is to do good and glorify God in their bodies and spirits, which are His, they need not be homesick nor look back, but first give themselves to the Lord and then to the work.

"We have had meetings every Sabbath since the commencement—had a visit from Bro. Betts [of Brownhelm]: he will preach for us every fourth Sabbath till you return. Bro. Leavenworth [also from Brownhelm] preached to us the first Sabbath after the brethren arrived from Vermont—and a blessed day it was, for the Lord was here. The people came in from the east, the west, and the south. The number from abroad was between twenty and thirty. . . .

"We trust you cease not to pray for us that we may be guided in every path of duty and usefulness, and above all that we may love one another with pure hearts, fervently. . . . Bro. Morgan, from Lockport, expects to move in to-morrow : we have built his house on the east side of the road, near the bank of Plum Creek ;* we live on the west side, opposite. We have commenced our clearing, beginning at the centre, and moving south and west; have about twenty acres now chopped—four cleared off ; are planting two of it to corn, more than one we sow to oats and grass for a little pasture. The remainder is occupied by two log houses and the site for the boarding-house and schoolroom. The school [college] will be in the upper loft; we have the timber all hewed, but one day's work. The delay of the mill we regret very much ; but as all things work together for good, we hope to acquiesce in all things, and shall endeavor to arrange all our affairs in accordance with the Divine will, believing that the Lord will accomplish His own purpose by us for time and eternity. . . .

"The brethren have mostly selected and procured their land and are now chopping their village lots, which will make a pleasant opening on the east side of the road. We have about fifty cords of wood cut for the engine. We can say 'Thus far the Lord hath helped us;' may we ever acknowledge Him! Dear brother, pray for the peace of the colony. We have a special prayer-meeting every Saturday evening, in which we remember you, and hope to be remembered by you."

The writers speak of four Sabbath-schools in neigh-

---

* MORGAN STREET, running along the north side of his farm, was named for him. He died many years ago.

boring settlements, which they had established or were about to open. This letter was signed by all the men then on the ground, as follows: Peter P. Pease, Brewster Pelton, Samuel Daniels, Philip James, Pringle Hamilton, Wm. Hosford, Asahel Munger, Harvey Gibbs, Jacob J. Safford, Daniel Morgan. Three or four women only were here at the time. Several of these colonists had come in advance of their families, to make ready for them. Several other families joined the colony during the season.

Mr. Shipherd returned early in September, and removed his family to Oberlin. He had engaged the number of families that he supposed it desirable to invite, had enlisted a considerable number of students who were to join the school at its opening in December or the following spring, had looked up and secured the appointment of the necessary teachers, and had raised a fund, in contributions and subscriptions, amounting to nearly fifteen thousand dollars. His journey back to Ohio was characteristic of the man and the times. Mrs. Shipherd had gone in the early summer, with a babe six weeks old in her arms, to her father's home in Ballston, N. Y. There Mr. Shipherd joined her in August, and in an open buggy, with a willow cradle at their feet, they made the journey to Ohio, remembered by Mrs. Shipherd, to the last, as the most pleasant journey of their lives. The last two miles of the road before reaching Oberlin was only a track cleared of underbrush, winding among the trees, the roots of which extend-ing across the track made it so rough that Mrs. Shipherd could not keep her seat, and she walked that portion of the way with her babe in her arms.

The first college building, afterward known as Oberlin Hall, was already enclosed; and in a room about fifteen feet square and seven feet high, in the basement of that building, Mr. and Mrs. Shipherd with their four little boys, and another family with three or four boarders, found their home.

The steam-engine, constructed at Cleveland, was brought on in October, and the saw-mill was soon in operation.

The teachers engaged at the East could not come on in time, and a student from Western Reserve College, at Hudson, Mr. John F. Scovill, was invited to take temporary charge of the school, at its opening; and on the third day of December, 1833, the school was opened. This opening was an occasion of solemn rejoicing on the part of the little community of colonists and students. The evening preceding, they were gathered to ask God's blessing upon the enterprise; and during the progress of the meeting young Scovill reached the place, and entered the little upper room where they were gathered together. After listening for a time to prayers and remarks he rose to speak, and his first words were, " Put off thy shoes from thy feet, for the place where thou standest is holy ground."

At this time there were eleven families on the ground. Several men who had spent a portion of the summer and autumn here, had returned East, expecting to bring on their families in the spring. Forty-four students were in attendance during this winter term—twenty-nine young men and fifteen young women. Half of them were from the East, the remainder from the neighboring towns. In addition, a primary school was organized as a department of the institution, embracing the children of the colony, about twenty in number, and taught by Miss Eliza Branch, now Mrs. Geo. Clark, of Oberlin. This primary school was in the original plan, but, after the first winter, it was judged better to leave the people of the place to provide for the elementary education of their children, in connection with the common-school system of the State.

This was the first practical trial of the system of education which was to be introduced at Oberlin. The students gathered here were, with few exceptions, mature, earnest young people, ready for any effort or sacrifice necessary in obtaining an education, and this continued to be their character through the years that followed. They entered into the work with enthusiasm, and identified themselves with the enterprise. The one wooden building, about thirty-five by forty feet in its dimensions, with two regular stories, and a third story called an attic, made by carrying up the central part about twenty feet in width, so that small windows could be inserted along the sides above the main roof—this one building contained the college with all its operations for more than a year. There was, however, an appendage in the rear, embracing the kitchen and apartments for the steward. Mr. and Mrs. Stewart presided in the steward's department, and had the responsibility of feeding the inmates. In the basement room, before mentioned, lived the corresponding secretary and general agent, Mr. Shipherd, with his family. His office, the centre of all business for the college and the colony, was in the room above, where also the principal of the school found his study. Across the hall or corridor was the dining-room, and above was the schoolroom, chapel, and church, all in one. This room, the scene of many interesting events and experiences during the two years following, was called in general "The Chapel." It was the place for the religious and literary exercises of the school, and for the gathering of the entire community on the Sabbath—a room about eighteen feet wide and thirty-five long. On every public occasion it was packed to its utmost capacity. The young women of the school family were closely quartered in this second story of the building, over against the chapel, while the young men were sent into the "attic," where each pair of them found a room eight feet square, with a window of six small lights, above the head of the student as he sat. This room was furnished with stove, table, two chairs, and turn-up bedstead. These occupied the entire area when the bedstead was let down, as at night; but during the day the bed was tilted up against the side of the room, and then there was space to spare.

Of course only sympathy with the enterprise could make such accommodations tolerable; but it is doubtful whether any body of students was ever more cheerful or better satisfied. A letter from Mr. Shipherd to his parents, dated December 13, 1833, gives his views of the situation at this time:

"The Lord is to be praised that we were enabled to open our institution at the appointed time, December 3d. We have now thirty-four boarding scholars, and expect forty for the winter. Applicants are without number, from Lake Erie to the Gulf of Mexico, and from Michigan to the Atlantic. The scholars study and work well. Five minutes after the manual-labor bell strikes, the hammers, saws, etc., of the mechanical students wake all around us, and the axe-men in the woods, breaking 'the ribs of Nature,' make all crack. Nearly all our visitors, and they are not few, express surprise that so great a work has been wrought here in so short a time. God be praised. I feel, as I said in my sleep the other night, 'Oberlin will rise, and the devil cannot hinder it.' This very sweet assurance, I hope, rests on God, without whom we can do nothing."

In February of this winter the college was chartered by the Legislature of the state, with university privileges, under the name of the Oberlin Collegiate Institute. Mr. Shipherd preferred this name as less assuming than Oberlin College, and because it was apprehended that it might be some time before regular college work would be done in the school. Yet such work and even more was in his plan. In a circular published March 8, 1834,—the first circular, probably, that was issued,—he thus states the work proposed:

"The grand objects of the Oberlin Institute are, to give the most useful education at the least expense of health, time, and money; and to extend the benefit of such education to both sexes and to all classes of the community, as far as its means will allow. Its system embraces thorough instruction in every department, from the infant school up through a collegiate and theological course. While care will be taken not to lower the standard of intellectual culture, no pains will be spared to combine with it the best physical and moral education. Prominent objects of this seminary are, the thorough qualification of Christian teachers, both for the pulpit and for schools; and the elevation of female character, by bringing within the reach of the misjudged and neglected sex all the instructive privileges which have hitherto unreasonably distinguished the leading sex from theirs."

The name Collegiate Institute was retained for many years, but as it led to much misapprehension, as implying that the school had not the full organization and work of a college, the trustees in 1850 secured from the Legislature a change of the name to Oberlin College.

The summer term opened May 7, 1834. Rev. Seth H. Waldo, a graduate of Amherst and of Andover, who had been elected Professor of Languages, with the duties of principal of the school until a full faculty should be constituted, had arrived a few days before, with his wife, recently married. Three days after the opening of the term, James Dascomb, M.D., from the Dartmouth Medical College, reached the place with his newly married wife. He had received the appointment of Professor of Chemistry, Botany, and Physiology. Mr. Daniel Branch and Mrs. Branch, a sister of Mr. Waldo, came about the same time. He too was a graduate of Amherst. He was afterward principal of the academy in Chester, Granger County, where James A. Garfield began his course of study. Mrs. Dascomb, who had been a pupil of Miss Grant of Ipswich, afterwards Mrs. Bannister, was soon made principal of the Ladies' Department. Mr. Branch became Principal of the Preparatory Department, and Mrs. Branch teacher of Latin, French, and of other branches as occasion required. Thus the new school was at once manned by a corps of enthusiastic and efficient young teachers, trained in the institutions of New England. Oberlin, therefore, as a community and a school, was the product of New England ideas and culture and life. The founders, the colonists, the students, and the teachers, were all from New England, most of them directly, the rest indirectly.

The day before this regular opening, under permanent teachers, many students having already come in, a meeting of the young men was held in the narrow passage hall of the "attic," each student bringing out his chair and sitting by his own door, and a literary society was organized, called the Oberlin Lyceum—the first literary society upon the ground. This lyceum existed about two years, and then gave place to other societies. It was not the same as the society afterward known as the Lyceum, and now as the Phi Kappa Pi. The old lyceum expired without any legal successor.

During this first summer term, there were one hundred and one students in attendance—sixty-three young men and thirty-eight young women. These

DR. JAMES DASCOMB.

MARIANNE P. DASCOMB.

filled every available corner of the building and the settlement, and many places which, under other conditions, would not be thought available. Everything was new and rough. The trees had been cut from the college square, but the stumps were still strong in the ground, and so numerous, that an agile boy might propose to cross the square by springing from stump to stump. The roads near the centre had been opened to the sunlight, but not thrown up or ditched, and teams were sometimes mired in front of the college building. At a greater distance the roads were still only tracks through the forest; and it was not an uncommon thing even for young women, coming to the school, to walk the last two or three miles of the way. Two came from Elyria, eight miles, in this independent fashion. The enthusiasm of the new enterprise made all things tolerable.

The colony kept even pace in its progress with the school. Mr. Pelton moved his hotel from the log house, first erected, to a comfortable frame building on the corner now occupied by the principal hotel. It was for a time a question whether the hotel under the colonial covenant could furnish tea and coffee to its customers; but it was at length concluded that to refuse would be carrying the principle farther than was "practicable." Such questions as this, in the social meetings, diversified the busy life of the colonists.

A small flouring-mill was erected, to be driven by the same engine which moved the saw-mill, also machines for cutting lath and shingles. These ma-

chines furnished labor for several students; and the
whole establishment was owned by the college—a
constant source, of course, of annoyance and expense, but a necessity of the new settlement. As
soon as opportunity offered the mills were sold, and
became the property of individuals.

To meet the growing necessities of the college,
another college building was erected, known in after
years as the Boarding Hall, or Ladies' Hall, the
main part forty by eighty feet, three stories high,
with two wings of two stories each. This was not
made ready for occupancy until the autumn of 1835,
a year, and more, from its commencement. Want of
funds, and the effort to have a large portion of the
work done by students, delayed the enterprise.

It was an encouraging fact to the students and
colonists that, in the midst of these labors and de-
privations incident to the settlement of a new country, no sickness prevailed among them. There was
some sickness among young children during the
warm weather of 1834, otherwise the health was un-
interrupted. Very satisfactory progress was made
in study; yet interruptions occurred such as would
be inadmissible under more settled conditions.
When the new boarding-house was to be "raised,"
the students were called out in a body, and all study
was suspended for three days. Now and then a
temperance man in some neighboring settlement,
not finding his neighbors ready to assist him in his
"raising," without the support of the bottle, would
send word in to the students, who would rally at
once in the good cause, and sacrifice a day's study

to their temperance principles. Oberlin was as aggressive and reformatory at this time as in after
years, only that the direction which its reformatory
efforts should take was not fully determined. Tea
and coffee were excluded from the tables in the
College Hall, and for the most part discarded in
private families. A plain, substantial diet was furnished, at a very moderate expense. The charge for
board in the Hall was seventy-five cents a week, for
a purely vegetable diet, and a dollar for the addition
of meat twice a day.

The first " Annual Report," published in November, 1834, estimates the entire expense of the student for all his requirements, except clothing, during
the forty weeks of term time, as ranging from fifty-
eight to eighty-nine dollars. This amount was
readily covered, in most cases, by the avails of the
labor required of the student, four hours each day,
for which he received, according to his skill and
power of accomplishment, from four to seven cents
an hour. The arrangement seemed a great success ;
the expenses were reduced to the minimum, and the
student's labor provided for this. To the apprehension of the more considerate, there was one draw-
back. This labor of the student was not made to
supply the constant expenditure. It yielded no
money to the college nor even food for the supply
of the tables. It was wholly expended in improvements, the erection of buildings, and the clearing of
the land. These improvements were needed, but it
was a question whether they could be afforded ; and

whence was to come the supply for this constant expenditure?

The arrangement of terms and vacations adopted
at this time involved continuous study through the
summer for the regular classes, with a winter vacation of twelve weeks, and continuous study through
the winter for the junior preparatory department,
with a long summer vacation. This arrangement
was intended to give the advanced students an opportunity to take schools for the winter, and those
in the beginning of their course opportunity for
summer work at their homes. This order, with some
variations, was continued until 1878.

The first college class was organized near the end
of October, 1834, consisting of four young men,
who came forward for examination to enter as
freshmen. Two of these had pursued their preparatory studies in an academy at Brownhelm, and in
the Elyria High School; another was from Phillips
Academy, Andover, Mass. They were all well prepared, for those times, and would have been admitted to any college in the country.

The first "commencement," or anniversary, was
held on the twenty-ninth of October. As there
were none to graduate, these entering freshmen were
brought upon the stage, and a few others of the
more advanced students. The trustees were present, and several visitors from neighboring towns.
The little chapel was crowded. The programme
presented, among other exercises, a Latin oration,
a Greek oration, and a colloquy, the aim of which
was to maintain the orthodox opinion on the sub-

ject of classical education. Thus closed the school year of 1833-34.

Early in September of this year a church was organized, called "The Congregational Church of Christ at Oberlin," now known as "The First Congregational Church of Oberlin." Sixty-two persons united at the organization, colonists and students. The confession of faith was Calvinistic in doctrine, after the New England type; and the church connected itself with the Cleveland Presbytery upon "The Plan of Union," after the fashion of the churches of Northern Ohio. Rev. J. J. Shipherd was at once called to become pastor of the church, but in consequence of pressing duties as corresponding secretary and general agent of the college, his acceptance of the call was delayed until the following year. Meanwhile he officiated as pastor while present, and in his absence Mr. Waldo, the principal of the school, usually preached.

Several houses were erected on Main Street and around the college square, during the year, giving the town quite the aspect of a village, and Mr. Hamilton's house, far in the woods, a mile south. At a colonial meeting the principles of the Oberlin Covenant were brought to bear upon the question, What color shall we paint our houses? It was clearly demonstrated that red was the most durable and least expensive color; and thus it was voted, not without earnest remonstrance on the part of some, that the houses of the village should be painted red. But a vote on such a question does not always settle it. Each man claimed the right to act according to his own judgment; and three dwelling-houses and the college shop were all the buildings that ever submitted to the coating of red, and these only for a few years. So early, under the Oberlin Covenant, did taste begin to prevail over stern utility.

Two years had now passed since Mr. Shipherd set out alone on horseback to realize his plan. The result thus far was a community of thirty-five families, a church of above eighty members, a college numbering a hundred students, with land and buildings and other property valued at seventeen thousand dollars, and such a movement toward the school that large numbers of applicants had to be turned away. Here and there appeared indications of disfavor toward the enterprise, partly because of the peculiar constitution of the school, opening its doors to both sexes, but chiefly because it seemed to come into competition with Western Reserve College, which had been established ten years before, and had pre-emption rights in the territory. Some of the trustees of Oberlin were warm friends of W. R. College, and Judge Brown, the first chairman of the Board at Oberlin, was a prominent founder and trustee of W. R. College; but at the close of this second year he resigned his connection at Oberlin, because, as he said, he could not "stand between two fires." The founders of Oberlin were in heart friendly to W. R. College, and had no thought of opposition or rivalry. In his first annual report Mr. Shipherd says: "Being distinctive in its character, it was thought by the principal of the nearest literary institution [Elyria High School] to be no more an interference with that or others in the neighborhood, than if located more remotely. It stands not as a *competitor*, but as a *sister* of all institutions of Christian science." A little consideration, however, would have suggested that the two colleges, less than fifty miles apart, must depend essentially upon the same constituency. The lines had already begun to be drawn between the friends of W. R. College and the friends of Oberlin.

CHAPTER III.

THE ACCESSION FROM LANE SEMINARY AND CONSEQUENT ENLARGEMENT.

THE college year had closed; the more advanced students had gone to their winter schools or their homes, and the less advanced had, according to the arrangement, resumed their studies for the winter term. Mr. Shipherd, under instructions from the trustees, set his face eastward again, to look for a president and a professor of mathematics, as well as to secure funds to meet the growing demands of the work.

In a season of fasting and prayer, his habitual preparation for a new movement, he received the impression that he must go by Cincinnati: an impression which he could give no account of, and which he at first resisted as unreasonable. He knew no one at Cincinnati, and he had special reasons, as he thought, for going directly eastward; but the impression increased upon him, until it ripened into a conviction which he dared not set aside; and thus he took his journey to the East by way of Cincinnati—a route to New York from Northern Ohio which no one perhaps ever took before.

Having reached Cincinnati, so worn out with the journey that he was obliged to take his bed for the day, he at length called on Rev. Asa Mahan, pastor of the Sixth Street Presbyterian Church, from whom

he soon ascertained the reason for his going by Cincinnati.

A movement had been inaugurated in Lane Seminary, a theological school at Walnut Hills, near the
city, which Mr. Shipherd saw at once might be
brought into connection with the Oberlin enterprise.
Of this movement there was no general knowledge
at Oberlin, and that Mr. Shipherd had heard of it
cannot be ascertained. The era of newspapers, rail-
roads, and telegraphs had not yet come. The facts
were these : Lane Seminary had been in existence
two or three years, and had collected a class of students of unusual ability and energy. Many of these
were from Oneida Institute, a school which enjoyed a
few years of vigorous life in Central New York. They
were manual-labor students, energetic and self-rely-
ing. As an indication of their spirit, it may be stated
that, in going from Oneida to Lane, some of them
went down the Alleghany and Ohio as hands on flat-
boats, and pocketed a handsome purse to begin their
studies upon at Cincinnati. Among these Oneida
students was Theodore D. Weld, a young man of
surpassing eloquence and logical power, and of a
personal influence even more fascinating than his
eloquence. Besides these Oneida students, there
were others at Lane, prominent actors in the movement, some of them, as James A. Thome and William T. Allan, sons of slaveholders, and linked to
slavery in all their worldly interests. The whole
number of students there at the time was above one
hundred. Many of these were not theological students, but were connected with a literary department

in preparation for theology, under the charge of Professor Morgan. The theological Professors were Dr. Lyman Beecher, Professor Stowe, and another gentleman unknown to fame.

About this time (as early at least as 1833) the quiet of Boston and New York, and some other Eastern cities, had been disturbed by the startling utterances of Wm. Lloyd Garrison and his *Liberator*. He had taken issue with the Colonization Society, and called on all honest men to stand aloof from it, as false in principle and pernicious in its influence. He enforced the duty of immediate and unconditional emancipation, as the only right and safe course. " Slavery is a sin, and ought to be immediately abandoned," was in those days the burden of his prophecy. Men of strong anti-slavery feeling were at once brought over by his facts and his logic. Weld, too, in the quiet of Lane Seminary, was moved, and others with him. The students requested of the Faculty the use of the public room occupied as a chapel for the discussion of slavery. The Faculty recommended quiet—rather discountenanced the discussion, but did not prohibit it. The students gathered in the chapel, and for eighteen successive evenings continued their debate. At the outset there was great diversity of sentiment, but in the end the antislavery view prevailed almost unanimously. We may well suppose that the discussion would be earnest and thorough, for there were men there whose course for life was to turn upon the result. It was not like an ordinary discussion in a literary society, where the main interest lies in the debate itself. Some of the young men well knew that the position they took might alienate friends, and prevent for many years, perhaps forever, a return to the homes of their youth. Yet even these were convinced, and took their stand against slavery at the sacrifice of friends and home.

As a result of the anti-slavery movement in the Seminary, the young men were stirred up to do something for the colored people in the city. They gathered them in Sabbath-schools, and established day-schools among them, and made use of all the means at hand to elevate and advance them. Some of the ladies of the city aided in the establishment and superintendence of the schools. The efforts were not limited to the colored people. Communications were sent to the religious journals, which elicited spirited discussions that attracted the attention of the city generally. Movements like these disturbed the quiet of the trustees of the Seminary, some of whom were wholly men of commerce, and understood better the pork market than the management of a literary institution. Others sympathized in the general apprehension of evil from the anti-slavery excitement.

The summer vacation of twelve weeks came on, and Professors Beecher and Stowe and Morgan had left for the East. The students, too, were mainly scattered. The trustees held a meeting at this juncture, and passed a law, without any consultation with the Faculty, except the single member who remained, prohibiting the discussion of slavery among the students, both in public and in private. They

were not to be allowed to communicate with each
other on the subject, even at the table in the Seminary commons.   At the same time the trustees
dispatched a message to Professor Morgan, in New
York, that his services were no longer required.
No reason was assigned him for so abrupt a termination of his relations.   Perhaps they already apprehended, what they soon realized, that his occupation
was gone.   But in the Seminary it was well understood that he was sacrificed on account of his sympathy with the anti-slavery movement.   The other
professors returned to swallow, as best they could,
the bitter pill which had been prescribed for them.
The students returned to enter their protest against
the oppressive gag law of the trustees, and to ask
dismissions from the institution.   Four fifths of them
left in a body, and Lane Seminary for many years
did not recover from the blow.

The protesting students, upon the invitation of
James Ludlow, a gentleman of property who resided
a few miles from the city, took possession of a
building which he provided for them; and for five
months they continued their studies together, with
such instruction as they could afford each other, and
a course of lectures on physiology given them
by Dr. Bailey, afterwards editor of the *National
Era*.   Arthur Tappan, of New York, sent them an
offer of $5000 for a building, and the promise of a
professorship, if they would establish a school under
anti-slavery principles and influences.   Mr. Mahan,
one of the trustees of Lane Seminary, had protested
earnestly against the action which had been taken,

and had resigned his place when he saw that the majority would pass and sustain the odious law pro-hibiting the discussion of slavery. He was in sym-pathy with the protesting students, and between him and Mr. Shipherd the plan was devised of add-ing at once a Theological Department to Oberlin, and bringing on the seceding students from Lane to constitute the first theological classes. Mr. Ship-herd's anti-slavery zeal was quickened by contact with the exciting influences there; and under date of December 15, 1834, he writes to the trustees at Oberlin, urging the appointment of Rev. Asa Mahan as President, and Rev. John Morgan, Professor of Mathematics. He also writes : " I desire you, at the first meeting of the trustees, to secure the passage of the following resolution, to wit : '*Resolved*, That students shall be received into this Institution *irre-spective of color.*' This should be passed because it is a right principle, and God will bless us in doing right. Also because thus doing right we gain the confidence of benevolent and able men, who prob-ably will furnish us some thousands. Moreover, Bros. Mahan and Morgan will not accept our invita-tion unless this principle rule. Indeed, if our Board would violate right so as to reject youth of talent and piety because they were *black*, I should have *no heart* to labor for the upbuilding of our Seminary, believing that the curse of God would come upon us, as it has upon Lane Seminary, for its unchristian abuse of the poor slave."

This letter was in care of the acting Secretary at Oberlin, and of course was communicated to the officers and teachers on the ground. The idea of receiving colored students was a new one, and the people of Oberlin were not prepared to embrace it at once. They knew no precedents in its favor. No such thing, so far as they knew, had been heard of in the land, or in any other land. There was earnest discussion and intense excitement. It was believed by many that the place would be at once overwhelmed with colored students, and the mischiefs that would follow were frightful in the extreme. Men who afterwards stood manfully in the anti-slavery ranks, when the battle was hottest, and whose lives had shown that they could face duty in its most forbidding aspects, were alarmed in view of the unknown and undefined evil which threatened. Young ladies who had come from New England to the school in the wilderness—young ladies of unquestioned refinement and goodness—declared that if colored students were admitted to equal privileges in the Institution they would return to their homes, if they had to "wade Lake Erie" to accomplish it. These same young ladies afterward showed their New England spirit, not in wading Lake Erie, but in stemming a torrent of abuse and reproach, which they encountered in their fearless advocacy of the cause of the oppressed. The excitement here was intense, and was not at all allayed by an arrangement on the part of the trustees to hold their session in Elyria, in the hope of finding a calmer atmosphere, more congenial to deliberation. This session was held at the Temperance House in Elyria, on the 1st of January, 1835. A petition was presented to the

Board, signed by the principal colonists, and by several students who remained during the vacation. It reads as follows:

To the Honorable Board of Trustees of the Oberlin Collegiate Institute assembled at Elyria:

Whereas, there has been, and is now, among the colonists and students of the Oberlin Collegiate Institute a great excitement in their minds in consequence of a resolution of Brother J. J. Shipherd, to be laid before the Board, respecting the admission of people of color into the Institution, and also of the Board's meeting at Elyria: now, your petitioners, feeling a deep interest in the Oberlin Collegiate Institute, and feeling that every measure possible should be taken to quell the alarm, that there shall not be a root of bitterness springing up to cause a division of interest and feeling (for a house divided against itself cannot stand); therefore, your petitioners respectfully request that your honorable body will meet at Oberlin, that your deliberations may be heard and known on the great and important questions in contemplation. We feel for our black brethren—we feel to want your counsels and instructions; we want to know what is duty, and, God assisting us, we will lay aside every prejudice, and do as we shall be led to believe that God would have us to do.

The trustees were in a state of doubt and perplexity, corresponding with the condition of the petitioners as here presented. Their action was conservative and non-committal. The record reads as follows:

Whereas, information has been received from Rev. J. J. Shipherd, expressing a wish that students may be received into this Institution irrespective of color; therefore, resolved, that this Board do not feel prepared, till they have more definite information on the subject, to give a pledge respecting the course they will pursue in regard to the education of the people of color, wishing that this Institution should be on the same ground, in respect to the admission of students, with other similar institutions of our land.

At the same session of the trustees President Mahan and Professor Morgan were appointed, according to the request of Mr. Shipherd, although the platform on which they had placed themselves was not adopted.

The report of the failure of the trustees to take the action he desired, reached Mr. Shipherd at New York, whither he had gone, in company with Mr. Mahan, to confer with Arthur and Lewis Tappan, and other antislavery men of the city, in reference to the proposal to bring to Oberlin the students who had left Lane Seminary, establish a theological department, and place the institution upon a distinctively antislavery basis. He was grieved, but not cast down. He wrote again to the Trustees, and especially sent a pastoral epistle to the people of Oberlin overflowing with faithful love to all, reviewing the way in which the Lord had led them, exhorting them to patient continuance in well-doing, and warning them against yielding to a worldly spirit and worldly principles. At length he reaches the matter which chiefly burdens his heart, and continues as follows:

"My fears are excited by your recent expressions of unwillingness to have youth of *color* educated in our Institute. Those expressions were a grief to me, such as I have rarely suffered. Although I knew that with some of you the doctrine of expediency was against the immediate abolition of slavery, because the slaves are not qualified for freedom, I supposed you thought it expedient and duty to elevate and educate them as fast as possible; that, therefore, you would concur in receiving those of promising talent and piety into our institution. So confident was I that this would be the *prevailing* sentiment of Oberlin, in the colony and institution, that about a year ago I informed eastern inquirers that we received students according to character, irrespective of color. And, beloved, whatever the expediency or prejudice of some may say, does not duty require this? Most certainly; for, 1. They are needed as ministers, missionaries, and teachers for the land of their fathers, and for their untaught, injured, perishing brethren of our country. 2. Their education seems highly essential, if not indispensable, to the emancipation and salvation of their colored brethren. 3. They will be elevated far more rapidly if taught with whites, hitherto far more favored, than if educated separately. 4. The extremity of their wrongs at the white man's hand requires that the best possible means be employed, and without delay, for their elevation. 5. They can nowhere enjoy needed education unless admitted to our institution, or others established for whites. 6. God made them of one blood with us; they are our fellows. 7. They are our *neighbors*, and whatsoever we would they should do unto us, we must do unto them, or become guilty before God. Suppose, beloved, your color were to become black, what would you claim, in this respect, to be your due as neighbors? 8. Those we propose to receive are the 'little ones' of Christ. We must take heed how we offend one of these little ones. 9. The objection to associating with them for the purpose of doing them good, is like the objection of the Pharisees against our Saviour's eating and drinking with publicans and sinners. 10. Intermarriage with the whites is not asked, and need not be feared. 11. None of you will be compelled to receive them into your families, unless, like Christ, the love of your neighbor compels you to. 12. Those who desire to receive and educate them have the same right to do it that Christ had to eat with publicans and sinners. 13. Colored youth have been educated at other institutions for whites. 14. They will doubtless be received to all such institutions by and by; and why should beloved Oberlin wait to do justice and show mercy till all others have done it? Why hesitate to lead in the cause of humanity and of God? 15. Colored youth cannot be rejected through fear that God will be dishonored if they are received. 16. However it may be with you, brethren, I know that it was only the pride of my wicked heart that caused me to reject them while I did. 17. If we refuse to deliver our brother, now drawn unto death, I cannot hope that God will smile upon us. 18. The men and money which would make our institution most useful cannot be obtained if we reject our colored brother. Eight professorships and ten thousand dollars are subscribed, upon condition that Rev. C. G. Finney become Professor of Theology in our Institute; and he will not, unless the youth of color are received. Nor will President Mahan nor Professor Morgan serve unless this condition is complied with; and they all are the men we need, irrespective of their antislavery sentiments. 19. If you suffer expediency and prejudice to pervert justice in this case you will in another. 20. Such is my conviction of duty in the case, that I cannot labor for the enlargement of the Oberlin Collegiate Institute if our brethren in Jesus Christ must be rejected because they differ from us in color. You know, dear brethren and sisters, that it would be hard for me to leave that institution, which I planted in much fasting and prayer and tribulation, sustained for a time by only one brother, and then for months by only two brethren, and for which I have prayed without ceasing, laboring night and day, and watering it with my sweat and my tears. You know it would be hard to part with my dear associates in these labors. And as I have you as a people in my heart to live and die with you, you know, beloved, that it would be heart-breaking to leave you for another field of labor; but I have pondered the subject well, with prayer, and believe that if the injured brother of color, and consequently brothers Finney, Mahan, and Morgan, with eight professorships and ten thousand dollars, must be rejected, I *must* join *them;* because by so doing I can labor more effectually for a lost world and the glory of God—and believe me, dear brethren and sisters, *for this reason only.*

"The agitation produced by my request, forwarded to the trustees some weeks since, was unexpected. I was sorry that it occurred, but happy that you fasted and prayed it down. I trust that season has prepared the minds of all who devoutly observed it for this communication, which I would have suppressed till my return had I not been under the

necessity of communicating the same to the trustees
for immediate decision; because our professors and
funds are all suspended upon that decision, and
myself also.   May God of His infinite mercy grant
that in this and all things right we may be 'perfectly
joined together in one mind.'"

The trustees and the colonists to whom these
appeals of Mr. Shipherd were addressed, were earnest
Christian men and women.   All their instincts and
convictions were opposed to slavery, but they had
given little consideration to their own practical relations to the subject.   Slavery they regarded as a
great evil—a curse; but the idea that they had anything to do about it, had not entered their minds.
The question of slavery had been discussed the summer previous in the "Oberlin Lyceum," which embraced both students and colonists, when it appeared
that the entire community, except Mr. Shipherd and
two or three students, were "Colonizationists."   The
prevailing sentiment was that it would never do to
"let the slaves loose among us"—that the free colored people should be "returned to Africa" as soon
as possible, and the slaves gradually made free, and
sent after them.   The Oberlin covenant contained
no allusion to slavery.   These good people would
not have hesitated a moment to go as missionaries
to Africa, if such a duty had been made clear to
them; but all their social prepossessions, not to say
prejudices, were against the idea of a mingling of
the two races in society here.   It required time and
consideration to make the thought acceptable.   Even
Mr. Stewart, stern reformer that he was, trained in

missionary service among the Choctaws, ready for anything that came as duty, however great the sacrifice required, was not prepared to take the step proposed by Mr. Shipherd, and, as a member of the Board of Trustees, cast his vote against it to the last. It was, however, simply a question of time with him. His mind naturally moved slowly, but at length he took his position with the foremost of the Abolitionists.

According to Mr. Shipherd's request, another meeting of the trustees was held at Oberlin, Feb. 9, at the house of Mr. Shipherd, which had been erected, the previous summer, on the north side of the College Square. Many of the good people had by this time become deeply interested in favor of the movement, and the results of this meeting were looked for with intense interest. Rev. John Keep, then of Ohio City [Cleveland, west side], was at the time president of the Board, having been elected the previous autumn, upon the resignation of Judge Brown.

The trustees convened in the morning, nine members being present, and the discussion was warm and long. Mrs. Shipherd was occupied with her household duties, but in her anxiety she often passed the door, which was ajar, and at length stood before it. Father Keep comprehended the case, and stepped out to inform her that the result of the deliberation was very doubtful. He greatly feared that the opposition would prevail. Mrs. Shipherd dropped her work at once, gathered her praying sisters in the neighborhood, and spent the time with them in prayer until the decision was announced. When the question was finally taken, the division of the Board was equal, and Father Keep, as the presiding officer, gave the casting vote in favor of the admission of colored students. The resolution which at length passed was not simple and direct, like the one proposed originally by Mr. Shipherd, but it seems the expression of timid men who were afraid to say precisely what they meant. It is as follows:

Whereas, there does exist in our country an excitement in respect to our colored population, and fears are entertained that on the one hand they will be left unprovided for as to the means of a proper education, and on the other that they will in unsuitable numbers be introduced into our schools, and thus in effect forced into the society of the whites, and the state of public sentiment is such as to require from the Board some definite expression on the subject; therefore, resolved, that the education of the people of color is a matter of great interest, and should be encouraged and sustained in this institution.

The logic of the resolution is not very luminous, nor is the conclusion entirely unambiguous, but the effect was decisive. It determined the policy of the institution on the question of slavery, and no other action has been needed on the subject from that day to this. It was a word of invitation and welcome to the colored man, as opposed to the spirit of exclusion which was then dominant in the land. That this decision was regarded as involving grave consequences, is manifest from the intense excitement which existed here at the time. There were no colored students at the door seeking admittance. Indeed there was but one colored person at the time resident in the county; but they were very generally

expected as the result of this decision; and when
at length a solitary colored man was seen entering
the settlement, a little boy, the son of one of the
trustees, ran to the house, calling out, " They're
coming, father—they're coming!"

At the same meeting of the trustees Rev. Charles
G. Finney, of New York City, was appointed Professor of Theology. He was then pastor of the Congregational Church worshipping in the Chatham
Street Chapel, formerly a theatre, and about to enter
the Broadway Tabernacle, which was building for its
reception. The Tappans and other prominent antislavery men were members of this church. They
had already become interested in the antislavery
movement in Lane Seminary, and were ready to
respond to the proposal of Messrs. Shipherd and
Mahan that Mr. Finney should become Professor of
Theology at Oberlin, and thus a refuge should be
afforded for the fugitives from Lane.

Arthur Tappan himself pledged a contribution of
ten thousand dollars to erect a building intended
primarily for the Theological Department, and engaged to secure a loan of ten thousand more for
other necessary buildings and improvements. Several other gentlemen united with the Tappans in
what was called " The Oberlin Professorship Association," engaging to pay quarterly the interest on
eighty thousand dollars, sufficient for the salaries of
eight professors, at six hundred dollars each. It was
intended finally to pay the principal, and thus secure the permanent endowment of the institution.
This was in the beginning of 1835, when all business

operations seemed prosperous, and the gentlemen forming the association were abundantly able to do what they proposed. On this foundation, and on the ground of the antislavery attitude of the college as determined by the final action of the trustees, Messrs. Mahan, Finney, and Morgan accepted their appointments, and arranged to come to Oberlin. Professor Morgan, however, was invited to the Chair of New Testament Literature and Exegesis, instead of that of Mathematics and Natural Philosophy, as at first proposed. These men were then in the prime of their manhood—Professor Finney forty-two years of age, President Mahan thirty-five, and Professor Morgan thirty-two. Professor Finney was born in Connecticut, removed early to Central New York, was trained for the profession of law, and entered the ministry after brief study with his pastor, Rev. George W. Gale. President Mahan was born in Western New York, pursued study at Hamilton College to the end of the junior year, and took his theological course at Andover. Professor Morgan was brought to this country from Ireland, at the age of eleven, was brought up in Philadelphia and New York, prepared for college at Stockbridge, Mass., and graduated at Williams. His theological studies were pursued privately in New York. Thus Oberlin experienced a sudden enlargement and took a new departure.

President Mahan came to Oberlin about the first of May, followed a month later by his family and a large number of the students from Lane. For the president's family, the first log house erected here

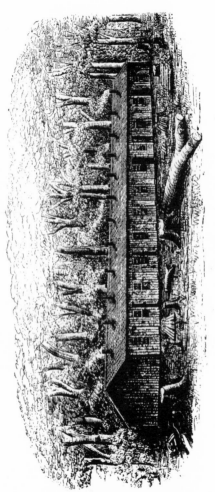

SLAB HALL.

was vacated and made ready, and this house they occupied several months, until the " President's House,"
at the south-west corner of the square, could be built.
For the students who came from Lane, special provision was made. A building was extemporized,
called " Cincinnati Hall." It was one story high,
one hundred and forty-four feet long, and twenty-
four feet wide. Its sides and partitions and ceilings
and floors were of beech boards fresh from the mill.
On the outside it was battened with " slabs " retaining the bark of the original tree, which gave the
building a decidedly rustic aspect. One end of the
" Hall " was fitted up as kitchen and dining-room,
and the remainder was divided into rooms twelve
feet square, with a single window to each, and a door
opening out upon the forest. This structure was
situated a little west of the site of the " Old Laboratory," its west side corresponding with what is now
the east side of Professor Street. This was then the
border of the forest toward the west. Two students
were assigned to each room. Oberlin strained a
point to give the new-comers a reception and accommodations worthy of their fame. The enthusiasm of the new enterprise lightened hardships and
made the rough places smooth. All were satisfied.
The number of students that came was about
thirty—not all theological students. Several were
from the literary course at Lane, in preparation for
theology, and entered a similar course here. A few
of those who had been most prominent in the movement at Lane, as Theodore D. Weld and Henry B.
Stanton, did not come to Oberlin to remain, but

were drawn at once into public antislavery labors in the country, and only dropped in at Oberlin from time to time as their work permitted. Among those who came and helped to make up a senior theological class were such men as Wm. T. Allan, of Huntsville, Ala.; John W. Alvord, more recently connected with the Freedman's Bureau; George Clark, known in the country for many years as an evangelist; Sereno W. Streeter, a well-known pastor in Ohio and Michigan; James A. Thome, of Augusta, Ky., professor at Oberlin, and afterwards pastor in Cleveland; George Whipple, twelve years professor at Oberlin, and for many years afterwards Secretary of the American Missionary Association; and others, fourteen in all—such a class as any seminary might be proud of.

The effect of this accession upon the institution and the place was, of course, decided and manifest. The school was at once transformed from a Collegiate Institute—as it had been modestly called—to a University, embracing the same departments as at present, with students in every stage of advancement. Hence the mistake has often been made abroad, of attributing the origin of Oberlin to the explosion at Lane Seminary. The Collegiate Department received considerable accessions, about the same time, from Western Reserve College, the trustees of which had been exercised, somewhat after the manner of the trustees of Lane, by the antislavery zeal of professors and students. Thus Oberlin incurred odium, not only by its antislavery position, but by becoming an asylum for discontented students. If these students had been such as could well be spared by the schools from which they came, the case would have been far .different; but the "glorious good fellows" of Lane, as Dr. Beecher called them, were well matched in the earnest and thorough-going young men from Hudson.

In June Professors Finney and Morgan came, and soon entered upon their work. The buildings provided for by the gift and loan of Arthur Tappan, were commenced and pushed rapidly forward. These were two dwelling-houses of brick, each two stories in height, one for President Mahan and the other for Professor Finney; and Tappan Hall, a college building of brick, four stories high, with four lecture rooms on the first floor, and dormitories above, intended first for the Theological Department, as far as required, and then for the general uses of the college. The colonists, though greatly pressed with the expense of building their own homes, and bringing their farms into cultivation, subscribed twenty-five hundred dollars to be applied in the erection of another college building, the lower story of which should be used jointly, by the college as a chapel, and by the church for its services. This subscription covered about half the cost of the building, and was made with the provision that the use by the church should be temporary, and that the claim should finally be transferred to the college. This building was three stories in height, the second and third stories furnishing dormitories for young men. In consideration of the subscription by the people, the building was called Colonial Hall. The frame was erected and the building inclosed before winter.

Meanwhile the congregation had outgrown the little chapel used the preceding year, and the dining-room of the new boarding-house, not yet occupied, was put in order every Saturday for the Sabbath services. In this room Mr. Finney did his first preach. ing in Oberlin, President Mahan usually taking the morning service, and Mr. Finney the afternoon. Both sermons were long—never less than an hour, often an hour and a half; but the congregation never seemed weary, and probably no one in the entire community, at that time, ever willingly stayed away. It was such preaching as the young people who heard it could never forget.

When Colonial Hall was erected and had received its roof and siding, loose boards were laid on the timbers and the service was held there, the whole interior being open to the roof, and the timbers of the successive stories being supported by studs, held in position simply by the pressure from above. At the first gathering in this building the service had just begun when the brick supports under the floor were crushed, and the props above, loosened by the sinking of the floor, fell one after another into the midst of the people. No one was injured, but there was considerable consternation, which Mr. Finney quieted by assuring the people that they could not possibly fall farther than the ground; and that if sinners were not in danger of falling farther than the ground, he would never preach another sermon. He then went on with a pungent and powerful discourse from the text, " He that turneth away his ear from hearing the law, even his prayer shall be abomination."

This rapid enlargement, involving the coming in of new men of commanding influence and new ideas, was not effected without some perturbations. Within a week of the arrival of President Mahan, the information was spread abroad, by some student who had " interviewed " him, that he was opposed to the study of the "heathen classics." He was at once invited by some committee to give a lecture upon the subject before the Oberlin Lyceum. Without due consideration, as he afterward used to admit, he consented, and stated freely and strongly, as was his wont, his views, not in opposition to the study of Latin and Greek, but of the classic authors commonly used in the college course, and indeed in opposition to so large an expenditure of time upon these studies. He was one of the earliest advocates of "the new education." Mr. Waldo, who was Professor of Languages, and who until this time had been principal of the school, felt called upon to defend the regular course, and gave notice that the next day, at four o'clock in the afternoon, he would reply to the views of President Mahan. The discussion thus opened continued several days, engaging the attention of the entire community. One evening, after an argument by the president, a student, who had never taken kindly to linguistic studies, entered the room of a fellow-student with his Virgil in his hand, and challenged him to join him in burning the obnoxious books. The student thus challenged took up an old volume of Virgil, careful to keep a better one safe, and together they went out in front of the building and lighted the leaves. A score or more of students dropped into the company, some of them bringing books to add to the illumination; and for half an hour they tossed them through the air like fire-balls. Some of the young men perhaps regarded it as a serious business, but to the majority it was mere sport. The young men who burnt the books prepared their lessons in Virgil for the next day, as usual. The boyish freak was widely published through the country as "The burning of the Classics at Oberlin," and was accepted very generally, not unnaturally, as a declaration that such studies were to be repudiated. No such impression prevailed at Oberlin, and no such result followed. The course of study remained unchanged, essentially the accepted American college course. But the discussion and the result disturbed Mr. Waldo's mind. He apprehended that he should not be able to realize at Oberlin his views of education, and at the next meeting of the trustees he tendered his resignation. Rev. Henry Cowles, a native of Connecticut, and an honored graduate of Yale, then pastor at Austinburg, was appointed to the vacancy, and entered upon the work in the autumn of this year.

One result of the discussion upon classical study was to awaken a temporary interest in the study of the Hebrew language, which it was proposed to substitute for a portion of the Latin of the course. To meet this demand, Prof. J. Seixas, a Jew, a teacher of Hebrew, from New York City, was employed the

latter half of the year, to give the students an introduction to this language. He was an enthusiastic
and successful teacher, and stirred up such an interest that his classes numbered, at one time, a hundred
and twenty-seven pupils. This interest soon sub-
sided, and the study of Hebrew was begun, at first
in the last term of the junior year, then in the first
term of the senior year, and finally was limited to the
theological course.

The commencement this year was held in July,
under the " Big Tent" which had been sent on from
New York by Professor Finney's friends, to furnish
him the means of holding protracted meetings
through the region, in places where no suitable house
for such meetings could be found. This tent was
for some years a conspicuous feature of the Oberlin
Commencement, and of other large gatherings. It
was a circular tent, a hundred feet in diameter—sufficient when closely seated to shelter three thousand
persons. Its first spreading on the college grounds
was an occasion of much interest. It was on Saturday afternoon, and the young men of the college all
entered into the work. The work, after some mis-
adjustments, was successfully accomplished, and the
long blue streamer floated out on the breeze, bearing
the millennial motto, in large white letters, " Holiness to the Lord." On Sabbath afternoon, at five
o'clock, the people gathered in the tent for a dedica-
tion service. Professor Finney was offering the ded-
icatory prayer, and asking that the tent might serve
the purposes intended, and might be protected from
the winds of heaven, when a sudden gale struck the

canvas on the west side; stakes yielded and chains broke, and the whole collapsed. The people were not seriously disturbed by the unpropitious omen. They strengthened the stakes and doubled the chains, and the Commencement was held in the tent.

There was no class to graduate, as those from Lane who composed the senior theological class had determined, on account of interruption of their studies, in changing from Lane to Oberlin, to take an additional year. The principal exercises were inaugural addresses from President Mahan and Professors Finney and Morgan.

The Annual Catalogue for this year, 1835, published after Commencement, presents the institution as fully organized in all its departments, with a total attendance of two hundred and seventy-seven students, thirty-five in the theological classes, thirty-eight in the college classes, and two hundred and four preparatory students. These were from all parts of the Northern States, with a few from the South—young men and women of mature age and earnest character, a large majority professed Christians, preparing for service in the different spheres of Christian labor.

A single colored student, James Bradley, once a slave, had come from Cincinnati, following the students from Lane, with whom he had become acquainted. All the resistance to the reception of colored students, which had been exhibited less than a year before, had disappeared. All seemed to have forgotten that they could have cherished such feel-

TENT.

ings, and the colored brother was made perfectly at home.

A few weeks before the close of the fall term Theodore D. Weld came to the place, and gave a series of more than twenty lectures on slavery, its nature and relations and bearings, personal, social, political, and moral: lectures of marvellous power, all charged with facts, with logic, and with fervid eloquence. To listen to such an exhibition of the system of slavery, was an experience to be remembered for a lifetime. It is doubtful whether any community was ever more profoundly moved by the eloquence of a single man. From first to last, through the evenings of three full weeks, the whole body of citizens and students hung upon his lips. Studies naturally suffered some interruption, but the opportunity was itself an education. Oberlin was abolitionized in every thought and feeling and purpose, and has been working out those convictions during the fifty years that have since elapsed.

During the following winter vacation a score or more of the students, equipped for the conflict by this course of training, went out as lecturers through Ohio and portions of Pennsylvania, under the auspices of the American Antislavery Society. Their experiences were sufficiently startling to meet all the requirements of an interesting campaign. They found bitter enemies and devoted friends, and encountered mobs which were sometimes amusing and sometimes terrific; and thus the abolitionism was diffused. The Western Reserve became, under these and other influences, a stronghold of antislavery sentiment and action ; and when at length the question of the relations of the government to slavery became the absorbing one in politics, the Western Reserve determined the position of the State of Ohio.

There were, during this year, hundreds of applicants for admission to the school who could not be received. The difficulty was to provide rooms and facilities for manual labor to the many who came. The prospect seemed to be that the only limit to the influx of students would be the necessity of providing for them room and work; but it was found that the labor could not be made immediately productive on the land not yet subdued, the roots of the original forest still alive in the ground. Hence during the winter the plan was matured of organizing subsidiary schools at convenient points, to provide for the overflow from Oberlin; and with the opening of the spring, in 1836, such schools were opened: one at Sheffield, about fifteen miles from Oberlin, and another at Abbeyville, in Medina County. The Grand River Institute at Austinburg was established about this time, and received a colony from Oberlin, and another colony was sent to the Elyria High School, already in existence. The school at Sheffield was provided for by Mr. Robbins Burrell, who devoted his fine farm and house to the enterprise, and took personal charge of its material and financial interests. The colonies sent to these schools were made up of volunteers. A popular teacher was selected, and his influence drew some, and these drew others. Lorenzo D. Butts, a Lane

Seminary student, was placed in charge at Sheffield, and Amos Dresser, another student from Lane, took charge at Abbeyville. The Grand River Institute became a permanency, because it had a field and constituency of its own. The schools at Sheffield and Abbeyville had scarcely more than a year of life; the impulse that originated them was soon exhausted, and the pupils drifted back to the centre.

A single church in Walton, N. Y., to provide for its young men who wished to come to Oberlin, built a hall of its own, called Walton Hall, on ground furnished by the college—a frame building of two stories, with twelve rooms for two students each. Individual students put up houses of their own on grounds leased from the college, which they occupied in company with some of their fellow-students— a privilege limited to young men. From the beginning the principle was adopted that young women, not provided for in the Ladies' Hall, must find homes in responsible families. Now and then a student, of somewhat monastic tastes and simple habits, would construct for himself a cabin in the woods; but this manner of life was never encouraged: the idea was inculcated that the culture arising from contact with fellow-students, in pleasant social relations, was an essential part of education.

Thus Oberlin was first established and then enlarged, and the enlargement was so conspicuous a fact that it has sometimes been mistaken for its origin. Professor Finney and the men from Lane joined a school already in existence, and numbering more than a hundred pupils.

CHAPTER IV.

THE EARLY SPIRIT AND THOUGHT AND LIFE.

THE Oberlin enterprise, in its very conception, was active and aggressive; it was the outgrowth of the great revival movement of 1830–31–32. It was no part of the plan of the founders to establish a community which should live within itself and for itself; to separate a group of Christian families and a collection of young people from the rest of the world for the sake of realizing certain ideas of the Christian life, with no thought beyond. The purpose was to concentrate Christian forces, and train Christian character, for effective operation upon the world without. To extend the influences of the Gospel throughout the " Mississippi Valley" was the constant idea in the minds of those who laid the foundations.

The revivals of those early years were connected with the presentation of the New School theology. Personal responsibility and immediate duty, on the part of saints and sinners, was the watchword. The world was in darkness, and those who had the Gospel were under solemn and pressing obligation to send abroad the light. These were the original ideas in the minds of Messrs. Shipherd and Stewart, and the early families which gathered in the wilderness. These ideas were strengthened and intensified by the accession of Mr. Finney and the men who came in connection with him in 1835. Mr. Finney had for years stood in the forefront of the great revival movement, and had but recently settled down in New York City as pastor of an aggressive, active church; from this point as a centre he hoped to move upon the country at large. *The New York Evangelist* had published his revival lectures delivered in this pulpit, and continued to publish his sermons; the country at large had, in a sense, become his field of labor. When he came to Oberlin, it was not simply with the thought of settling down in quiet, to give a class of theological students his New School views and the benefits of his experience as an evangelist: this he intended to do; but he hoped to find at Oberlin a new centre, from which he might operate more effectively upon the country and the world. The record of the action of the trustees in his appointment, discloses his purpose in this respect. It includes the following proviso: "Resolved, that with the view of the increased influence of Mr. Finney in the church at large, he have liberty to be absent four or five months of each year, when, on consulting with the Faculty, and with them making the arrangement so as to secure the best interests of the institution, he shall deem it to be his duty."

The "Big Tent" was another indication of his thought and purpose. It was not possible that a man of such restless energy, with an apostle's baptism upon him, should have his influence circumscribed by the woods that environed Oberlin; and he was not alone. His associates were men of similar purpose and power, acting under the same inspiration. The colonists had joined the enterprise under a kind of missionary impulse, and the students were largely of the same spirit—young men and women of mature age and earnest character, expecting to find in the world some work to do.

Such a concentration of power and purpose is rarely secured in any community; and this power was not quiet and dormant: it was vitalized and energized by contact with the great questions and movements of the day. It was not primarily or chiefly an antislavery excitement that animated the community: it was a "zeal for the Lord," ready to move in any direction where a way should open, to benefit mankind and honor God.

Such restless activity must find a field of action— objects upon which to expend itself; and upon the wise direction of this activity the question of a wholesome result must turn. A calm observer, contemplating the scene, would have been in doubt whether to expect a conflict of forces, divisive and self-destructive; a union of force in some eccentric or extravagant form of action, involving a blind enthusiasm, or more likely a malignant fanaticism; or a well-considered and well-regulated work, operating beneficently at home and abroad. The first and the second were often predicted, often affirmed to exist; the last was to a great extent realized. The zeal and impulse of some was happily balanced by the considerate conservatism of others, and all blended in a movement essentially harmonious. No one ever attained to such authority in the community that his opinion was accepted as conclusive; all opinions were freely discussed, and accepted or discarded acccording to the apparent reason of the case. The range of investigation was very broad, embracing questions practical and abstract. Dietetics and the foundation of moral obligation were discussed with equal interest; and every conclusion capable of application in practical form was brought to the test of experiment.

For a time many of these discussions gathered about the Oberlin Covenant. That document was supposed to contain principles by which the Christian life should be ordered; but when it was brought to bear in a practical case, it was found quite as difficult to determine what the covenant prescribed, as to settle the question on independent grounds. This was no valid objection to the covenant; nothing more could properly be asked of it; but it proved less useful in the adjustment of practical questions than some had hoped. Such general terms as "economy and Christian self-denial," "necessary personal and family expenses," "plain and wholesome food," "expensive and unwholesome fashions of dress," "plainness and durability in the construction of houses, furniture, carriages, and all that appertains to us," were found to be just as broad as the Scripture injunction, "Whether, therefore, ye eat or drink, or whatsoever ye do, do all to the glory of God." The whole ground of Christian life and duty was traversed, and all questions were vigorously discussed; but the community settled down upon the catholic basis, of leaving to each one's personal judgment and conscience the determination of his own conduct. The Oberlin Covenant thus became a general confession of the obligations of the Christian life. More than this would have proved a hindrance instead of a help. But such an interpretation of the covenant did not set aside investigation and discussion. The Oberlin enterprise was undertaken as a new departure, and all the questions of life and godliness invited to a reconsideration. One of the first questions before the community pertained to eating and drinking. The covenant was measurably specific as to the use of strong drink and tobacco, and these indulgences were generally discarded. The use of tea and coffee was regarded as questionable, under the covenant; but how far it was "practicable" to dispense with them, was never perfectly ascertained. Simplicity of diet was at the beginning maintained on the ground of economy. The aim of the school was to bring a liberal education within the reach of all; and Mr. Stewart, the first manager of the college boarding hall, had very positive ideas on the subject of table economy. To diminish the cost of living without detriment to health or vigor was his constant aim. Mr. Finney brought with him from New York ideas on diet which had been set forth by Dr. Mussey of Dartmouth, Dr. Hitchcock of Amherst, and such popular writers as Graham and Alcott. These views were based on the question of health, and in general involved the disuse of animal food. The dietetic reform at Oberlin was thus placed on the double foundation of economy and health, and was sustained by impulses from without as well as within. Students at Amherst, under the lead of Dr. Hitchcock, were weighing out their fourteen ounces of food a day, while students at Oberlin were experimenting on Graham bread and crust coffee. Both experiments were short-lived, but that at Amherst soon passed out of thought, while that at Oberlin was accepted as characteristic, and became historical. The facts were that after two years Mr. Stewart left the boarding hall, and a steward was called from Boston, who held radical views on the subject of a vegetarian diet; and for two or three years longer the students were furnished at the Hall with "Graham" fare. They were not restricted to this. A table was still set for those who preferred a different diet; and there was never any constraint or compulsion in the case. Tea and coffee were not introduced into the college boarding hall until 1842 —possibly a little later.

The dietetic experiment in the community, or colony, as it was called, was similar to that in the college. Many of the families discarded tea and coffee, and a few adopted the vegetarian diet; but as the years passed on, these peculiarities disappeared, and the present generation know of them only as traditions of the early days. The dietetic experiment was attended with vigorous discussion, and the dogmas of vegetarianism were often publicly controverted as well as supported; and a final blow was given to the extreme vegetarian views, as presented by Sylvester Graham, by two young men, T. B. Hudson and S. D. Cochran, in a public discussion before the "Society of Inquiry."

Abstract and philosophical questions were investigated with no less interest. In the year 1839 the foundation of moral obligation was discussed in the college chapel, by President Mahan and Prof. J. P. Cowles of the Theological Department, now of Ipswich, Mass. Professor Finney presided, and a large audience of students and citizens was in attendance. President Mahan maintained the popular view, of an intuitive principle of right as ultimate in thought, out of which all obligation springs, and to which all questions of duty must be finally referred—the rational faculty determining, more or less distinctly and directly, the rightness or wrongness of every action. Professor Cowles had been educated at New Haven, and held the modified Paleyan view as presented by Dr. Taylor. The discussion was earnest and vigorous, occupying two or three hours each day, and adjourned from day to day through the week. As is usual in such discussions, neither of the disputants was able to convince the other of his error; but Professor Finney, who occupied the chair, and who had not distinctly formulated his theory of obligation, was able to combine the strong points of both theories, and at the close of the discussion set forth his view, afterwards elaborated in his work on Systematic Theology as the " Benevolence theory." From Professor Cowles he accepted the idea of happiness, well-being, as the ultimate good, and from President Mahan the fact that obligation is intuitively or rationally seen and affirmed; but this obligation is only seen or affirmed in the presence of the good, and rests on the perceived value of happiness, or ultimate good, as its ground. This was the genesis of the Oberlin philosophy of obligation, the resultant of the utilitarian scheme, and the theory of ultimate, abstract right. It may not differ in any essential feature from the view of Edwards and Samuel Hopkins; but so far as Mr. Finney was concerned, it was undoubtedly an original and independent investigation.

The pronounced antislavery position of Oberlin naturally brought here, from time to time, the prominent apostles of Abolitionism, both such as were in full harmony with the conservative political and ecclesiastical attitude of the people here, and such as seemed to themselves to have reached a better and more advanced position. Wm. Lloyd Garrison and Frederick Douglass came, at one time, to convince us that the proper antislavery position involved a withdrawal from all political action; that the Constitution of the United States was pro-slavery and corrupt, and all who voted under it shared in its wickedness, and that those only were bearing a proper testimony against slavery who came out from all political organizations, and refused to take any part in the affairs of government. President Mahan, as usual, led the discussion on the Oberlin side, sustained by Professor T. B. Hudson, and perhaps some others. The result was that Oberlin people continued to vote, Mr. Garrison went on his way, and Mr. Douglass, then or soon after, joined the voting abolitionists.

Stephen Foster and his wife, Abby Kelly Foster, came to Oberlin on a similar errand of " come-outer-

ism," to persuade the people that they were com-
promising their antislavery position, weakening
their testimony, and sharing in the guilt of slavery,
by maintaining any correspondence or fellowship
with the churches of the land. The continuous
chain of fellowship united the church at Oberlin
with the slaveholding churches of the South, and,
no matter by how many links, ten or ten thousand,
bound all together in one " covenant of hell." The
doctrine was not an abstract one in its bearings. It
was dividing the churches of the land and alienating
Christian men from each other. They were invited
to present their views before the people in the college chapel, but, as usual, with the provision that
half the time should be given to a presentation of
the other side. The evenings of a full week were
given to the discussion, with President Mahan in
the forefront of the battle. The atmosphere waxed
hot and lurid with the fire and smoke of the conflict,
but the sky soon cleared, and the church arrangements continued undisturbed.

Rev. Charles Fitch, of Newark, N. J., came to
preach the doctrine of the immediate second coming
of Christ. He was a man of much personal mag-
netism, intensely in earnest, profoundly convinced
of the truth of his message, and called, as he felt, to
bring the better light to the good people of Oberlin.
He was welcomed to the chapel, with the inevitable
condition of an open and free discussion. He had
half the time, and President Mahan and Professors
Morgan and Henry Cowles reviewed his Scripture
interpretations, his logic, and his rhetoric. The work

was done so thoroughly that it sufficed for a generation. The people lived quietly through 1843, and
all the other periods subsequently designated by the
Adventists.

Every such question was hospitably entertained,
but was required to give a reason for its claim to attention. The people had broken away from many
old ideas, and there was no such presumption
against a new doctrine that they could set it aside
without examination. This temper of mind exposed
them to the approach of every would-be reformer
who had some new theory or scheme of life to prop-
agate. He expected sympathy at Oberlin, if nowhere else; and constant vigilance was the price of
security from imposition.

But the Oberlin idea was first Christian and evangelical, and afterwards reformatory. It was not to
realize some special fancy, or to accomplish some
particular outward change, that the people came and
planted their institutions in the wilderness. Their
aims were as broad as the Gospel itself, and all proposed reforms were at once tested by their bearing
upon the general Christian life and work. The pre-
dominance of this idea saved them from any wild
fanaticism. An intelligent Christian earnestness
is the best security against the extravagances of
social reform.

The situation at Oberlin was remarkably favorable to earnestness and unity of action, in every line
of duty and of thought. There was but a single
congregation, composed of citizens and students,
during the first twenty years and more; and of this

congregation Mr. Finney was the pastor, preaching once every Sabbath and often twice. In the early days, Mr. Mahan was accustomed to preach in the morning and Mr. Finney in the afternoon. Mr. Mahan was a preacher of no ordinary power.

It was natural that with such a concentration of religious forces here, with a predisposition on the part of the people to religious activity and inquiry, the religious life should have been always earnest and often intense. With a powerful sermon from President Mahan or Professor Morgan in the morning, not less than an hour, and an hour and a half of Mr. Finney's fervid eloquence in the afternoon, the Sabbath was an occasion of strong impressions and "great searchings of heart." Mr. Finney never preached but with a definite aim and a purpose of immediate results. There were times when his object was to present some doctrine or truth as a part of the gospel system ; but in the presentation he addressed himself to the audience before him with the intention of securing their acceptance of the doctrine. Oftener his aim was to stir up Christians to greater effort and fidelity, or to move the thoughtless and the worldly to undertake a life of duty and religion. If there was evidence of a solemn and profound impression upon the audience, he was accustomed to call for an open decision, on the part of those whom he particularly addressed, at times asking them to rise in their places in testimony of their purpose, or at other times to come forward to seats that were vacated for their occupancy. Sometimes a hundred, and even hundreds, responded to his appeal, coming forward and kneeling while he in prayer besought for them light and strength.

Such Sabbaths extended their influence to the daily thought and life, and induced a general religious activity rarely found. All the duties and possibilities of the Christian life were thoroughly considered, and outward and inward activity greatly stimulated. It was under such a pressure that the inquiry arose, as to the possibility of a life of full obedience or entire consecration to the will of God. The duty of such a life was granted by all, and the absolute possibility of it was involved in the New School theology, which maintained that ability was the condition of obligation.

The first attempt at a practical application of this principle to the Christian life was made by a few young men in the summer of 1836. They had formed a missionary circle, and held a weekly prayer-meeting to secure a better preparation for their chosen work. In conference upon the consecration needed and required, they were led, one after another, to promise the Lord, in prayer, not to grieve Him any more by sin; and they left the meeting with the feeling that they were pledged to a life of entire obedience to God, assuming that the Lord would afford deliverance in every time of need. It was a contemplation of a life of entire obedience, chiefly from the side of duty—the obligation and the possibility of it. The step which these young men supposed they had taken, attracted some attention in the community, and was met with disapprobation. Mr. Finney himself announced in a sermon that he would creep a hundred miles upon his hands and knees, to see a man who was living without sin. The young men went quietly on their way, making no profession, in public or private, as to their success in the life they had undertaken.

The same season a few numbers of *The Perfectionist*, published in New Haven, were circulated in the community, and while the doctrine they inculcated was in general disapproved, they seemed to stimulate inquiry. In the autumn of the same year, the entire community of citizens and students was profoundly moved in a religious quickening, and the chief burden of thought and of prayer was, a higher spiritual life, a more full consecration on the part of Christians. At one of the daily meetings a student arose and asked what Divine help he might expect, in his effort to live the Christian life. Did the Gospel contain provisions and promises, of which he might avail himself, sufficient to secure him from sin and enable him to stand under all temptations? President Mahan at once answered yes, and his answer served to fasten his own thought upon the subject, until he seemed to enter upon a new experience and a higher life. According to his own expression of it, it was coming out of darkness into light. Others were similarly wrought upon, and new experiences were received, until the idea became prevalent that there was a somewhat definite experience, open to all Christians, by which they could rise to a higher plane of living, and maintain unbroken communion with the Saviour. This experience was variously named "the blessing," "sanctification," "perfect love," "Christian perfection." The theory of the experience, so far as a theory was presented, was that it was a passing from a state of imperfect obedience to perfect obedience—perfect, not in the sense of freedom from mistakes and involuntary imperfections, but in freedom from voluntary failures, positive and present sin—a passing from partial to entire consecration.

The view was essentially that of the Wesleyan experience of perfect love, and biographies of Wesleyans were eagerly sought for, in which these experiences were portrayed, as of the Wesleys, Fletcher, Carvosso, Hester Ann Rogers, as well as the experiences of President and Mrs. Edwards and J. B. Taylor. Mr. Finney was about leaving for his winter in New York, but these new ideas went with him, and gave tone to his experience and his preaching there. Mr. Mahan's preaching was in the direction of this experience, and many were greatly moved by it.

The question of sanctification in the present life became very prominent, and the possibility of it was generally accepted. Those who entered into the special experience involved were comparatively few. Many others sought the experience, with more or less earnestness and anxiety. But the prevailing opinion probably was, that while the experience was genuine and valuable, it was not to be attained at will; and that true Christian wisdom dictated a life of fidelity and duty, and the acceptance of whatever experience should fall to one's lot. This certainly was true, that those who in the earlier part of the movement came into this special experience were often greatly and permanently quickened in their spiritual life, and acquired an energy and efficiency as Christian workers which had never before characterized them. To numbers of them it proved a life-long elevation of soul, a vision of spiritual realities that sustained them many a year. There was, on the part of these persons in general, no profession of sinlessness; but a humble acknowledgment of God's faithfulness to His promises, a constant joy in the Saviour as a present help in every time of need. It was inevitable that in such a movement there would be superficial imitations of the genuine experience—mere excitement of feeling, with no permanent result in character or life. Such cases must occur in all earnest and effective movements. There is the substance and the shadow, and the shadow is often the more showy.

As months and years passed on, the first impulse of the movement seemed in a measure to exhaust itself, and experiences became less intense. There was time, too, to examine more carefully the doctrinal force and relations of the experience itself; especially the idea that the ordinary Christian experience involved only a partial consecration, which in the higher experience, became entire consecration. This view was soon found to be unscriptural and unphilosophical. No partial consecration could be in any sense acceptable to God; nor indeed could such a partial consecration exist. The idea of the necessary simplicity of moral action became developed in the Oberlin theology, and the doctrine of sanctification was brought into harmony with this principle. It was found that the very beginning of the

Christian life involved entire consecration, and that the difference, in moral attitude, between the mature and the immature Christian, is in the continuity or permanency of obedience, and not in the heartiness or genuineness of obedience while it exists. This view of the case made no provision for the Christian passing from an unsanctified to a sanctified state, by a single act of faith, or by any special experience. All experience in the Christian life must tend to greater stability, but there is no clear dividing line between sanctified and unsanctified Christians; and there can be no experience which should be called sanctification, as distinguished from other experiences which precede or follow. Conversion is a turning from sin to holiness, and the subsequent work of the Christian is, to resist temptation, to return to obedience when he has fallen, and to become established in righteousness.

This view of Christian character was generally accepted by the leaders of thought at Oberlin, practically if not theoretically; and the doctrine of sanctification by special experience, gradually gave place to a presentation of the baptism of the Spirit as a condition of a more efficient and permanent Christian life.

At the height of the interest in these questions of Christian duty and the Christian life, near the close of 1838, *The Oberlin Evangelist* was established as an organ of communication with the Christian world, and soon attained a circulation of five thousand copies. It was a semi-monthly paper of eight quarto pages. The principal contributors to it were Profes-

sors Finney and Cowles, President Mahan and Professors Morgan and Thome.   An office editor was
employed, who received compensation.   The labor
of the other writers was entirely gratuitous, and
whatever income there might be, was devoted to the
educational work at Oberlin, chiefly in aid of young
men preparing for the ministry.   The publication of
The Evangelist was continued twenty-four years,
until, during the war, it failed for want of support.
Almost every number contained a sermon of Mr.
Finney, reported for the paper, often a letter from
him, and various other communications upon doctrine and duty.   The whole series of twenty-four
volumes embodies a large amount of valuable Christian literature, and in its day the paper commanded
a wide influence.

In 1845 the *Oberlin Quarterly Review* was established, with President Mahan and Professor Wm.
Cochran, and afterward Professor Finney, as editors.
The leading aim of the *Quarterly* was the more extended and thorough discussion of these questions
of doctrine and duty, and of others which occupied
public attention.   It was issued only four years, and
never secured an adequate support.

In such activities of thought and life, the community and the college were constantly exercised and
trained.   The regular work of the college was carried forward without material interruption, and the
colonists pushed forward the improvement of their
lands and the various enterprises of the community.
There were periods, oftener near the close of the
year before the winter vacation, when the religious

interest became deepened and intensified in connection with the Sabbath services, and almost spontaneously the people would gather upon the following day ; and thus the meetings would be continued from day to day, for a week or two, or even three, with a suspension of the ordinary work of the college, and of the community.   On one such occasion there was a beginning of some complaint on the part of a few students not in sympathy with the general feeling, that they were here to study, and not to attend meetings—that they were here on expense, and it was not reasonable that their work should be interrupted. The complaint would seem to have some foundation ; but Mr. Finney met it in a discourse in which he told them that the first thing they needed was to become reconciled to God ; that neither study nor anything else was of any account to them until this great question of life and duty was settled ; that Oberlin was founded by the servants of God for the promotion of His cause in the world, to prepare teachers and preachers for His service ; that the funds by which the college was sustained were given by Christian men for this purpose, and they had no right to avail themselves of these opportunities to prepare themselves for their own selfish and worldly schemes. He besought them to give their hearts to God, and no longer abuse His forbearance or the privileges afforded them by His people.   The appeal was overwhelming, and silenced if it did not satisfy.

With all this intensity of the religious life, the prevalent piety of the place was never ascetic, never noisy or demonstrative.   A general cheerfulness pervaded the community; and the broad culture which was encouraged and maintained, and the varied interests and occupations which engaged the attention of citizens and students, were incompatible with any narrow or extreme type of religious manifestation. There were, of course, instances of a self-centred and introspective pietism, but in general the spirit of the place was active, aggressive, practical, bringing everything to the test of reason, and experience and the Scriptures. Mr. Shipherd's idea of an isolated Christian community, by its very position sheltered from the influences of the world, was scarcely realized. Hundreds of young people from every part of the land were continually drawn in, and were again sent forth to find their place and their work in the world. The connections were too vital and wide-spread to permit the development of any very peculiar life.

CHAPTER V.

THE families first gathered at Oberlin were of the New England training and culture, and were thus inclined to the Congregational order in church arrangements. This was true also of Messrs. Shipherd and Stewart, the original founders. But all New England ministers, coming to the West in those days, connected themselves with the Presbytery under the "Plan of Union;" and all the churches organized among the New England emigrants of the Western Reserve, while Congregational in their internal constitution, maintained their outward fellowship through connection with Presbytery. Messrs. Mahan, Finney, and Morgan were Presbyterian in their church connections before coming to Oberlin, and had no special leaning to the Congregational order. The two brothers, Henry and John P. Cowles, were original Congregationalists, but Henry had been some years a pastor in Ohio, and was connected, as usual, with Presbytery. Nothing was farther from the thoughts of the founders than the idea of a new departure in ecclesiastical matters, or any action not in harmony with the established order and arrangements of the churches of the region.

The organization of the Oberlin church was begun

on the 3d of September, 1834, nearly a year and a half after the first colonists came upon the ground. The ministers present at the organization were John J. Shipherd; Seth H. Waldo, principal of the school; John Keyes, pastor of the church at Dover; J. H. Eells, pastor at Elyria; and Oliver Eastman, of Oberlin. The people assembled in the little school chapel, the only gathering place, at half-past ten in the morning, and listened to a sermon from the young Elyria pastor. In the afternoon sixty-one persons came forward with letters and credentials, and were approved as members. The completion of the organization was accomplished on the 13th of September, when those who had been approved " Resolved that those who are examined and accepted do now consider themselves as members, and that the church is legally and completely organized." At a preliminary meeting it had been voted that the name of the church should be " The Congregational Church of Christ at Oberlin."

The first act of the church after the vote of organization was to pass the following resolution : " Resolved, that this church apply to the Presbytery of Cleveland for admittance and membership, and that Bro. J. J. Shipherd represent this church in Presbytery, and that Bro. P. P. Pease accompany him as a delegate." A confession of faith had been adopted at the preliminary meeting, orthodox in the New England Calvinistic sense, setting forth the doctrines of God's existence and attributes, the Divine authority of the Scriptures, the Trinity, Divine Sovereignty, the Fall, Total Depravity, Atonement, Regeneration by the Holy Spirit, Election, Perseverance, and Free Agency. A missing leaf of the record has taken away the articles on the Ordinances of the Church, the Resurrection, and the Future Life, which undoubtedly belonged to the confession.

The church at once gave a unanimous call to Mr. Shipherd to become their pastor. After some delay, on account of pressing duties connected with the establishment of the college and the oversight of its interests, he accepted the charge, and, with some interruption from ill-health and his other duties, he held the position until June, 1836. He then tendered his resignation, giving as his reasons his poor health, which disqualified him for the work, and the fact that the Lord was calling him to the establishment of other schools which, like Oberlin, should aid in supplying laborers for the great field. This resignation was accepted, and Mr. Finney was called to take "temporary charge" of the church. The relationship was at length made permanent, and Mr. Finney continued pastor of the church, in connection with his professorship in the seminary, until 1872. Much of this time Professor Morgan was associated with him as his assistant.

In August of this year, 1836, the church appointed a delegation to meet with the representatives of other churches at Hudson, for the purpose of organizing a Congregational Association for the Western Reserve. The organization was consummated at an adjourned meeting held at Oberlin the following month, when there were present nine ministers and thirty-four lay delegates representing twenty

churches.   The Oberlin church at this time with-
drew from the Presbytery, and became connected
with the W. R. Association.   Only two Oberlin
ministers took part in forming the Asssociation—
President Mahan and Professor Jno. P. Cowles.
Others preferred to hold back with the purpose of
still maintaining fraternal relations with their Presbyterian brethren.   Professor Henry Cowles joined
the Association six years later, and Professors Finney
and Morgan eight years.

There is no record of the motive of the church in
this movement of separation from the Presbytery.
Those who united in forming the Association put
on record their purpose in the organization as follows :

1. "That this Association has originated in an
honest attachment to the principles of Congregation-
alism ; in a wish to carry out our Saviour's laws of
Christian union ; and in a regard for the welfare of
many churches, both on the Reserve and in the
region south of us, that have not been connected
with any ecclesiastical body, and have been waiting
for and desiring an organization of this sort."

2. "This Association entertain a high regard for
the Presbyterian ministers and churches on the Reserve, and would most cordially cherish their Christian fellowship ; and our movement in forming ourselves into a distinct organization has not originated
in any lack of confidence in those brethren, nor in
any wish to be dissociated from their communion."

Some months before this change of ecclesiastical
relations the church had appointed a committee to

revise the "articles of faith:" apparently not because of any change of theological opinion, or any serious dissent from the confession as it stood ; but there was in the church a growing sense of the importance of such an organization of the church that no Christian should be necessarily excluded from it. For a long time, apparently, no other church would be required on account of numbers, and it did not seem desirable that any subordinate difference of views should make another church necessary. The aim in the revision, therefore, was to secure a creed which should commend itself to all evangelical Christians. As the result of the deliberation the following articles were adopted, and have ever since stood as the confession of the church :

1. We believe that the Scriptures of the Old and New Testaments are given by inspiration of God, and are the only infallible rule of faith and practice.

2. We believe in one God, the Creator and Ruler of the Universe, existing in a Divine and incomprehensible Trinity, the Father, the Son Jesus Christ, and the Holy Ghost, each possessing all Divine perfections.

3. We believe in the fall of our first parents, and the consequent entire apostasy, depravity, and lost condition of the human race.

4. We believe in the incarnation, death, and atonement of the Son of God ; and that salvation is attained only through repentance and faith in His blood.

5. We believe in the necessity of a radical change

of heart, and that this is effected through the truth by the agency of the Holy Ghost.

6. We believe that the moral law is binding on all mankind as the rule of life, and that obedience to it is the proper evidence of a saving change.

7. We believe that credible evidence of a change of heart is an indispensable ground of admission to the privileges of the visible Church.

8. We believe that the ordinances of Baptism and the Lord's Supper, together with the Christian Sabbath, are of perpetual obligation in the church.

9. We believe in a future judgment, the endless happiness of the righteous, and the endless misery of the wicked.

There is testimony that the words "*the resurrection of the dead*" were omitted from the last article by a clerical error in entering it upon the record; but the article stands as it was recorded. For many years care was taken by the pastors, at every public reading of the Confession, to announce that it did not contain all that the church believed, but what was regarded as necessary to membership.

For twenty years and more this was the only church in Oberlin. At one time a Methodist class existed here, but there seemed to be no call from within the community itself for another church, until the members had so increased as to make the church unwieldy. Doubtless Mr. Finney's powerful ministry had much to do with this persistent unity. The church increased in numbers with the growth of the town and the college until it numbered probably twelve hundred resident members.

The first place of worship was the small upper room in Oberlin Hall, the first college building. In 1835 it became impossible to crowd the people into it, and Sabbath services were held in the new college boarding-hall, still in an unfinished state; and after it was completed the dining-hall was occupied as a place of meeting. The same year the "colony" united with the college in the building of Colonial Hall, with the arrangement that the first story should be finished as an audience-room, and be used as a college chapel, and audience-room for the church. This was completed in the spring of 1836, and furnished, closely packed, eight hundred sittings. For several years this provision was adequate to the demand; but at length the place became too strait, and in 1840–41, during the pleasant part of the year, a subsidiary service was held on Sunday in one of the lecture-rooms of the college—generally the laboratory or the music-hall. In the summers, of 1841 and 1842 the "Big Tent" was spread, on the north-east corner of the square, every Saturday afternoon, for the Sunday service. The labor involved was considerable, and the comfort of the place depended upon the weather. After much deliberation the church resolved to build a house, larger than the usual congregation required, sufficient to meet the necessities of commencement occasions. The walls were erected, and the building was inclosed in 1842, and the commencement was held in it, still unfinished, in 1843. The building was a great undertaking for the community at that time. The expense of building their homes and bringing their farms under cultivation still bore upon them, and no returns had as yet been received beyond the absolutely necessary cost of living. The professors were all in straitened circumstances, depending on precarious salaries. The students, with rare exceptions, were self-supporting. But the people had a mind to the work, and with a little aid from friends abroad, who were interested to help the college to a suitable place for the gatherings at commencement, the required amount, $12,000, was raised. At the time it was built it was as desirable an audience-room as any in the West, and it is difficult now to find a better. It furnishes permanent sittings for sixteen hundred persons, and can be made to accommodate five hundred more. It was thought to be larger than the ordinary uses of the church required, but this impression was soon done away. It was never too large. The house failed to receive a definite and formal dedication. It was occupied by the church at various times during the progress of the work, and as one part after another was completed, it was recognized with thanksgiving on the following Sabbath. Thus the work and the dedication went on together; and when the house was completed the people found themselves already domesticated there.

This was the church home for the Oberlin people as a whole for many years. No college church has ever been organized at Oberlin. It has been thought that it was better for all concerned that students and citizens should be associated in church relations; that with this arrangement they would better

FIRST CHURCH.

understand and appreciate each other, and the danger of hostile feeling between the college and the town would be avoided; that a more wholesome religious culture would thus be secured to the students, and a general interest in the progress of religion in the world be better maintained among them. The result has seemed to justify the plan.

There was naturally among the people at Oberlin a somewhat settled repugnance to the establishment of other churches here. This repugnance did not have its seat in denominationalism, for this was comparatively weak among the people; but rather in the feeling or conviction that church unity was important to the prosperity of the enterprise. There was more or less anxiety among the different denominations round about that this vacant territory should be occupied. A town of two or three thousand people, with only a single church, was in some quarters regarded as proof of a destitution of religious privileges. Our friends of the Protestant Episcopal Church seemed to be the first to awake to the necessities of the situation; and the voice of a missionary was soon heard in the Eastern churches setting forth the call for the establishment of gospel institutions in Oberlin. The Episcopal Church was organized in the year 1855, and was received with a degree of hospitality, in spite of the repugnance to the division of the church interest. When Bishop McIlvaine first came to look after his little flock, the Oberlin First Church was opened to him, and he held the service there with his people.

When once the line was broken, other church organizations soon followed: the Methodist Episcopal, the Baptist, and a Methodist Church for the colored people—all organized between 1866 and 1869.

The congregation of the old church was still very large, and it was difficult for new families to find comfortable seats in the house, or to make themselves fully at home among so many. After full deliberation it was voted by the church, with only one dissenting voice, to encourage a part of the church to withdraw and organize a Second Congregational Church. This was done in the spring of 1860; and the new church, taking about one hundred members the first year from the old church, set up for itself, holding its services in the college chapel. Those who volunteered for the new enterprise were dismissed with a benediction, and only fraternal feelings have ever existed between the two churches.

Up to this time there had been no pastor in the old church exclusively devoted to the work of the church. Mr. Finney and his assistants held professorships in the college.

The Second Church after a few months called a pastor, Rev. M. W. Fairfield, to give himself exclusively to the work. He remained four years, when the church returned to the old habit of employing the professors, which continued until February, 1876, when Rev. Wm. Kincaid was called, and filled the position until 1882, when failing health compelled him to retire.

Mr. Finney resigned the pastorate of the First Church in 1872, and Rev. James Brand was called in 1873, and still continues in the work. The First and Second churches have been about equally prospered as to numbers, reporting 870 and 624 respectively in the Year-book for 1883.

The war coming on soon after the organization of the Second Church, absorbed all the means and energy of the people, so that, for six or seven years, nothing was done toward building a house. In the autumn of 1870 the Second Church was dedicated. The audience-room furnishes eleven hundred sittings, and in the basement are the Sunday-school room, prayer-room, and parlors.

The other churches of the place all have comfortable houses, so that the church destitution of the early days has passed away. There is work and room for all; and it would be difficult to find a community in which the different denominations have a better understanding with each other, or are more ready for all reasonable co-operation. The colored church came into existence, not because the colored people were not welcomed to all the churches, nor because a separate organization was desired by those who had been most favored with education and culture, but because considerable numbers of them felt more at home with a style of service and instruction more like that with which they had been familiar from their childhood.

The college is not organically denominational. It has no connection with any ecclesiastical organization. The trustees invite the State Congregational Associations of Ohio and Michigan to send visitors annually to the theological seminary. The board of trustees is a self-perpetuating body, and there is nothing in the charter, nor even in the by-laws, limiting the choice of trustees in any respect whatsoever. The nine corporators named in the charter, as granted by the Legislature, were pastors and members of churches under the Plan of Union, a considerable portion of them decidedly Presbyterian in their leanings. Of their successors the majority have been Congregationalists; but there have always been members of the Board who were connected with other denominations. There is no regulation requiring that professors and instructors shall have any church connections whatever. There is no creed to which theological professors even are required to assent in their inauguration. All these things regulate themselves under the organic forces that have controlled the movement; and no embarrassment, no question even, has ever arisen upon the subject. The college is Congregational, not because of the definite purpose of the founders, or of any of the earlier framers of its polity, but because the seed that was planted thus grew. For the first two years it seemed an even question under what influences it would at length develop. If the surrounding Presbyterianism had been able to welcome the new enterprise, Oberlin might have been Presbyterian.

The students of the college determine for themselves with what church they will worship; but they are required to make a selection, and to attend that church continuously for a term.

POLITICAL ACTION.

The early inhabitants of Oberlin, those who came as colonists, were New Englanders, immediately or remotely, and hence were members of the Whig party. There was probably no exception to this rule. The Whig party, as they knew it, was the party of order and progress and intelligence, and they felt it almost as necessary to be Whigs as to be Christians. People of other views in politics soon appeared, but they were not of the original stock. Until 1837 nothing occurred to indicate that the people of Oberlin would ever do anything else than vote the respectable Whig ticket. They had become abolitionized, but they were just as good Whigs as ever. In the autumn of that year there was an election in the county for representative to the State Legislature. The day before the election a report was circulated in Oberlin that the Whig candidate was not careful in his observance of the Sabbath. A spontaneous gathering of the voters was held, and Mr. Finney and others were invited to give their suggestions as to the duty of the hour. The result was that a large proportion of the Oberlin voters "threw away their votes." The two parties were closely balanced in the county, and the Oberlin vote turned the scale. The next evening, as the returns came in at Elyria, the county seat, the shouters of the two parties were drawn up on opposite sides of the square, and the returns were cried out from the court-house steps. The balance inclined now in one direction, and now in the other; but the Whigs were full of hope until the returns came in from Russia township, which contained the village of Oberlin. These returns threw their whole calculation out of balance, and the Whigs retired in disgust. It was currently reported on the streets that a dozen men volunteered, and teams were offered, to go to Oberlin and "tar and feather Mr. Finney." Probably a sober second thought suggested that the proceeding would scarcely be in keeping with the claims of the party of law and order. They never appeared at Oberlin. From this time Oberlin was reckoned an uncertain quantity in the matter of political action. The antislavery question began to have a practical bearing both in state and general politics; and the Oberlin vote could always be depended on where it would tell against the pro-slavery attitude of the government. If "black laws" for the state of Ohio were in question, the representative from Lorain County had before his eyes the Oberlin vote, which still turned the scale in the county. The time came at length when three men in the Legislature—of whom the representative from Lorain, Dr. N. S. Townshend, a trustee of Oberlin College, was one—held the balance of power between the two parties, and sent Salmon P. Chase to the Senate of the United States. Thus the antislavery sentiment of the Oberlin people became an active force in politics. At the Presidential election in 1840, a Liberty candidate for the Presidency was put forward, and the majority of the people of Oberlin voted for him. There was some

division of sentiment at this time—a portion of the
people still hoping for antislavery action from the
Whig party. In 1844 almost the entire Oberlin vote
was cast for the candidate of the Liberty party,
James G. Birney. In 1848 there was still some dis-
traction, but a large majority voted for Van Buren,
the Free Soil candidate, and afterward the Oberlin
vote was with the Republican party. It will thus
appear that the aim at Oberlin in the matter of political action has always been practical. The men
voted for were not always satisfactory representatives of the Oberlin sentiment, but they occupied
such a position that a vote for them would bear
most directly upon the great end. Those who
claimed to be, during these years, the true, radical,
abolitionists, were either not voting at all, like the
followers of Mr. Garrison, or were voting for Gerrit
Smith, because he was right on all questions pertaining to slavery. The people at Oberlin voted for Van
Buren, for Fremont, for Lincoln, because these men
represented a movement which bore directly upon
the power and extension of slavery in the land.

There were other things to be done at Oberlin, in
an antislavery way, besides the use of the ballot.
The decision to receive colored students, made when
there was no such student probably within a hundred miles, soon brought forth results. The first
colored student was James Bradley, from Cincinnati,
who followed the Lane Seminary students to Oberlin. Others soon came, but not in large numbers.
From 1840 to 1860 the proportion of colored students was four or five per cent. Soon after the war

the ratio rose to seven or eight per cent, but has fallen again to five or six in a hundred. No adaptation of the course of study to the special needs of colored pupils was ever made. It was not a colored school that was proposed, but a school where colored students should have equal privileges with others. No record of colored students has been kept distinct from the general record. No distinctive mark appears in the catalogues. The only reliance for the past is the knowledge and memory of instructors and others.

Among the 20,000 different pupils that have been in attendance from the beginning probably 1000 have been colored. Sixty have completed a course —thirty-two young men and twenty-eight young women. Some of these were brilliant scholars, some have attained to distinction, and most are occupying positions of usefulness in the land.

The chief benefit of the open door for the colored people at Oberlin, however, has probably not been in this direct result, nor even in the indirect effect in opening other schools in a similar way. These results are important, but above all there is the reaction of the arrangement upon the large number of young people who have received their education, more or less, at Oberlin. These came from all parts of the land, and scattered as widely when they left. It mattered little what were their views on slavery, or their feelings toward the colored people, when they came. They might at first look scornfully on the colored fellow-student, but soon a kindly feeling grew upon them, and they became friends of the colored people, and champions of their rights; and thus the anti-slavery influence was diffused. It is probable that the arrangement was more important to the white students than to the colored. The great question of the times arrested their attention, and they became settled in their attitude and action in regard to it. A single colored student in each class, unconsciously to himself, accomplished the work. He stood there in his own right, "a man and a brother," more effective than all the antislavery sermons that Oberlin could have brought to bear. No such sermons were called for. Every student was left to determine for himself whether he would recognize his colored fellow-pupil. Nothing in this respect was required of him. He was not permitted to abuse him, and that was the limit of the obligation imposed. Classes were never seated alphabetically in the recitation-room or in the chapel; hence no one was required to sit next a colored student. He must consent to be in the same class with him, or forego the opportunities of the school; but to this he had made up his mind when he came. No difficulties in discipline, so far as is remembered, ever arose from the arrangement. In a few rare instances a colored and a white boy have had a quarrel, and occasionally a colored student has imagined that some disrespect was shown him by a fellow-student; but in general each one has found the place that belonged to him, in the regard of his fellows, irrespective of color.

The same action which brought colored students to the school, brought colored families to the town to find their homes. At first, some of the more properous of the free colored people of the Slave States came in to secure privileges for themselves and their children. Some of the more enterprising of the slaves at length heard of Oberlin, and crept in stealthily to see whether what they had heard was true. Some of these found courage to remain, and thus the colored element gradually increased until it has become a fifth part of the population. There are among the colored people several prosperous business men and successful mechanics. A larger portion are day laborers. They are a quiet and peaceable people in general, anxious for education for their children, and on the whole gradually improving.

Oberlin was, of course, an important station on the Underground Railroad; and a volume might be written of incidents and experiences, pathetic, amusing, and exciting, which befell the people in meeting their responsibilities in regard to this business. The fugitives who came through Oberlin were generally shipped for Canada, at some neighboring port on the Lake, between Cleveland and Sandusky. There were captains of sailing vessels and steamers, many of them, who, it was well understood, would never observe when a group of timid fugitives crept aboard their ships, and hid themselves away in some dark corner; and there were men at all these ports ready to despatch a trusty messenger to Oberlin when such a ship came in. It was a convenience in the transaction of the business that it mattered little to what port in Canada the vessel was bound. The emigrants could be dropped at any point between Windsor and the Welland Canal, to their entire satisfaction. It was free soil they were in pursuit of, and it was of no account what other qualities the soil possessed. If it yielded no fetters nor masters, it was the soil for them. Some of these fugitives found themselves so comfortable at Oberlin, that they lingered here, and made a permanent home. There was risk in this, and it was not generally encouraged. But there were always numbers of this class among the colored people, and the appearance of a suspected slave-catcher in the community produced consternation. Every device for concealing fugitives was resorted to ; every movement for transporting them to the point of embarka- was carefully planned. Sometimes the ruse was adopted of starting off a load of pretended fugitives toward the Lake, with great show of carefulness, while the real fugitives were quietly taken away in another direction. In one instance a student escorted a colored man, attired and veiled as a woman, on horseback, across the country to Huron.

It was not regarded as legitimate to go into the Slave States and entice the slaves from their masters; not because of scruples in regard to the master's real ownership, but because it would be a reckless undertaking, involving too much risk, and probably doing more harm than good. One person, Calvin Fairbanks, went from Oberlin to Kentucky for this purpose, in 1845, against the remonstrance of several who knew his intention. He soon found himself in the penitentiary, and served out a term of eleven years. There was abundant sympathy for

him, but no approval of his undertaking. Another, George Thompson, who had been a student
at Oberlin, but was at the time a member of Mission
Institute at Quincy, Ill., for an effort to aid a slave
to escape from Missouri, served a term of five years,
with two companions, in the Missouri Penitentiary.
Not to deliver to his master the servant that had
escaped from his master, seemed to the people of
Oberlin a solemn and pressing duty. This attitude
exposed the college and the community to much
reproach, and sometimes apparently to serious danger. Threats came from abroad that the college
buildings should be burned. A Democratic Legislature, at different times, agitated the question of
repealing the college charter. The fourth and last
attempt was made in 1843, when the bill for repeal
was indefinitely postponed in the House, by a vote
of thirty-six to twenty-nine.

The people in neighboring towns were, at the
outset, not in sympathy with Oberlin in its antislavery position. They agreed with the rest of the
world in regarding it as unmitigated fanaticism.
The feeling was often bitter and intense, and an
Oberlin man going out from home in any direction
was liable to be assailed with bitter words ; and if
he ventured to lecture upon the unpopular theme,
he was fortunate if he encountered words only. Of
course the self-respectful part of the community
would take no part in such abuse, but fellows of the
baser sort felt themselves sustained by the common
feeling. On the Middle Ridge road, six miles north
of Oberlin, a guide-board put up by the authorities,

stood for years, pointing the way to Oberlin, not by the ordinary index finger, but by the full length fig-ure of a fugitive running with all his might to reach the place. The tavern sign, four miles east, was ornamented, on its Oberlin face, with the representa-tion of a fugitive slave pursued by a tiger. Where the general feeling yielded such results, not much could be expected in the way of sympathy for the fugitives. But even among these people the slave-catcher had little favor. They would thwart his pursuit in every way, and shelter the fugitive if they could. Only the meanest and most mercenary could be hired to betray the victim. Now and then an official felt called upon to extend aid and comfort to the slave-hunter who claimed his service, but he could expect no toleration from his neighbors in such a course. A whole neighborhood would sud-denly find themselves abolitionists upon the appear-ance of a slave-hunter among them; and by repeated occurrences of this kind, as much as by any other means, Lorain County, and all Northern Ohio, be-came at length intensely antislavery in feeling and action.

It was not often that a slave was seized in Oberlin, and no one, during all the dark years, was ever carried back to bondage. Violent resistance, in the form of personal assault upon the kidnapper, was not encour-aged, and no instance of bloodshed or personal harm ever occurred; but the people would rally in a mass and hinder the captor from proceeding with his vic-tim, and oblige him to exhibit his authority, and repair at once to the nearest court to establish the

legality of his proceedings. Often the illegality of
the process was so marked that the slaves would be
at once discharged ; and once discharged, they were
soon beyond danger.

In the spring of 1841 an arrest took place, one
Friday evening, at a house then standing in the
forest one mile east of the centre. Some public
meeting was in progress in the college chapel when
the alarm reached town. A committee of citizens
and students was appointed to follow the kidnap-
pers, and do whatever could be legally done to rescue the two victims, a man and his wife, from their
clutches. The people turned out in committee of
the whole, entirely unarmed, and without definite
thought as to what could be done. They overtook
the company on the State road, two or three miles
south-east of the village, and effectually interrupted
their progress for the night. In the morning the
slave-claimants were induced to go to Elyria and
have their process reviewed in court. Their papers
were found to be irregular, and the two fugitives
were placed in jail until the claimants could return
to Kentucky and obtain the required evidence. At
the same time a warrant was served upon the claimants for assault and battery with deadly weapons,
and threats of violence toward members of the family that had sheltered the fugitives, and they were
bound over to appear in the same court in their own
defence. Before the day of trial came, one of the
two received a summons to appear before the Judge
of all the earth. The other returned sad and de-
jected to the twofold trial, to find that the slaves

had broken jail and escaped. The Kentuckian, too, was released without trial. It did not appear that any force from without had been used in behalf of the slaves. A basket-maker in the jail had been furnished by the jailer with the implements of his trade with which he opened a way for himself, and the others followed.

Under the notorious fugitive-slave law of 1850, a case of attempted recovery of a fugitive occurred in September, 1858. The case appeared in the U. S. Circuit Court at Cleveland the following spring, and excited much interest in the country as the " Oberlin-Wellington Rescue Case." It was nearly the last instance of an attempt to execute the fugitive slave law in Northern Ohio, as well as in the country. John Brown came a few months later, then Lincoln and Sumter and emancipation. A young black man, John Price, supposed to be a fugitive from Kentucky, had been some months at Oberlin, when a group of four strangers came into town and took up their quarters at an obscure tavern where they would attract little attention, and where, if at all, they would find some sympathy with their undertaking. About four miles from town they found a man ready to afford them advice, and with a young son of this man, about thirteen years of age, they laid a plot for the seizure of John. The scheme was arranged on Sunday, and Monday morning the boy came into town with a horse and buggy, looked up John, and offered him large wages to go with him into the country a mile or two to dig potatoes. A mile or more out of town, as they were driving very leisurely, they were overtaken by a carriage containing one of the parties from Kentucky and two others, a deputy U. S. marshal and a deputy sheriff from Columbus, O. Two of these men stepped out, seized John, hurried him, with threats and a show of weapons, into their carriage, and took the diagonal road, two miles east of Oberlin, which leads to Wellington, nine miles south. At Wellington they would soon find a train for Columbus and Cincinnati. For this treachery the boy, as he afterward testified in court, was paid twenty dollars.

Two men coming from Pittsfield met the carriage which was bearing John away, and reported the fact in town. Some of the colored people had had suspicions and alarms the previous week, on account of inquiries made, and were ready at once to accept the idea that John had been carried off. The news spread through the town, and under a common impulse, without concerted action, large numbers of the people, white and colored, citizens and students, were soon on the road to Wellington. Every form of conveyance was pressed into service, and probably two or three hundred people in all went from Oberlin to Wellington that afternoon. Others fell in along the way, and Wellington furnished its share of the crowd. John and his captors, the two officers from Columbus and the two men from Kentucky, were waiting at the hotel for the first train going south. The crowd soon swarmed about the house, and John was taken to a room in the garret for safe-keeping. Quite a number of guns appeared in the crowd—some of the witnesses

in court put the number as high as fifty ; one of the
Kentuckians estimated it at five hundred. No gun
was fired, and it is not certain that one was loaded.
The crowd acted without concert and had no leader,
but persistently kept their place around the house,
and filled the rooms below and above. They were
not harmonious in their views of what ought to be
done ; the more conservative were disposed to ascertain that the proceedings had been regular under
the fugitive-slave law, and on that condition to allow the party to go on its way. The larger portion
probably had no respect for the infamous law, and
held it their duty to rescue John, whatever the authority by which he was held. No one seemed to
take responsibility on one side or on the other.
Different persons, among them a magistrate and a
lawyer of Wellington, were shown the warrant in
the hands of the marshal for the arrest of John, and
this warrant was read to the crowd ; but it brought
no relief. The train for the south passed, but did
not take John and his captors. Finally, near sun-
set, a little group that had gathered about John in
the upper room started him down the stairs, and
the crowd passed him on to a buggy standing near,
lifted him in, and the buggy was driven rapidly
toward Oberlin. John found refuge in Oberlin two
or three days, and was then sent on to Canada. It
was a flagrant case of resistance to the execution of
the fugitive law ; and if it were allowed to pass
without serious animadversion, the law, which was
supposed to be vital to the maintenance of the
Union, would fall. The machinery of the govern-

ment was set in motion, and a trial in the United States Court at Cleveland was determined on. Judge Willson brought the case before the grand jury in an elaborate charge, from which the following is an extract:

" There are some who oppose the execution of this law from a declared sense of conscientious duty. There is, in fact, a sentiment prevalent in the community which arrogates to human conduct a standard of right above, and independent of, human laws; and it makes the conscience of each individual in society the test of his own accountability to the laws of the land.

" While those who cherish this dogma claim and enjoy the protection of the law for their own life and property, they are unwilling that the law should be operative for the protection of the constitutional rights of others. It is a sentiment semi-religious in its development, and is almost invariably characterized by intolerance and bigotry. The leaders of those who acknowledge its obligations and advocate its sanctity are like the subtle prelates of the dark ages. They are versed in all they consider useful and sanctified learning. Trained in certain schools in New England to manage words, they are equally successful in the social circle to manage hearts; seldom superstitious themselves, yet skilled in practising upon the superstition and credulity of others— false, as it is natural a man should be whose dogmas impose upon all who are not saints according to his creed the necessity of being hypocrites; selfish, as it is natural a man should be who claims for himself the benefits of the law and the right to violate it, thereby denying its protection to others. . . .

"Gentlemen, this sentiment should find no place or favor in the grand-jury room. . . . The fugitive-slave law may, and unquestionably does, contain provisions repugnant to the moral sense of many good and conscientious people; nevertheless, it is the law of the United States, and as such should be recognized and executed by our courts and juries, until abrogated or otherwise changed by the legislative department of the government."

This is a favorable specimen of the manner in which the doctrine of "the higher law" was dealt with in those days. A ruder statement of the same idea was made by Judge Leavitt, of Cincinnati, the same year. In a charge to the jury he said: "Christian charity was not within the meaning or intent of the fugitive-slave law, and it would not, therefore, answer as a defence for violating the law."

The grand jury, moved by this charge, made out thirty-seven indictments against twenty-four citizens of Oberlin and thirteen of Wellington. Among the Oberlin men were Prof. H. E. Peck, of the College Faculty; J. M. Fitch, superintendent of the large Oberlin Sunday-school; Ralph Plumb, a lawyer; and other prominent citizens and students, good men and true. Among the men from Wellington were several of their leading citizens, pioneers of the town, and pillars in society.

The same day, Marshal Johnson appeared in Oberlin to arrest these violators of law. He called first on Professor Peck and made known his errand, and asked of him the favor of an introduction to the other parties. He accepted from each one the promise to appear at Cleveland in court the next day. According to promise, these men appeared in court Dec. 7th, and asked for immediate trial, but at the instance of the prosecuting attorney the case was adjourned first to March 8th, and again to April 5th. The defendants declined to give bail, and were sent away upon their own recognizance of $1000 each. On the 5th of April the trial commenced, and continued with slight interruptions until the middle of May, when the cases were put over until the July term. At this time two of the alleged rescuers, Simeon Bushnell, a white man, and Charles H. Langston, a colored man, had been convicted and sentenced. Messrs. Spalding, Riddle and Griswold, prominent lawyers of Cleveland, had volunteered to conduct the case for the defence without charge. They had done their work with great ability, but the conviction seemed a foregone conclusion. Bushnell was sentenced to sixty days' imprisonment, a fine of six hundred dollars and costs of prosecution—understood to be about two thousand more. Langston, when asked if he had anything to say for himself, made a manly and eloquent address, which thrilled the court and indeed the country. The closing paragraph was as follows:

" But I stand up here to say, that if, for doing what I did that day at Wellington, I am to go in jail six months, and pay a fine of a thousand dollars, according to the fugitive-slave law, and such is the protection the laws of this country afford me, I must take upon myself the responsibility of self-protection; and when I come to be claimed by some perjured wretch as his slave, I shall never be taken into slavery. And as in that trying hour I would have others do to me; as I would call upon others to help me; as I would call upon you, your Honor, to help me; as I would call upon you, [to the district attorney], and upon you [to the counsel for prosecution] and upon you [to his own counsel], *so help me* GOD! I stand here to say that I will do all I can for any man thus seized and held, though the inevitable penalty of six months' imprisonment and one thousand dollars' fine for each offence hangs over me. We have a common humanity. You would do so; your manhood would require it: and, no matter what the laws might be, you would honor yourself for doing it; your friends would honor you for doing it; your children to all generations would honor you for doing it; and every good and honest man would say you had done right."

The court seemed impressed by this appeal, and sentenced Langston to a fine of only one hundred dollars and twenty days' imprisonment, with costs of prosecution.

In pronouncing the sentence upon Bushnell the judge indulged in various arguments in support of the action of the court, of which the following is a specimen:

" A man of your intelligence must know that if the standard of right is placed above and against the laws of the land, those who act up to it are anything

else than good citizens and good Christians. You
must know that when a man acts upon any system
of morals or theology which teaches him to disregard
and violate the laws of the government that protects
him in life and property, his conduct is as criminal as
his example is dangerous."

This is an illustration of the logic and the spirit in
which the fugitive-slave law was defended in those
days. It would be admitted that there might be a
conflict between this law and the law of God, and
then the principle was boldly announced that man's
law was to be obeyed rather than God's.

The political aspect of the trial was very distinct.
The judge, the prosecuting attorney and assisting
counsel, and every member of the jury in Bushnell's
case belonged to the party of the administration,
while every one of the defendants and their counsel
were of the opposition.

At the close of Langston's trial, when the cases
were to be deferred from the middle of May to the
July term, several of the indicted from Wellington
entered a plea of *nolle contendere*, and were sentenced to pay a fine of twenty dollars each and costs
of prosecution, and to remain in jail twenty-four
hours. One old man from Wellington was almost
entreated to leave the jail and go home. He at
length consented. Thus all that remained, including
the two convicted parties, were fourteen Oberlin
men. These had been in jail since April 15th, and
were to continue in jail through the recess of court.
—two long summer months, and how much longer
no one could foresee. They continued in jail upon a

CLEVELAND JAIL.

point of honor. At the beginning of the trial they had been allowed to come and go upon their recognizance, giving their personal pledge for appearance when called for. At the conclusion of Bushnell's trial there was a ruling of the court so unjust, that they gave notice that they would dismiss their counsel, call no witnesses, and make no defence; and their counsel approved their decision. Thereupon the prosecuting attorney demanded that they should be taken into custody, and they were taken in charge by the marshal, and declining to give bail they were committed to jail. The unjust ruling was afterwards recalled in fact, and they were notified that their own recognizance would be accepted as before; but a false record had been made—a record which put the defendants in the wrong, and the court refused to correct it. They therefore declined to renew their recognizance or to give bail, and therefore they lay in jail from the 15th of April on. The sheriff to whom they were committed, and the jailer, and indeed a large portion of the people of Cleveland, were their warm friends, and in hearty sympathy with their course.

During the recess of court an attempt was made to obtain relief by an appeal to the State courts. A writ of *habeas corpus* was granted by one of the judges of the Supreme Court, commanding the sheriff to bring Bushnell and Langston before the court, that the reason of their imprisonment might be considered. The case was ably argued before the full bench, at Columbus, for a week; but the court, three to two, declined to grant a release.

This was a severe blow to the men in jail. They had counted with much confidence upon relief from that quarter. It is idle to speculate upon possible results, if a single judge had held a different opinion. Salmon P. Chase was governor at that time, and it was well understood that he would sustain a decision releasing the prisoners, by all the power at his command; and the United States Government was as fully committed to the execution of the fugitive-slave law. This would have placed Ohio in conflict with the general government in defence of State rights, and if the party of freedom throughout the North had rallied, as seemed probable, the war might have come in 1859 instead of 1861, with a secession of the Northern instead of the Southern States. A single vote apparently turned the scale; and after a little delay the party of freedom took possession of the government, and the party of slavery became the seceders. Of course those who urged Ohio tо the conflict did not anticipate war with the general government. They expected the general government to retire from the execution of the fugitive-slave law, and thus remove the occasion of the conflict.

During this recess of court, on the 24th of May, a mass meeting was convened in Cleveland, gathering the people of Northern Ohio by thousands, to express their sympathy with the rescuers, and their intense condemnation of the fugitive-slave law. There was great enthusiasm—an immense procession with banners passing through the streets, and around the square, and in front of the jail. The crowds were addressed by Joshua R. Giddings and

Salmon P. Chase, with other distinguished men. Mr. Giddings was bold and defiant:

"I have no hesitation as to the means for acting upon this great matter which is now before us. I would have a committee appointed to-day to apply to the first and nearest officer who has the power, that he shall issue a writ for the release of those prisoners, and I want to be appointed on that committee, and if so I will promise you that no sleep shall come to my eyelids this night until I have used my utmost endeavors to have these men released. I will, if such a committee be appointed, apply to Judge Tilden [at his side], and if he flinched in the exercise of his duty, and refused to issue this writ, I would never speak to him again, or give him my hand. If he failed I would go to another and another, until death came to close my eyelids. I know that the Democratic press throughout the country has represented me as counselling forcible resistance to this law, and God knows it is the first truth they have ever told about me."

Governor Chase was more wary and circumspect, with a sense of immediate responsibility:

"If the process for the release of any prisoner should issue from the courts of the State, he was free to say that so long as Ohio was a sovereign State that process should be executed. He did not counsel revolutionary measures, but when his time came and his duty was plain, he, as the Governor of Ohio, would meet it as a man."

The resolutions adopted by the meeting were decided and radical, and, read at this day, sound as if

they had emanated from some State-rights convention.   The last scene was a gathering of the crowds
around the jail yard, to listen to brief addresses from
Messrs. Langston, Peck, Fitch, and Plumb in behalf
of the prisoners.   Their words were earnest and determined, without railing or bitterness.   The meeting yielded no immediate result in behalf of the
prisoners, and no such result was anticipated.   It
amounted to a notice that the fugitive-slave law was
to be no farther executed in Northern Ohio.

The rescuers, after this, settled down to prison
life, without any distinct anticipation when or how
the end was to come.   Some of them were mechanics, of various crafts, and their friends furnished
them the tools and materials for prosecuting their
business.   Two of them were printers, and a print-
ing-office was soon established in the jail, and a paper
named the "The Rescuer" was issued.   Five thousand copies of the first number were sent out, and it
was promised every alternate Monday.   The two
students in the group were furnished with books,
and set themselves to the work of their classes.
Visitors from all parts of the land came to the jail,
and letters of sympathy and funds to meet expenses
poured in upon them.

One of the most interesting occasions at the jail
was a visit of four hundred Sabbath-school children from Oberlin—the school of which Mr. Fitch
had been superintendent sixteen years.   They were
invited and entertained by the Sabbath-school of
the Plymouth Church, Cleveland; then they filed
into the jail, filling all its corridors and open spaces,

and an hour was given to brief addresses from their superintendent and others, with music interspersed. This was on the 2d of July. Four days later, the jail doors opened and the rescuers came forth, and were escorted with jubilations to their homes.

The occasion of the release was this : The four men who were engaged in the seizure of John at Oberlin had been indicted in Lorain County for kidnapping, and their trial was set for the 6th of July, six days before the resumption of the trials in the U. S. court at Cleveland. The indictment was not without apparent foundation. The description given of John, in the power of attorney under which the seizure was made, was grossly deficient and in-accurate, and there was no sufficient proof of title to John in the claimant who issued the power of attor-ney. These indicted men were abroad on bail until near the time of trial at Elyria. Then a writ of *habeas corpus* was obtained from a judge of the U. S. court, and an attempt was made to deliver up the four men to the sheriff of Lorain County, that the writ might be served upon him, and his prisoners be released by order of the U. S. judge. An accumulation of hindrances prevented this delivery, and the hour of trial was just at hand when the writ would be useless. The men were alarmed. They interceded with the U. S. attorney to propose to the counsel for the rescuers that the suits on both sides should be dropped. To this the rescuers consented. The marshal went to the jail and announced that they were free. They were escorted from the prison to the train by several hundred of the citizens of

Cleveland, to the music of Hecker's band, while a hundred guns were fired on the square. The last tune from the band as the train started was " Home, Sweet Home." The *Plain Dealer* of that evening announced the result with great disgust: " So the government has been beaten at last, with law, justice, and facts all on its side, and Oberlin, with its rebellious, higher law creed, is triumphant."

At Oberlin the rescuers were met at the station by the whole mass of the people, and escorted to the great church, where for hours, until midnight, the pent-up feeling of the people found expression in song and prayer, and familiar talk over the experiences of the preceding weeks. It was a costly price to pay, but it secured to Oberlin, from that time on, freedom from the incursions of the slave-catcher, and Northern Ohio largely shared in the immunity.

CHAPTER VI.

EARLY MISSIONARY ACTIVITY.

OBERLIN was itself a missionary enterprise. It was the purpose to carry the Gospel to the regions beyond that had brought Mr. and Mrs. Shipherd, under appointment from the American Home Missionary Society, to the regions of Northern Ohio. Mr. and Mrs. Stewart had been engaged for years as missionaries among the Choctaws in the State of Mississippi, and, while resting from those labors for the recovery of health, they pledged themselves for five years to the work of laying the foundations at Oberlin, without any compensation but food and clothing. The families that came to find their homes in the wilderness had no visions of improved outward circumstances and growing wealth. They came to aid in establishing a community and an institution which should contribute to the evangelization of the Mississippi valley —then the " New West." The students, for the most part, came with the same purpose, their hearts full of the earnest impulses which had been begotten in the great revival movement of those years. One of the earliest associations organized among the students was a Missionary Society, embracing such as contemplated a life-work in the foreign field.

The first among the students to enter upon missionary service was Miss Angeline Tenney, who married Mr. S. N. Castle, a missionary of the American Board, and went to the Sandwich Islands, in 1836. But from this time on, for many years, the earnest antislavery feeling on the part of Oberlin students, and the somewhat dubious attitude of the American Board on the subject of slavery, combined to prevent men and women from Oberlin receiving appointments from the Board. The distrust seemed to be mutual. The conservative fathers at the East looked with apprehension upon what seemed to them, in the distance, the religious and reformatory fanaticism of Oberlin, and wisely, as they thought, concluded not to open the way for its extension to their field. An Oberlin young woman was now and then sent out, without objection, as the wife of a missionary, whose only connection with Oberlin was by marriage. There were two or three instances of young men, with sufficient conservative endorsement, receiving appointments from the Board. But in general Oberlin students were disinclined to seek such appointments, although there was at that time no other missionary organization to which they could look for support. The church at Oberlin, with rare individual exceptions, did not contribute to the funds of the American Board, but found other channels for their missionary gifts, until the Board attained a more satisfactory attitude on the subject of slavery.

Under these conditions the idea of self-sustaining missions was very generally favored, and a large amount of independent missionary work was accomplished. Much of this, very naturally, was expended among the colored people, at home and abroad. Teachers of colored schools went to Cincinnati, and to other towns of Ohio, where the colored people were found in sufficient numbers to call for such services—sometimes encouraged by the promise of aid from some philanthropic person in the neighborhood, often without compensation except the little that the colored people themselves could afford. Missionaries and teachers in considerable numbers went to the colored fugitives in Canada, led by Hiram Wilson, of the Theological Class of 1836, one of the Lane Seminary men. Funds were raised among the antislavery people of Ohio, and at the East, to sustain this Canada mission.

In the winter of 1836–7, David S. Ingraham, another of the Lane students, finding it necessary for his health to seek a warmer climate, went to Havana, Cuba. He was a skilful mechanic, and finding that he could sustain himself there without difficulty, he conceived the idea of establishing a self-supporting mission among the colored people of Jamaica, recently emancipated. He returned to Oberlin, was ordained as a missionary, and in the autumn of 1837, with his wife and several other recruits to the mission, he left for Jamaica. Thus the American mission to the freed people of Jamaica was established. Other Oberlin students followed, during the next fifteen years, until nearly forty in all, young men and young women, had shared in the work of the mission. Several of these died in the field. Mr. Ingraham, after four years of very exhausting labor, lived to reach this country, but died three days after land-ing at New York. His young daughter was edu-cated at Oberlin, and gave her life to the work which her father had left, dying, as he did, soon after her re-turn to this country. During the first few years of the mission, the missionaries relied almost wholly upon their own field for their support, and to a considerable extent upon the work of their own hands. They built their own mission houses and school-houses and chapels. Some aid came to them from the London Missionary Society, and from school funds provided for the education of the freed-men. After a time a "West India Committee" was established at New York, to receive and forward contributions to the work. One of this band, Rev. James A. Preston, in 1841, having recently com-pleted his theological course, wrote to the officers of the "Union Missionary Society," then just organ-ized at Hartford, Conn., asking an appointment for himself and his wife to the mission in Jamaica, and thus presented his case and expectations: "Money we have not ; our friends who love Zion are poor; the American and other education societies have assisted in defraying the expenses of my education; should I make application for aid in behalf of myself and assistant—a female teacher, each of us having the requisite recommendations and testimonials, would the directors of your society—thanks to the God of the oppressed that it has been formed—feel disposed to grant us the money necessary for our outfit and passage ? After that we will trust, under God, to the generous gratitude which glows in the breast of the disenthralled. I should expect to raise funds in this vicinity sufficient to defray our expenses to New York." Preston was sent out upon the conditions proposed, and after six years of labor returned to this country to die. As the years passed on it became evident that the work in Jamaica might properly be left to English Christians, and no more reinforcements were sent to the American mission, and most of the missionaries that survived returned to this country. Two still cling to the work to which they gave their lives more than forty years ago: Rev. Julius O. Beardslee, of the first college class that graduated at Oberlin; and Mrs. Seth B. Wolcott, whose husband was a graduate of 1841. She buried her husband there in 1874, and their son, Henry B. Wolcott, of the class of 1870, is carrying on the work which his father left. The field upon which this hearty and exhausting labor was expended, though in some aspects inviting, was on the whole a hard one, exhibiting in a strange combination the superstitions of African heathenism, and the vices engendered by West Indian slavery.

In the year 1839, a Spanish ship, the Amistad, came into port at New London, Conn., having on board nearly fifty native Africans who had been brought to Havana, in Cuba, and sold to two slave-traders, to be transported to Principe, three hundred miles distant. On the passage they were told by the ship's cook that they were to be killed and eaten on reaching Principe. This so excited them that they rose upon the crew, killed the cook, put their owners in irons, and dealt out to them bread and water in such rations as they had received from them, and ordered the pilot to take them to Africa. He brought them to the American coast. Their owners, backed by the Spanish Government, claimed the Africans as slaves, and the government at Washington, with decided pro-slavery tendencies, was ready and rather eager to favor the claim. But the antislavery sentiment throughout the country was intensely moved ; prominent men in New York and Boston, and elsewhere, took up the case, and after a series of trials in the United States courts, the last at Washington, where the case of the captives was powerfully supported by John Quincy Adams, they were declared free. They were kidnapped Africans, and not slaves.

This decision was awaited with intense interest, and the news would naturally spread over the country with great rapidity. It came from Washington to Oberlin in nine days. These Africans had been in the country somewhat more than two years, while their case was before the courts. They were kept in jail, but Christian people were permitted to see them and give them daily instruction. It was ascertained that they were all from a limited region of West Africa, called Mendi, about one hundred miles south of Sierra Leone, and forty to sixty miles from the coast, and six or seven degrees north of the equator. They used different dialects of the same language, and could understand one another. They seemed a bright and amiable people, and the plan was formed of making them the nucleus of a mission to West Africa. As it was to be an antislavery mission, Oberlin was naturally called on to furnish the pioneer missionaries. James Steele, of the Theological Class of 1840, was chosen as the leader of the enterprise; and Wm. Raymond, who had been drawn from Amherst College to Oberlin by his antislavery sympathies, and afterward to the fugitives in Canada, was called as his associate. The company of Africans, which numbered fifty-three when they were shipped from Havana, had been reduced by death to thirty-nine. With this company, Mr. Steele, Mr. and Mrs. Raymond, and Mr. and Mrs. Wilson—colored—sailed from New York for Sierra Leone, Nov. 27, 1841; and thus the Mendi Mission was begun. A "Mendi Committee" was established at New York, of which Lewis Tappan was treasurer, to solicit and appropriate funds for the mission.

The Mendians, when they left this country, seemed interested in the establishment of the mission in their country; but they lacked stability and character, and their connection with the mission was a doubtful advantage. Three or four of them were steadfast and faithful to the missionaries, but the rest fell back to their old heathen life upon reaching the country. Mr. Steele was taken with the fever at Sierra Leone, and was obliged to return to this country; but Mr. Raymond went on to the Mendi country, established the mission, and after six years of exhausting but effective work, died at Sierra Leone in the spring of 1848.

George Thompson, of Oberlin, who had learned to endure hardness as a good soldier, in a mission of five years in the Missouri State Prison, succeeded to Mr. Raymond's work, going out in April, 1848. There followed him Dr. and Mrs. Tefft, Mr. and Mrs. Arnold, and others, until fifteen in all had gone from Oberlin to the Mendi Mission. Of these, eight died at the mission, and the rest were compelled, sooner or later, to return to this country for their health. The site of the mission was unfortunate, not being far enough interior to escape the fatal malaria of the lowlands of the coast. The mission has been carried on with more or less success until the present time, but during the last twenty-five years none have joined it from Oberlin. The precious lives which were sacrificed there might seem too great a price to pay for the work accomplished; but no word of regret was ever heard from those who died, or from those who lived to labor. "Except a corn of wheat fall into the ground and die, it abideth alone; but if it die, it bringeth forth much fruit."

The Indians of the great West early attracted the attention of Oberlin students. As early as 1837 or 1838 several families left Oberlin with the thought of missionary work among the Indians—some to stop on this side of the Rocky Mountains and some to pass beyond into Oregon. The whole United States territory beyond was then Oregon, and the Rocky Mountains themselves were more difficult to reach than the heart of Africa to-day. Yet these persons went out little knowing whither they went, with limited means of their own, and with no expectation of aid from home. They were practical men, capable of making homes for themselves in any land that could sustain human life, and no special apprehension was felt for them here. Mr. Finney announced, about that time, that a man was not fit for a missionary who could not "take an ear of corn in his pocket and start for the Rocky Mountains."

The only ordained minister who struck out from Oberlin on this distant mission was John S. Griffin, of the Theological Class of 1838. He still survives, a citizen and minister of Oregon.

These missionary families were able to do very little for the Indians, because they could not follow them in their wanderings; but they were pioneers in carrying Christian civilization to those remote lands, and made at length comfortable homes for themselves and their children.

In 1841 two young men, students of Oberlin, took appointments from the American Board, and went with their wives as missionaries to the Cherokee Nation, in the Indian Territory, where they spent some years as teachers.

Early in 1843 several students had become interested in the Indians of the remote north-west—the Ojibwas, about the head-waters of the Mississippi. The American Board had a few missionaries in that region, and these young men made application for appointments to that mission. But the Board was not then prepared to extend the work in that direction. Accordingly, on the 15th of June of that year, at a meeting of the Western Reserve Association of Congregational Churches, held at Akron, upon the representation of these young men the "Western Evangelical Missionary Society" was organized, and within two weeks ten missionaries, men and women, were on their way to their distant field. There is probably no missionary field to-day, on the face of the earth, more difficult to reach than this was at the time. There were two different routes, presenting about equal difficulties. One was by the lakes to the most western point of Lake Superior, known as Fond du Lac, and then by an overland journey of several weeks on a trail made by fur-traders, through swamps and along streams and lakes, by canoe and by portage, exposed to insatiate swarms of mosquitos, not to speak of beasts of prey which were abundant but far less formidable, to a group of lakes in the northern part of what is now Minnesota, —Leech Lake, Cass Lake, and Red Lake,—around which the Ojibwas were gathered. The other route was by the Mississippi, which was reached either by Cincinnati and the Ohio River, or by the lakes to Chicago, and an overland journey to Galena. The Mississippi was navigable, in some form, to Crow Wing, a little below where the Northern Pacific Railroad now crosses. Then followed the tedious succession of swamps and lakes and streams and portages, to the group of lakes already named. More than twenty in all went out to this mission. The names most naturally recalled, as connected with the mission, are Bardwell, Barnard, Wright, Spencer, Lewis, Adams, Coe, Fisher, and Johnson.

The work was carried forward through a period of sixteen years, until 1859, when it was discontinued in consequence of the breaking in of the advancing tide of emigration upon the region. The

United States Government still provides for schools and other work of civilization on the Indian reservations in the same region, and Rev. S. G. Wright, one of the missionaries in the first company sent out in 1843, is still at work among the Indians at his old station, Leech Lake.

The hardships of the work were more than usually fall to the lot of missionaries. In that high latitude the productive part of the season was brief, and the winter was long and terrible. The Indians had no permanent dwelling-place, but cultivated a little land in one place, made sugar in another, and hunted and fished in another; and their teachers were compelled sometimes to make a journey of five hundred miles in the winter, that they might not be separated from their flock. Then the Western Evangelical Missionary Society was often short of funds, and it was very difficult and expensive to forward supplies to the mission. Thus the missionaries were thrown greatly upon their own resources. They must raise their own provisions, saw their own lumber by hand, build their own houses, and help the Indians do all these things for themselves. Sometimes, to avert starvation, they were obliged, in the dead of winter, to make an expedition with oxen and sledges to the Selkirk settlement, four hundred miles to the north. They were obliged to see their provisions stolen and their cattle killed by starving Indians, and sometimes to divide their last potatoes with them. Yet there were compensations in the wonderful transformations of character witnessed in individual cases, numbers dying in hope in the new light which had come to their darkened souls, and in the general advancement toward a settled and civilized life.

Amid all their hardships the missionaries generally came through without breaking down in health. Mrs. Barnard died at her post, and Mrs. Spencer was shot through the window of her cabin at night, by a roving band of Indians on the war-path; but the work of her life is continued by her daughter, Miss Charlotte D. Spencer, a missionary of the American Board in Turkey, and her son, David B. Spencer, a preacher of the Gospel in Ohio. Forty years have passed since these missionaries went out into the wilderness. Slavery has been blotted out within that period, but the problem of civilizing the Indians is still before us.

In 1846 a convention of the "Friends of Bible Missions" met at Albany, N. Y., and organized the "American Missionary Association," to take the place and work of three organizations then existing —the West Indian Committee of New York, the Union Missionary Society of Hartford, and the Western Evangelical Missionary Society of Oberlin. Mr. Lewis Tappan was elected treasurer of the new society, and the office of corresponding secretary was filled the next year by the appointment of Prof. George Whipple, of Oberlin College, a member of the first theological class from Lane. He held the place until his death in 1876—almost thirty years.

In 1864, on account of the great extension of the work of the society by reason of emancipation, Rev. M. E. Strieby, of the college and theological classes of 1838 and 1841 at Oberlin, pastor at the time at Syracuse, N. Y., was elected as the associate of Mr. Whipple, and under their joint administration the great work in the Southern field has been carried forward. Oberlin students have been connected with this work in large numbers, as preachers, and as teachers both in elementary schools in city and country, and in the institutions for higher education, such as Berea College, Ky.; Fisk University, Nashville, Tenn.; Talladega College, Ala.; Atlanta University, Ga.; Straight University, New Orleans, La.; Emerson Institute, Mobile, Al.; Howard University, Washington, D. C.; and other similar schools for the colored people.

Such enterprises as these absorbed for many years the missionary activity of Oberlin men and women, and it is only within the last few years that the work of the American Board has come distinctly before them in such a way as to enlist their interest and command their service. During all the years there have been individual cases of young men and young women entering the service of the Board in different foreign fields, as Turkey in Europe and in Asia, India, Siam, China, Japan, South Africa, the Sandwich Islands, and Micronesia. Some, too, have engaged in foreign missionary work in connection with other societies in different parts of South America, in Hayti, in India, and in Burmah.

Within the last two years there has been a revival of interest among our students in the foreign work, and six have gone to South Africa, four to West Africa, two to India, and seven to China.

These seven that have gone to China are the pioneers of what is called the "Oberlin China Band,"
to whom the province of Shansi has been assigned
by the Board as a special field.

The great body of the young men that went out
from Oberlin to preach in the early days went as
home missionaries—with this exception, that they
looked to no society to aid the churches in paying
their salaries. It was not difficult for them to find
needy churches to welcome them. Such churches
were numerous in Western New York, in Northern
Ohio, in Michigan, in Northern Illinois, and to some
extent in New England. A few of the stronger
churches were open to Oberlin ministers; but for
the most part they were the weaker churches—such
as at that time, and at the present, would look for
home-missionary aid. But such aid came only
through the advice and recommendation of committees of associations and presbyteries—under the
Plan of Union, chiefly presbyteries; and such was
the prevalent ignorance and apprehension in regard
to Oberlin men, that the most they could look for
was the privilege of working in some needy field
without molestation. Thus each man was obliged
to find a place for himself, and slowly secure recognition. To give an illustration of the general suspicion: in 1842 the Presbytery of Richland, fifty
miles from Oberlin, sent up as an overture to the
Synod of Ohio the inquiry, "Is baptism, administered by the preachers of the Oberlin Association,
to be regarded as valid?" This inquiry was referred
to an able committee, who reported in substance

that "as the efficacy of Christian ordinances does not depend on the character of those who administer them, but on the grace of Christ," so their validity does not depend on the character of the administrator. The report went on to speak of the errors of the Oberlin Association as exceedingly dangerous and corrupting, and urged that "these preachers should not be received by the churches as orthodox ministers, nor their members be admitted to communion." An animated discussion upon this report followed, but finally the opinion prevailed "that Oberlinism was not yet sufficiently developed to justify the synod in coming to a decision on this important question," and the report was laid on the table. At this time the *Oberlin Evangelist* had been published four years, and Oberlin preachers and teachers were well scattered over the State.

Under these conditions Oberlin men found their work and waited for a brighter day. Some would make their way with little difficulty, and soon found a warm welcome—and this was the more frequent result. Others were less favored, and had somewhat trying experiences before presbyteries and councils. A year or two of self-denying and efficient labor with some needy church, without aid, was the usual probation to a recognized ministerial standing. Thus the work of the early Oberlin preachers was mainly missionary work in the weak churches and in the newer regions, where there was abundant room. Theological students going out to preach during the long vacation, found no home-missionary society to guide them to open doors and to secure them compensation for the service. They went where the preaching seemed to be needed, and often returned to the seminary as empty-handed as they went, except for the friendship and gratitude of those to whom they had carried the word of the Gospel. They were manual-labor students, and could make their way through another year of study. The situation had its advantages. The Oberlin man secured a theological standing of his own—a birth-right of liberty. No one was responsible for his or-thodoxy. If he talked like the Westminster Confes-sion, it was a surprise and a satisfaction. If he did not, it was only what was to be expected, and at all events he must have the privilege of talking in his own way. This freedom may have come at a heavy price, but it was worth the having.

In educational work there was a similar mission-ary enterprise. The common schools of Ohio at that time generally afforded two terms of instruc-tion in the year, called the summer and the winter school. In the more favored communities, these continued four months each; in others, but three. The manual-labor arrangement at Oberlin made it necessary that the college should continue in session during the summer, and have its long vacation in the winter. The winter schools through the coun-try called for young men as teachers. Thus the way opened for large numbers of the students to find employment in teaching. The intense prejudice against Oberlin, so widely diffused, was an obstacle in the way; but before this prejudice was fully estab-lished, Oberlin teachers had made a reputation for themselves and their successors, and a place from which the growing prejudice could not exclude them. There were dark places to which they found no access. In only rare instances did they pass " Mason and Dixon's Line;" and students from other parts, going over into Kentucky to find schools, were sometimes confronted with an Oberlin catalogue, which the people kept for their own protection. The majority of Oberlin students, young men and young women, during the first forty years, taught in these schools more or less during their course. At one time, when statistics were taken, it was found that five hundred and thirty students went out to teach in a single year. These teachers not only earned the means to sustain themselves in their study, and supplied the great want of competent teachers; they were also bearers of a wholesome and elevating influence wherever they went, inculcating the principles of temperance, morality, and religion, and leaving a leaven of antislavery sentiment in the communities which they visited. They were also a recruiting force for the school from which they went out ; and thus, through all the years of obloquy and reproach, the number of students was constantly sustained.

There were special educational enterprises of a missionary character, in which the colony shared with the college. The first of these was led by Mr. Shipherd himself, who had laid the foundations here, and had a longing to continue work of the kind. In providing men for Oberlin, the church and the college, he had not been careful to reserve a place for himself, and thus, after ten years, while still a young man, he found himself, with improved health, free from responsibility in the college except as a trustee. Having occasion, in the autumn of 1843, to pass through the State of Michigan, his mind occupied with the thought of another Oberlin, he chanced upon a place in Eaton County that impressed him as possibly the appointed field. After spending the night at a cabin in the neighborhood, he went on his way. On his return, intending to take a different road, by mistake he came back to the same locality, and spent another night. Returning to Oberlin, he gathered a few of the men who had joined the Oberlin colony upon his invitation, and proposed to them the new enterprise. After some weeks of deliberation and prayer, in the spring of 1844, Mr. Shipherd took his wife and six boys into a wagon, with such household goods as could be readily transported, with a young man or two to drive his cows and sheep, and made his way overland to the new wilderness home. A half-dozen families from Oberlin followed, and two young men, graduates of the preceding year, Reuben Hatch and Oramel Hosford, joined them as teachers; and thus the foundations of the town and the college of Olivet, in Michigan, were laid.

The new settlement had its experiences of hardship and trial. The breaking up of new lands, and the flooding of other lands for a mill site, brought sickness to many, especially to Mr. Shipherd and his family, and in September Mr. Shipherd died. It was a sad blow to the enterprise, but there was no looking back. The work went on, and after many days, and through many trials, prosperity came.

One of the young men especially, who left his studies at Oberlin to help Mr. Shipherd and his family on their journey, Albertus Green, from Lancaster, N.Y., proved himself a most enterprising and efficient business manager; and the little community again and again assessed upon themselves the cost of some new extension or addition to the advantages of the college, thus proved their vitality, and secured the confidence of the people of the State. For many years they drew their teachers almost wholly from Oberlin, but at length they could call men from Eastern colleges, and have now reached the stage where they find satisfactory professors among their own alumni.

A few families went out from Oberlin to Southwestern Iowa, in 1848, with the purpose of establishing a Christian settlement and Christian institutions in advance of the tide of emigration which was turning in that direction. They first settled upon the Missouri bottom, a few miles north of the State line. They had no minister, and only at rare intervals preaching of any kind; but they maintained religious meetings and a Sabbath-school, organized a temperance society, and sought the co-operation of their neighbors. These neighbors were interested in the new style of immigrants, and to express their appreciation, called the little settlement by the river side "Civil Bend."

These families drew others from Oberlin and the neighborhood, and among them Rev. John Todd, who had graduated at Oberlin, and was then pastor of the church at Clarksfield, Huron Co. These joined the colony in 1851. Meanwhile it had been discovered that the Missouri River bottom was too uncertain and unstable a foundation for a town, and the colony of Civil Bend found a new site fifteen miles away, on the bluff, and called it Tabor. Here the germ of Tabor College was planted, and has proved its vitality by a slow but steady growth during thirty years, under a heavy pressure of difficulties and embarrassments. The faith and courage and self-sacrifice of the surrounding community have saved it in one crisis after another, until now the day of its prosperity seems to have come. All these years it has been a fountain of educational and spiritual forces to a wide district of country. The families that have sustained it, by their faith and their contributions, were mainly of the original colony from Oberlin, and the instructors that have labored in hope, and given their lives to the work, have been Oberlin graduates.

Oberlin students have aided in the establishment of many other Western schools and colleges, among them Hillsdale College, Michigan; Ripon College, Wisconsin; Iowa College, Grinnell, Iowa; Drury College, Springfield, Missouri; and Carleton College, Northfield, Minnesota; not to mention again the schools at the South already referred to. The impulse of a new college, growing from small beginnings, has seemed to impress many Oberlin students, and they have gone forth with the thought of undertaking a similar enterprise. Such an impulse would scarcely be felt among the students of an old and fully equipped college. It comes where college-building is a part of the education.

CHAPTER VII.

OBERLIN IN THE WAR.

THE conflict which Oberlin had waged with slavery was essentially a moral one—a conflict of ideas and principles. The purpose was to diffuse abroad correct ideas as to the wrongfulness and unprofitableness of slavery, in the full expectation that in the end the truth would prevail, and slavery would give way before it. The example of emancipation in the West Indies was naturally accepted as an illustration of what it was reasonable to expect. Thus, from time to time, instances appeared in our own country of individual slave-owners who had become dissatisfied with their position, and under great difficulties and at great expense had set free their slaves. It was thought that all that was necessary was to continue this moral pressure, and slavery would at length yield to the power of truth. There was more or less apprehension of violence and bloodshed, but it was supposed that this would arise between the slaves and their masters, in the form of insurrections and repressions. No emancipation was thought to be desirable which did not involve the consent and co-operation of the holders of the slaves—not that the rights of slaveholders were of any special force, but because there could be no satisfactory result without such co-operation.

In the early days of the antislavery movement there was a very sanguine expectation of rapid progress in this moral revolution, and the people of Oberlin shared in the hope. Occasionally one would make a journey through the Southern States, and return with his views greatly changed as to the hopefulness of the prospect. The entire civilization of the South rested on slavery, and all investigation or inquiry or discussion upon the wrongfulness of the system was effectually precluded. Such was the impression from the inside view. But to the average antislavery man it seemed impossible that slavery should survive the growing agitation which would at length bring to bear upon it the protest of the civilized world. A conversation is recalled which took place at an Oberlin tea-table, about the year 1840. A young man asked of Father Keep, who was present, how long a time he thought would pass before slavery would come to an end. "About twenty years," was his deliberate answer; and no one present seemed to think the expectation unreasonable. It is true that after twenty years the end was just at hand; but to human apprehension it was no nearer than twenty years before.

But while "the irrepressible conflict" was thus regarded as a moral one, it was not the teaching nor the practice at Oberlin to omit any opportunity of effective testimony or action against slavery, social or political or religious. All that was required was that the action should be in harmony with Christian principle, and should have some probable bearing upon the end to be attained. The monthly concert of prayer for the termination of slavery was maintained for many years. The fugitive from slavery was sheltered, and helped on his way; not only as a service to him personally, but because such an escape was believed to have a wholesome reaction upon public sentiment at the North and at the South. The idea of maintaining a testimony by abstaining from the use of the products of slave-labor, such as sugar and cotton, obtained only a slender and very brief following. The more practical view was that the money expended for the maintenance of the principle could be used more wisely in direct action upon public sentiment.

The extreme doctrine of " non-resistance," which pervaded antislavery circles quite extensively, was never prevalent at Oberlin. The right to repel by force injustice and outrage, under proper conditions, was vindicated in the Oberlin philosophy, and maintained as a practical principle; but there was no expectation that the antislavery struggle would afford occasion for any general application of the principle. The most that was apprehended was that the violent measures of slave-catchers, who invaded the community, might some time call for the defence of property, or liberty, or life; and a patrol was sometimes organized to guard the community from such invasions. A proposal to operate, in either an open or clandestine way, upon slave territory, for the release of slaves, was never regarded with favor. The effort would bring danger and violence, without useful result.

When, in 1854, Congress declared the Missouri

Compromise act "inoperative and void," in relation to Kansas and Nebraska, the people of Oberlin, in common with many communities at the North, were profoundly moved. They organized an emigrant-aid society, and sent forward several companies of emigrants from Oberlin and the surrounding country, to pre-empt Kansas as a free State. These emigrants went prepared for the rough times of the "border-ruffian" war that followed, and helped to organize Kansas as a free State. Several Oberlin ministers were on the ground through all the conflict, and were sometimes driven from their homes and hunted like wild beasts over the prairie. But the day was won at length, and Kansas came forth one of the most prosperous and progressive of the free States.

John Brown, of Harper's Ferry, was not a stranger at Oberlin. His father was a trustee of the college as early as 1835. His younger brothers and a sister were students here, and he himself had rendered service in the survey of lands belonging to the college in Western Virginia. He was more or less associated with Oberlin men in Kansas; but his raid at Harper's Ferry was as great a surprise to the people of Oberlin generally as to any other community in the land. Two young colored men from Oberlin were with Brown's company, one of whom, Leary, was killed in the fight, and the other, John Copeland, died on the gallows a few days after his leader.

It was not unnatural that, in pro-slavery circles, Oberlin men should be suspected of complicity in the affair at Harper's Ferry. The following extract from *The Pennsylvanian*, of Philadelphia, gives the average Democratic impression of that day: "Oberlin is located in the very heart of what may be called 'John Brown's tract,' where people are born abolitionists, and where abolitionism is taught as the 'chief end of man,' and often put in practice. . . . Oberlin is the nursery of just such men as John Brown and his followers. With arithmetic is taught the computation of the number of slaves and their value per head; with geography, territorial lines, and those localities of slave territory supposed to be favorable to emancipation; with history, the chronicles of the peculiar institution; and with ethics and philosophy, the 'higher law' and resistance to Federal enactments. Here is where the younger Browns obtain their conscientiousness in ultraisms, taught from their cradle up, so that while they rob slaveholders of their property, or commit murder for the cause of freedom, they imagine that they are doing God service."

The actual, responsible sentiment of Oberlin men is expressed in the following extract from an editorial in the *Oberlin Evangelist* upon the Harper's Ferry tragedy: "We object to such intervention, not because the slave-power has any rights which mankind, white or black, are bound to respect, and not therefore because it is properly a moral wrong to deliver the oppressed from the grasp of the oppressor; but entirely for other reasons. We long to see slavery abolished by peaceful means, and as a demand of conscience, under the law of rightousness, which is the law of God. Such a result would be at once glorious to Christianity, and blessed to both slaveholders and slaves. It is especially because an armed intervention frustrates this form of pacific, reformatory agency, that we disapprove and deplore it. Perhaps the day of hope in moral influence for the abolition of slavery is past already; we cannot tell. If so, it is a satisfaction to us to be conscious of not having unwisely precipitated its setting sun. If a mad infatuation has fallen upon Southern mind, and they will not hear the demands of justice, nor the admonitions of kindness, let the responsibility rest where it belongs. We would not have it so. 'We have not desired the woful day, O Lord, thou knowest.'"

But the woful day was hastening on, and Oberlin was to have its full share of responsibility and sacrifice. Fort Sumter was surrendered April 13, 1861. The call of the President for seventy-five thousand volunteers followed, and the question of responding to the call came before the students of Oberlin. Friday evening, April 19, they held a meeting in the college chapel, where members of the different classes appealed to their fellows to rally to the defence of the Union, and committees were appointed to receive the names of volunteers. The next evening a meeting was called in the church, which was addressed by Professor Monroe, who was at the time a member of the Ohio Senate, and had returned from Columbus to stir up the students and people of Oberlin to the duty of the hour. The roll was laid upon the desk, open to enlistments, and a large number rushed at once upon the platform, and entered their names. The company was half filled that evening, ten thousand dollars were pledged to furnish and sustain the volunteers, and the people retired to ponder the question of duty during the hours of the Sabbath. It was a time of solemn and absorbing interest. In many rooms there were gatherings for prayer during the day, and there were many consecrations to the service of God and the country. The term of enlistment was for three months, but those who closed their books, and turned from the recitation-room to the tented field, in general regarded themselves as enrolled for the war.

Numbers sent in their names before the close of the Sabbath, lest there should be no room for them if they waited until Monday. These were not mere boys who acted from the impulse of the hour; they were serious, mature young men, from all departments of the college, who had their cherished plans of life, and had pursued them through years of toil and study. They could not drop these plans, distinctly apprehending that they might never resume them, without earnest self-inquiry, and solemn thought. Oberlin has witnessed during its history many memorable Sabbaths, probably few that left a deeper impression upon character than this.

Monday morning found one hundred and thirty names enrolled, while it was supposed that only eighty-one could be accepted. The faculty of the college did not feel at liberty to encourage enlistments. They maintained a conservative position, restraining the ardor of the impulsive, and requiring all under twenty-one years of age to wait the approval of parents or guardians. It was soon ascertained that a single company of one hundred members would be accepted from Oberlin, and this was organized, and furnished with such an outfit as could be provided in two days, in a country town. For these two days the college exercises were suspended, and the lecture-rooms were occupied with groups of women, from the college and the town, in the preparation of such articles as soldiers were supposed to need, not omitting the sadly suggestive work of scraping lint. Teachers of literature and science were at a discount, and every old man who had seen a squad of soldiers on the march or in bivouac was brought to the front. Thus, with very meagre resources, was commenced that education in the ideas and facts of warfare, which was to continue through a period of four years, until every detail of military life and movement became familiar, even to children.

There was a vigorous and rapid growth in the virtue of patriotism. Less than two years had elapsed since Oberlin, with its antislavery ideas and practices, had been in conflict with the general government, and numbers of citizens and students had gone to prison under its authority. There had been no enthusiasm for the flag: it was the symbol of oppression. An antislavery man had found it difficult, for many years, to maintain his loyalty. He could rejoice in his country, but his chief interest in the government was in the hope and purpose that it should one day be redeemed from its degradation. Now all was changed. Lincoln, the representative of freedom, was at the head, and slavery was in rebellion against the government. Oberlin men did not stop to ascertain what was to be the outcome of the war, in regard to slavery. They saw that, standing with the government, they would be on the side of liberty against slavery, and they could not hesitate. Whatever the result, freedom must gain, and slavery must lose, in the conflict. There was a very general conviction that slavery must go down in the struggle, whatever might be the ostensible policy of the government. Thus the loyalty of the people, which had been suppressed or overborne for years, at once found free scope, and the national flag was thrown aloft. Oberlin fairly blossomed out with the stars and stripes, and it was a great relief to know that these were the symbols of righteousness and liberty, and not of oppression.

Two days of preparation sufficed to provide the young men their uniforms and general outfit, and on Thursday, April 25th, the company were attended to the railroad station by almost the entire population of the town. Amid various demonstrations, and sad farewells, they took the train for Cleveland, where they went into Camp Taylor, and became Company C, of the Seventh Regiment of Ohio Volunteer Infantry. Its captain, G. W. Shurtleff, was a member of the theological school and tutor in Latin, and a large majority of the members were students. A few were young men from the town. The company remained at Camp Taylor about ten days, waiting for orders, and during this time received many visits from friends at Oberlin. On the 5th of May, their regiment was ordered to Camp Dennison, near Cincinnati. Here they built their first barracks, and continued in drill and general discipline until the 26th of June. Here, too, they came to be known as "the praying company." Each mess had its chaplain, who was responsible for a service of daily family worship. A daily prayer-meeting was established by the company, usually held in the open spaces between the barracks, to which members of other companies were frequently attracted. The daily family service was maintained in most of the messes during their entire connection with the army, a period of more than three years. Such peculiarities exposed them at first to sneering remark, implying an expectation that they would fail in the sterner work of the soldier's life; but after the first few marches and the first battle, these remarks lost their point, and were no longer heard.

The enlistment thus far was for three months—a time scarcely sufficient, at the beginning of the war, to bring untrained men into the field. At Camp Dennison the question of enlistment for three years was brought before the company, on the 23d of May. If any of them had acted from impulse or the spirit of adventure, the two months had given them time to cool. The rough experience of the camp had given them a better understanding of a soldier's life, even without the sight of the battle-field. A portion of the company decided that duty did not call them to this further sacrifice; but the large majority accepted the call, and turned away from their classes and their books, with little prospect of ever returning to them. The company was soon filled, by other volunteers, to a maximum, and

retained the officers with which it was first organized.

It was natural that this first company sent out
should be followed with special interest by the people of Oberlin. Other companies went out, and
many others, students and citizens, volunteered; but
Company C was the first contribution of Oberlin to
the war, and had the first experience of its hardships.

The Seventh Ohio was ordered from Camp Dennison to Western Virginia on the 26th of June, and
then began, for Company C, the marches and the
battles, which continued until they were mustered
out of service, at Cleveland, just three years later.

The company first came under fire at Cross Lanes,
in Western Virginia, where the Seventh Regiment
was surprised by a large force of the enemy; and for
a time Company C stood alone, unsupported, and
without any field officer, until they were at last compelled to retreat, leaving five of their number severely wounded on the field, two mortally wounded,
and two uninjured to look after them. In their retreat through the woods they fell in with a regiment
of the enemy, and the captain and those near the
head of the company, twenty-nine in all, were taken
prisoners. The rear of the company was saved
from this misfortune by the rather unmilitary order
of the lieutenant, E. H. Baker, "Skedaddle, boys."
Thus in the first encounter with the enemy the company was sadly broken, and was never entirely re-
united. The prisoners were first marched one hundred miles with their elbows tied together behind

their backs, and were then taken by rail to Richmond, Va., where they were confined in the somewhat famous tobacco factory. The captain was
here separated from his company, and spent a year
in various Southern prisons, at Richmond, Salisbury,
Charleston, and Columbia. After exchange in
September, 1862, he was placed on the staff of General Wilcox, and passed through the battle of Fred-
ericksburg; was soon after commissioned as Colonel
of the 5th U. S. Colored Troops, and fought with
them through the remainder of the war in the
trenches before Petersburg, in June, July, and August, 1864, and at New Market, Va., where he lost
nearly half his regiment, and was himself severely
wounded; and was honorably discharged at the close
of the war as brevet brigadier-general. Many of the
officers of his regiment were young men who had
been his friends and fellow-students at Oberlin.

The rest of the prisoners from Company C were
soon taken in open cars, through the whole length of
the Confederacy, to New Orleans, where they were
placed in the parish prison, without any care for their
clothing, and a very inadequate supply of food; and
at night they were thrust together into a cell, without
blankets or any bedding, where only half could lie
down at once, while the other half sat upon the stone
floor, leaning against the wall, a small opening in the
door and a smaller opening in a flue in the wall,
being the only arrangements for ventilation. Their
Yankee ingenuity enabled them to add to their resources by the manufacture of various trinkets, rings,
watch-chains, crosses, and pen-holders, from the bones

which came, in ample proportion, with their allowance of meat. By the sale of these they supplied
their more pressing wants. The more studious
among them pursued their French, German, Greek,
or Theology. A " Union Lyceum" was organized,
a semi-monthly paper, " The Stars and Stripes,"
issued, and prayer-meetings and Bible-classes were
maintained. Two of their number died in this
prison, of typhoid fever. They remained there from
October, 1861, to February, 1862, about five months,
when they were removed to the prison at Salisbury,
N. C., where they were kept until near the end of
May; when, after taking the oath not to bear arms
against the Confederacy until regularly exchanged,
they were sent down the Tar River under a flag of
truce, and were placed on board a Union steamer,
over which floated the Stars and Stripes. As they
stepped upon the deck it is reported that "they
danced and wept, and even kissed the mute folds
of those loved colors." Some of them were discharged as not fit for further duty, and the rest,
after exchange, reported themselves to their company, and served out the three years of their enlistment. Little was heard at Oberlin of these men
during their captivity. A few scraps of intelligence
came by roundabout methods, and occasionally a
letter on tissue paper came through, packed under the
covering of a brass button on the uniform of a soldier
who, for some reason, was sent through the lines.

The news of the battle and disaster at Cross
Lanes reached Oberlin in the midst of the commencement exercises, and gave a sad interest to the

occasion. The programme that day bore the names of twenty-nine members of the Senior Class, nine of them marked with a star referring to a marginal note, "In the Federal Army." These nine received their degree with the rest; but Burford Jeakins was lying, mortally wounded, on the field, and Wm. W. Parmenter died soon after in the prison at New Orleans.

The portion of the company remaining from the Cross Lanes disaster, more than two thirds of the whole, soon rallied, reorganized by the appointment of officers in the place of those lost, and had their numbers at length replenished by the enlistment of recruits, in part from Oberlin, and in part from other sources.

During the remaining years of the war, they held on their way, leaving their dead on many a hard-fought field, marching twenty-four hundred miles, and carried by rail and by steamer forty-eight hundred more. Among their battle-fields are Winchester, Port Republic, Cedar Mountain, Chancellorsville, Antietam, Gettysburg, Lookout Mountain, Mission Ridge, Ringgold, and Resaca. During these three years one hundred and fifty students were at various times members of Company C. Of these, only three died from disease, two of the three from typhoid in the prison at New Orleans. Twenty-eight fell in battle, and fifteen were discharged on account of serious wounds. That their sound principles and temperate habits had much to do in securing their freedom from disease, and their power of endurance, there can be no reasonable question. Of their fidelity to the principles with which they enlisted, Prof. J. M. Ellis, of the college, after a visit to the camp, thus testified: "When their ranks had been thinned by capture and death, and they had passed through all the corrupting tendencies and temptations of their new life for a year, surrounded with godless men and officers on every side, I saw them in their tents in the heart of Virginia; and nightly from the six tents of Company C went up the voice of song and of prayer, as they bowed themselves around their family altars. It was a strange sound in a camp of thirty thousand men. They were known as the 'praying company,' and the fame of their meetings was spread through all that army."

But Company C was not the only contribution of Oberlin to the war. A company from Oberlin joined the 41st O. V. I.; and about the same time, a considerable number of students and citizens joined the Second Ohio Cavalry, and followed the line of war from the Mississippi to the Indian Territory, and back through the whole length of the Confederacy to Danville, Va., and still back again to the western border of Missouri. One of these, A. B. Nettleton, rose from the rank of a private to the command of his regiment, fought under Sheridan the campaigns of the Shenandoah, and helped win the final victory at Five Forks.

In 1862, another company went from Oberlin to join the 103d O. V. I. Its captain, P. C. Hayes, was a graduate of the college, and a member of the Theological School. He soon rose to the command of his regiment, and at length became Provost-Gen-

eral of Schofield's army, with his regiment as guard.
The same year, when Cincinnati was threatened by
Kirby Smith's army, and the "Squirrel Hunters"
were called out, our recitation-rooms were given up
almost wholly to the young women, while the young
men, upon a few hours' notice, rushed with such
arms and ammunition and provisions as they could
gather up, to the point of danger. When the danger was past they returned to resume their work.
For this service there was no compensation—only
the approval of the authorities of the State, and the
Squirrel Hunter's diploma. The same year, when
Washington was in danger, a company of "three-
months men" went from Oberlin directly to the
"front," held several posts to relieve veterans,
shared in various skirmishes, and at last were involved in the surrender by Gen. Miles at Harper's
Ferry. In 1864, when Gen. Grant was concentrat-
ing all his forces upon Richmond, and Ohio sent,
within the space of two weeks, forty regiments of
"hundred-days men" into the field, Oberlin sent a
second "Company C" to the 150th Regiment; and
though in general these short-time soldiers were
sent to garrison forts, that veterans might be sent
forward to the front, this company, occupying the
fortifications near Washington, had a taste of actual
warfare, in repelling Gen. Early's movement upon
the city.

Numbers of young men in the college went to
their homes in this and other States, and enlisted
there, to help make out the quotas for their own
towns. Thus it was difficult to determine how

many of our students were in the army, or to follow their fortunes. The alumni of the college, scattered through the land, responded to the call of the country in the same spirit as the undergraduates. They went in command of companies and of regiments, many of them as chaplains, and some as privates. One, J. Dolson Cox, attained the rank of major-general. He went into the army from the Ohio Senate, at the first call, commissioned as brigadier-general; took charge of the Department of Western Virginia, and held it to the Union; led the Ninth Army Corps and the Twenty-third with McClellan and Burnside; and fought through the Georgia and Tennessee campaigns with Sherman and Thomas.

Taking graduates and undergraduates together, it was estimated that not less than eight hundred and fifty were in the army, at some time during the four years. The annual attendance of students was reduced from thirteen hundred and thirteen in 1860, to eight hundred and fifty-nine in 1862—a loss of nearly thirty-five per cent. This loss, after the first year of the war, was wholly on the part of the young men. The number of young women was greater in 1864 than in 1860, and for the first time in the history of the college they became the majority, while before they had been less than two fifths of the whole. The system of co-education thus helped to keep the college in good working order during these years, while so many young men were taking their discipline in the army. Still several classes were greatly demoralized, in the military sense of the word, by the loss of nearly half their numbers.

In the first excitements and anxieties of the war, the work of the class-room was maintained with some difficulty. The telegraph or the morning paper often brought news so distracting that neither teachers nor pupils could give their full strength to the work of the hour ; but at length all learned to possess their souls in patience. Still there were often sad interruptions, as when one who had fallen was brought back to be buried from among us— Danforth and Worcester from Winchester, Kenaston from Gettysburg, Ells from Washington, and others from other fields. There were also pleasant interruptions when paroled prisoners came back after a year's captivity, almost as from the dead.

The recreations of the students took on an unusual form. In the spring of 1861 they had built a gymnasium on the campus, by voluntary contributions, and had called a teacher of gymnastics from the East, to inaugurate the new dispensation. Great enthusiasm was shown in the exercises, but from the day of the fall of Fort Sumter, the gymnasium was deserted. The teacher returned to his own State to enlist in the army, and the students organized companies and practised the military drill instead of gymnastics. The gymnasium was sometimes utilized as an armory, but at length it became utterly desolate, and before the close of the war was removed from the campus as a useless incumbrance. Two or three entire generations of students passed away before any demand arose for a new gymnasium.

Of those who went forth from Oberlin to the war, about one in every ten never returned, and the soldiers' monument, erected in 1870, bears the names of one hundred citizens and students who fell on the field, or died in prison or in hospital. A special sadness attaches to the memory of those who fell at the last hour, when all the dangers seemed to be past—of Tenney, of the Second Ohio Cavalry, who was killed by almost the last shell that exploded in the neighborhood of Richmond; and of Trembley, member of Company C, who had fought in every battle, except one, in which his regiment had been engaged, and had suffered no harm. The time of his discharge had come; he had written to his mother to dismiss her anxiety for him—that his fighting was over and he would soon be with her. On the deck of the steamer a few miles below Cincinnati his foot slipped and he was drowned. His comrades recovered the body and bore it to his mother.

When the war was finished, all show of military life at Oberlin disappeared. The experience of war had been too real and serious to leave any taste for its pastime or its pageantry. No military companies survived among the students, and no military drill was adopted as a college arrangement. The classes gradually filled up, the advanced classes more slowly than the others, and in 1873 the numbers in attendance were greater than when the war began.

SOLDIERS' MONUMENT, AND OLD LABORATORY.

CHAPTER VIII.

SPECIAL FEATURES: CO-EDUCATION—MANUAL LABOR—MUSIC.

THERE are several features in which Oberlin has been distinguished from most of the older colleges, peculiarities which, to some extent, were in the original idea and plan, and which have given it a degree of notoriety, and sometimes of reputation. The most prominent of these is doubtless the principle and practice of

CO-EDUCATION.

This word seems to have come into use within the last twenty years—an Americanism, made necessary by the existence of a special feature in the later American education, in which Oberlin was called to lead the way. Co-education, as far as schools for primary and secondary education are concerned, is not a modern arrangement. The common-school of New England has always brought boys and girls together, except to a limited extent in cities and larger towns. The ordinary New England academy has involved the same arrangement; and it was almost inevitable that the two original founders of Oberlin, who had received their education in such an academy, should embrace this arrangement in their ideal school.

It does not appear that they regarded themselves as introducing any innovation, or any questionable principle. They did not realize that they were lay-ing the foundations of a college. Mr. Stewart dis-tinctly discarded the idea, and Mr. Shipherd seems to have accepted it as an afterthought. Their "Collegiate Institute" grew into a college on their hands, after the announcement had been made that the doors should be open to young men and young women. There seems to have been no discussion of the question of introducing co-education into a higher institution of learning. The founders and colonists had many principles to discuss and settle, but this was not one of them. The concentration of spiritual and intellectual forces to move upon the ' Mississippi Valley" necessarily carried with it the education of men and women. To what extent they should be brought together in this preparatory education, was probably not clearly determined, even in idea. The earliest circular thus sets forth the plan: "The several departments of instruction in the Institute are thus arranged : Preparatory or Academic School; Female Department; Teachers' Seminary ; Collegiate Department; and Theological Department." Then follows a brief description of each department or school, giving the idea of the female department thus : " The Female Department, under the supervision of a lady, will furnish instruc tion in the *useful* branches taught in the best female seminaries; and its higher classes will be permitted to enjoy the privileges of such professorships in the Teachers', Collegiate, and Theological Departments,

as shall best suit their sex, and prospective employment." In a subsequent paragraph of the same circular, we read : " Pupils may enter the Female Seminary for one term only, but none can enter the
higher departments without expressing the determination to pursue such a course as the Faculty shall
direct. . . . . The Preparatory School, and the
Female Seminary, may be entered at any age above
eight. The Teachers' and Collegiate Departments
cannot be entered under fourteen." Such statements manifestly contemplate a separate school for
girls, with the privilege of attending upon instruction in the other schools or departments. This condition of things was never realized at Oberlin. Whatever the intention in the planting, the growth never
brought out this form. There has been no female
department, except in relation to general management and discipline, not as related to scholastic instruction. In a letter written in May, 1834, by Mrs.
M. P. Dascomb, the first principal of this department, giving to her friends a view of things as she
found them at Oberlin, this sentence occurs : " I
spend three or four hours daily in hearing classes
recite. Mrs. Waldo also assists in school. The females are very interesting—most of them from other
States, and many from a distance. That department is not yet distinct from the other." The same
state of things would be found by a visitor to-day.
The fact seems to be that women came in because
they belonged to the enterprise, as they come into
the household, with no special theoretical views on
the subject, but with a prevalent conviction that

every necessary adjustment could be made. The founders certainly held no new or special views of the rights or the sphere of woman: they only sought for her such an education as should fit her for highest usefulness in her own appropriate work.

Thus young women were invited to the school, and came; and the required adjustments and arrangements were made as the years went on. The first year, out of one hundred and one pupils in attendance, thirty-eight were young women; and these were of mature years and character. No children, boys or girls, were received. Provision was soon made by the community, in connection with the common-school system of the State, for the elementary education of their children. The proportion of young women in attendance slowly advanced, being at the end of the first decade thirty-seven per cent of the whole; at the end of the second, forty-three per cent; of the third—in the midst of the war—fifty-one per cent; of the fourth, forty-seven per cent; and of the fifth, fifty-three per cent. No special educational arrangement was made, the first year, for these young women, except the appointment of a lady principal. Their instruction was provided for in the general classes.

The announcement for this department in 1835 was as follows:

"Young ladies of good minds, unblemished morals, and respectable attainments are received into this department, and placed under the superintendence of a judicious lady, whose duty it is to correct their habits and mould the female character. They board at the public table and perform the labor of the steward's department, together with the washing, ironing, and much of the sewing for the students. They attend recitations with young gentlemen in all the departments. Their rooms are entirely separate from those of the other sex, and no calls or visits in their respective apartments are at all permitted.

"This department is now full, and many applicants have been necessarily rejected. Such, therefore, as may wish to enter hereafter, would do well to send us their application, accompanied with the requisite testimonials, and hear from us before they make the journey in person."

For the years 1836–7, no change in the organization of this department appears; but in 1838 the catalogue presents a "Ladies' Course, introduced with a single sentence: "The following is the course of study for young ladies." This course was based upon a common-school education of that day, as a preparation, and was extended through four years. The course in the best female seminaries of the period was for three years. This course was, for the time, thorough in mathematics, natural science, English literature, history, and philosophy, but afforded no language, ancient or modern, except the "Greek of the New Testament." The only strictly "ornamental" branch was linear drawing. A significant remark concludes the presentation: "Whenever the course of study admits of it, the young ladies attend the regular recitations of the College Department." There were several studies not found in the College Course, which required separate classes, but the tendency was, as a matter of economy, and of general wisdom, to diminish the number of separate classes, and bring the two courses into harmony. "The Ladies' Course" stood thus side by side with the College Course for many years, modified and strengthened from year to year as experience suggested, or the general advancement of education in the country required. Greek was made optional in 1839, but was frequently studied by young women, and Latin and Hebrew as well. Latin was introduced as a required study in 1849, and French in 1852.

The principal of this department was reinforced by a "Ladies' Board of Managers" in 1836, an institution which has continued from that time. This Board has been made up of the lady principal and several ladies of mature experience, wives of members of the Faculty, or of others connected with the management of the college. To them was committed the general ordering and discipline of the department, and the provision of such special instruction as might be necessary. This arrangement was intended to secure to the young women the watchful guardianship of ladies of experience and culture, and save them, in any case of inquiry or personal discipline, from the publicity of appearing before the general Faculty of the college. The service of this Board has been without compensation, and has unquestionably contributed much to the success of the "experiment" of co-education at Oberlin.

In 1837 four young women came forward with a

full preparation for college, having pursued Latin
and Greek in the various classes of the preparatory
department, and asked admission to the Freshman
Class, as candidates for graduation. Young women
had already been reciting with all the college classes,
and more or less in all the studies; still, the idea of
their taking the full College Course, instead of the
course designed for them, raised a new question.
There was a little hesitation, but the application was
granted, and three of the four graduated in 1841—
the first young women in this country to receive a
degree in the arts. No announcement of this new
departure appears in the Catalogue. For the years
1838–9 the names of these young women appear
after the names of all others under a separate head-
ing, "College Course, Freshman Class." In 1839
their names and classification lead the names in the
Female Department, and in 1840 they are placed,
with the college classes to which they belong, after
the names of the young men; and this arrangement
has been retained until the present time. But to
guard against misapprehension as to the relations of
these young women the following remark was introduced and kept standing in the Annual Catalogue
until 1855: "Young ladies in college are required
to conform to the general regulations of the Female
Department."

In 1847 two young women who had completed
their literary course applied for admission to the
Theological Course. They were received and regis-
tered as "resident graduates, pursuing the Theological Course;" and thus their names appear for three

years. The next lady applicant for the Theological Course appeared in 1873. She was received and catalogued with her class.

When the first class of young women had completed the Ladies' Course, they were not brought before the great congregation at Commencement to read their essays. They called together their friends, by tickets of invitation, the evening before Commencement, and read their essays in their own assembly-room, receiving no diplomas. The two following years this anniversary was held in the college chapel the evening before Commencement, and the young ladies read before as large an assembly as the chapel could contain. Theoretically this was the Ladies' Anniversary and not a part of the Commencement proper, which was held the next day in the large tent. The next year, 1843, the Commencement was held in the large new church not yet completed, and the young women of the Ladies' Course read in the same church the preceding afternoon, and received their diplomas. From this time onward the anniversary of the Ladies' Department was reckoned as a part of the Commencement, but the arrangements were designed to indicate that it was the day for the ladies specially. The platform was occupied by the Ladies' Board of Managers, and the announcements were made by the lady principal, the president of the college being at hand to open with prayer and to present the diplomas.

When the first young women came to graduate, having completed the full College Course, they naturally felt some anxiety as to the place that should be given them at Commencement. It was proposed to them that they should read their essays on the preceding day, with the young women of the Ladies' Course, it being announced that they had taken the full College Course, and should come forward the following day with the class to receive the degree. This was not thought to provide a suitable discrimination, and to avoid the impropriety of having the young ladies read from a platform arranged for the speaking of young men, and filled with trustees and professors and distinguished gentlemen visitors, the essays of the lady college graduates were read by the professor of rhetoric, the young women coming upon the platform with their class at the close to receive their diplomas. This arrangement was continued eighteen years, but became less and less satisfactory, and in 1859, for the first time, the young women were permitted to read their own essays with the graduating class, and in 1874 a young lady graduate who desired it, was permitted to speak instead of reading an essay, and this liberty is still accorded.

In 1875 the "Ladies' Course," which had appeared in the catalogue for forty years, was transformed into the "Literary Course," and opened to young men ; and the two courses thus presented became parallel courses in the School of Philosophy and the Arts—the Literary Course requiring one year of preparation, and the Classical three years. Thus a distinctive Ladies' Course disappears. For the Literary Course no degree has yet been granted. It has been suggested that a year be added to the preparation required, and that a degree be conferred.

Thus it appears that co-education at Oberlin was not undertaken as a radical reform, but as a practical movement in harmony with the prevalent idea of woman's work and sphere, and thus it has been carried forward, carefully adjusting itself to the new conditions, as they have arisen. There was no attempt to put young men and young women upon the same footing, regardless of their diverse natures and relations. While they were members of the same class, and received, in general, the same instruction, their duties were not identical. There has been no effort to train young women as public speakers. Declamations, orations, and extemporaneous discussions have been required of young men—not of young women. Their elocutionary training has been in the direction of reading rather than of speaking. Nor has there been an aim to place young men and women upon the same footing in regard to the general regulation of conduct. The general judgment of the world has been accepted in regard to the proprieties of womanly conduct, and the college regulations have conformed to these principles. That young women should be less conspicuous on the street, and in public generally, than young men, is a requirement of general society, and the college regulations have recognized this fact.

The Ladies' Hall is the headquarters of the Ladies' Department, furnishing private rooms for a hundred young women who choose to occupy them, also principal's office, reception rooms and parlors. The dining-room of this hall furnishes seats at table for nearly as many young men who choose to take their meals there; and thus they meet at meals and recitations. Social calls upon these young women are in order during the early evening hour. A large number of young women board in families in the village, under the general supervision of the lady principal, and young men are received to the same families as boarders, with suitable arrangements in regard to rooms. This has been the order from the beginning.

In the organization of Literary Societies, the principle of separation has always been maintained. The young men have their own societies, and the young women theirs; and there has never appeared any desire for a different arrangement. At least this established order has been cheerfully accepted,

The aim has been to have the restrictions few and simple, such as commend themselves to the good sense of the reasonable and well-disposed, and to depend greatly upon this good sense and reasonableness; but the point has never been reached where it seemed wise or safe to dispense with all restrictions, and leave the young people to their own free judgment. The young need and expect such guidance. Older people often need it, but there is no one to afford it.

There is no place in these pages for an argument upon the system. A historical statement of the arrangements, and the results, is all that can be given. The plan has been in operation fifty years, and the work is as satisfactory and hopeful to-day as it has ever been. It cannot be claimed that there have been no anxieties connected with the system, or

that there have not been occurrences, at rare intervals, that were painful or even shocking. Such things
belong to human society in every form, and no arrangement or vigilance can afford complete security.
Those who have been intrusted with this work, during the years that are past, have been trained in the
best schools of the land, and are familar with the
results in these schools. They have sometimes
come to the work with some apprehension ; but without exception, so far as is known, they have grown
into a hearty approval of the system.

It is not necessary to say that in scholarship the
young women have held an honorable place. Whenever a comparison has been made, it has been found
that the young women are a little above the average
in regularity of attendance and in general scholarship ; and that the best scholar, in any branch of
study, is just as likely to be a young woman as a
young man. There is a probability that intense competition tells more upon the nervous endurance of
the young woman than of the young man, and that
anxieties and apprehensions in general take a stronger
hold. Some care is called for in these respects ; yet
it is not observable that a larger proportion of young
women, who enter upon a full course, are turned
aside, from failing health, than of young men.

During the history of the college, one hundred
and thirty-three young women have taken the full
College Course, of whom nineteen have died since
graduation—exactly one in seven. Seven hundred
and two have taken the Literary Course, of whom
ninety-five have died, or one in seven and four tenths.

Eight hundred and fifty young men have graduated, of whom one hundred and eight have died, or one in seven and nine tenths. These proportions are not sufficiently divergent to afford an argument unfavorable to co-education, nor are the numbers sufficiently large to establish a favorable conclusion. The general impression of those who have watched the experiment is a safer reliance.

That the system of co-education, as here pursued, tends to bewilder young women with false ambitions, or to draw them away from their proper work, no indication whatever has appeared. Those educated here, like other educated women of the land, are found filling the places which belong to such women. For a large proportion, probably four fifths of the whole, their work centres in the home life. Others are filling responsible positions in this land and abroad, doing a work which the world needs. Amid all the changes in the outward form of the work, which the fifty years have brought, the spirit and aim of the young women gathered here remain the same as in the early days.

In reviewing the early announcements and catalogues, among other changes which time has wrought, a change of nomenclature is observable, to which the adjustment is not yet complete. The English use of the terms "lady" and "gentleman" is prevailing over the American, in our land, and Oberlin is in the transition state. Young ladies have become young women; but we still retain, as relics of the early day, Ladies' Department, Ladies' Hall, Ladies' Literary Society, and Ladies' Board of Managers.

Fifty years more may help us through this formal inconsistency.

MANUAL LABOR.

The idea of Manual Labor as a feature in the life of the student was not original with the founders of Oberlin, nor peculiar to the Oberlin plan. Several schools at the West founded fifty years ago, more or less, undertook a provision for manual labor. In Ohio, Western Reserve College, Marietta College, Lane Theological Seminary, and other schools later than these, adopted the arrangement. Oneida Institute, of Central New York, from which quite a number of students came to Oberlin, through Lane Seminary and otherwise, was a manual-labor school; and doubtless schools still farther east had tried the experiment. Probably in no case, except perhaps a few of the distinctively agricultural or mechanical schools of a later date, has there been so earnest and thorough and persistent an effort to maintain the system. The founders of Oberlin believed in the arrangement as fully as they believed in any form of education, and all their plans were formed in view of it. The five hundred acres of land secured as a gift from Messrs. Street & Hughes, of New Haven, were not secured mainly for the sake of providing ample grounds for the college site, nor for the purpose of selling at a profit for the advantage of the college. They were designed as a college farm, and were given by the proprietors, as the deed states, because of their " interest in a literary, manual-labor institution," to be held inalienably by the college. Three hundred acres in addition were bought to enlarge the farm. The Circular issued in 1834, near the close of the first year of the college work, contains the following statement:

"MANUAL LABOR DEPARTMENT.—This department is considered indispensable to a complete education. It is designed first to preserve the student's health. For this purpose, all of both sexes, rich and poor, are required to labor four hours daily. There being an intimate sympathy between soul and body, their labor promotes, as a second object, clear and strong thought, with a happy moral temperament. A third object of this system is its pecuniary advantage; for while taking that exercise necessary to health, a considerable portion of the student's expenses may be defrayed. This system, as a fourth object, aids essentially in forming habits of industry and economy, and secures, as a fifth desideratum, an acquaintance with common things. In a word, it meets the wants of man as a compound being, and prevents the common and amazing waste of money, time, health, and life.

"To accomplish the grand objects of this department, a farm of eight hundred acres has been secured, some fifty of which are cleared and seeded; other clearing is in progress, and teams, cows, sheep, and swine, with agricultural implements, have been procured according to present wants, to be increased as necessity requires.

"This department is also furnished with a steam-

engine of twenty-five horse-power, which now pro-
pels a saw-mill, grist-mill, shingle and lath saw, and
turning-lathe, to which will be added other machinery
as experience shall prove expedient. One work-
shop is now erected and supplied with tools. Others
are to be added as necessity requires, and funds allow. The agricultural system is much more extensive than the mechanical, because it is more condu-
cive to the student's health and support. A few
apprenticed and a few natural mechanics may be well
employed, but a large majority can work in mechan-
ism to but little pecuniary profit; while on the farm
they can secure more health and earn much of their
support."

The first year four hours' daily labor was required
of every student. The manual-labor bell was rung
at one o'clock in the afternoon, and each young man
repaired to the field or the forest, the shop or the
mill, for his work, for which he received from four
to seven cents an hour, according to his efficiency or
his skill. The young women performed the domes-
tic labor in the boarding-hall, for which they received
three to four cents an hour. To equalize matters
somewhat, the price of board was seventy-five cents
a week for young women, and a dollar for young
men. Tuition was twelve dollars a year for young
women, and fifteen dollars for young men. Incidentals were one dollar for young women, and two dollars for young men.

The Circular of the first year adds, in a closing
paragraph: "The testimony of one year's trial is,

that students, by four hours' daily labor, may preserve their health, clear and invigorate their minds,
guard against morbid influences, earn their board,
and yet facilitate instead of retarding their progress
in scientific attainments. The most delinquent in
manual, have been the most deficient in mental
labor."

The second year the number of students was increased nearly threefold, although "more than half
the applications for admission were refused." The
Circular for the year states that "students, both
male and female, and in all the departments, are *expected* to labor three hours daily." The abatement
in the hours of labor seems to have arisen from the
difficulty of providing remunerative labor for the increasing numbers. There was no end of work to be
done—forests to clear away, stumps to eradicate,
fields to subdue, and buildings to erect, besides all
the work involved in feeding and caring for the hundreds of students. But all this was expenditure
instead of income. There could be no profitable
agriculture until the roots of the original forest which
filled the soil had time to decay. Most of the labor
on the fields for some years must be in the shape of
permanent investment for remote returns; and it
was labor not well adapted to young men and boys
who must work a few hours a day to pay for their
board. It was easy for the superintendent of manual labor to measure off a half acre of forest for a
youth to fell the trees upon it, and cut them into
cord-wood. The work would be sufficient for the
season; and if he were paid by the acre and the

cord, the college would be safe, but the student would find the balance sadly against him; while if he were paid by the hour, even at the lowest price, the college had little or nothing to show for its investment. Only inexhaustible resources on the part of the college could solve the problem, and no such re sources existed.

The founders were sanguine men, fruitful in devisings, and various schemes for furnishing remunerative labor to young men and women were tried. Mr. Shipherd, in one of his letters, suggested spinning and weaving for the girls; but the factory era was just at hand, and the spinning-wheel and the family loom were giving way before the march of civilization. A dream of the production and manufacture of silk in the country was producing some excitement, and was taken up by the managers here. Large quantities of mulberry trees were brought on from the East, and the young men were excused from study for a week to change the college farm into a mulberry plantation. The unsubdued soil and the unskilled labor combined, gave a discouraging result. A few scattering trees survived, and were visible for twenty years perhaps, but the college never produced a cocoon, even for the Cabinet. A single family in the colony fed a few silk-worms for a year or two. Other experiments were tried, less expensive than this, but they brought no relief. The college employed, at times, a general business manager to bring things into shape, and again a college farmer was appointed to organize and direct the agricultural labor, but with the wisest arrangement every bushel of corn produced cost twice the market price. These experiments were repeated through a series of years, in hope of a better result; but long before the effort was relinquished, the college ceased to require labor of the students, or even to promise it to those who desired it. The Catalogue of 1838 says: "At present no pledge can be given that the Institute will furnish labor to all the students; but hitherto nearly all have been able to obtain employment from either the Institute or the colonists. It is thought that the same facilities for available labor will be continued." From that day to this the college has held out no pledge to furnish labor, and of course the requirement has never been revived. In 1840 the announcement was as follows: "The number of students is now so great that the Institution cannot engage to furnish labor to all; yet it does employ many. In the village the demand for labor both agricultural and mechanical is continually increasing, as improvements and wealth advance, and may be expected to keep pace with the growing number of the students. The demand for school-teachers during the winter vacation is constantly beyond the means of supply, many applications being made to the Faculty which cannot be met. Students in the advanced classes receive from eighteen to twenty-six dollars per month and board." The following was the announcement for 1850: "The Institution cannot pledge itself to furnish labor to all the students. However, *diligent and faithful young men* can usually obtain· sufficient employment from the Institution or from the inhabitants of the village. Many, by daily labor, have been able to pay their board ; others have not been able to do this ; while others still have paid their board, washing, and room-rent. The long vacation gives an opportunity to those who are qualified to engage in teaching, by the avails of which many pay a large part of their expenses."

In 1851 a successful effort to raise an endowment, by the sale of scholarships through Northern Ohio and the adjacent regions, brought the college into general notice, so that the number of students was doubled in a single year. The attempt to maintain a superintendent for the organization of the manual-labor department had been abandoned some years before, and students were left to find employment for themselves as they were able. The college farm had been temporarily leased in parcels, and thus afforded some employment to diligent and faithful young men. It was found by experience that the best opportunity for students' labor was afforded by families, in the care of yards and gardens, in the preparation of fuel, and in other chores which pertain to every household. It was ascertained that a single family, as a rule, afforded as much employment to students as several acres of farm land, managed as the college had been able to do it, and this without any expense or supervision on the part of the college. After mature consideration, and the best legal advice attainable, it was decided to lease permanently the inalienable lands of the college, with the provision that the leaseholders should furnish a certain amount of labor to students, proportioned to the quantity of land held. Thus the college farm was opened to occupation for residence, and is now covered by that part of the village lying between Lorain and Morgan streets, and west of Main Street. The care of the gardens and lawns affords more and better employment for students than the original farm could do; and this employment is available to those who seek it, without any attention on the part of the college.

This certainly is a wide departure from the original idea of a manual-labor school. The college seal still bears the motto, "Learning and Labor," with a college building in the foreground, and in the distance a field of grain; and it is the aim and purpose of the managers to encourage all efforts at self-support among the students, and to maintain a public sentiment in sympathy with the working life. The school, in some of its arrangements, still bears the impress of the original manual-labor plan. In the higher departments all recitations and lectures are in the forenoon; so arranged originally to have the afternoon open to manual labor. Monday, instead of Saturday, is the open day of the week, because Monday was the washing day in the early college life, as in all well-ordered families. Until very recently the long vacation was in the winter instead of the summer, because summer rather than winter is the time for manual labor. Another and stronger reason finally operated to hold the long vacation to the winter, namely, the opportunity it afforded for school-teaching. These somewhat unusual arrangements are relics of the manual-labor system.

There are obvious and inevitable difficulties connected with the systematic provision of labor for students. It is proposed as a means of self-support, and probably could not be sustained without affording compensation to the student. But the necessary expensiveness of the system more than absorbs the profits. The investment of capital is essentially the same for a student working three hours a day as for an ordinary laborer. The expenditure for superintendence is probably even greater, because the average student acquires no stability or momentum in his work. Then, again, the work is far less effective even for the time it continues, because the student does not get fairly adjusted to his work before he drops it for the day. He never gets fairly into the harness; and finally, his heart is not in it: study is his occupation, and the work is incidental. He cannot throw himself into it, so as to become an effective laborer. It is not his life. There are exceptions to this general fact, but not enough to affect the result. Hence student labor can never enter the market in competition with ordinary labor. The reaction of the labor upon the student would be most wholesome, if a motive could be found to hold him to it, without compensation in the form of wages. This would involve the idea of making the labor a part of the education, like practice in the gymnasium or in the laboratory, a privilege for which the student pays, instead of receiving pay; and this is the principle maintained in most industrial schools, but this was not the thought of the founders of Oberlin. The expectation which they cherished could not possibly be realized, but it was a part of the impulse which sustained them in laying their foundations. The building is, in this respect, different from their planning, but in regard to its great purpose it probably transcends their expectations.

MUSIC.

The musical interest at Oberlin appeared early in its history. The announcement of 1834, the first exhibition of the plan and purpose, contains no reference to the subject, and during the first year of the college work there was no indication of special interest in that direction. Deacon Turner, one of the colonists, organized whatever musical talent the community afforded, and led the singing in the Sabbath services.

The Catalogue of 1835 gives the name of Rev. Elihu P. Ingersoll as " Professor of Sacred Music." To the special work of his professorship, the oversight of the Preparatory Department was added. The musical instruction, given at this time, was limited to the training of classes in singing ; and this instruction was free to students in all departments. The new interest came in with the advent of Professors Finney, Morgan, and Cowles. These men were all passionately fond of music, and had strong convictions of its value as a force in Christian education, as well as of its importance as an element of worship. Their views doubtless had much to do with the growth of the interest at Oberlin.

Mr. Ingersoll was enthusiastic in his work, but he

occupied the position only a single year. The narrowness of the resources of the college was doubtless the reason for his retirement. Instruction in music formed no definite part of the course, and when retrenchment must be made it naturally took effect here. The Catalogue of 1836 gives a blank in place of the name of the Professor of Sacred Music; but the same Catalogue states that " particular attention will be paid to the cultivation of sacred music," and this item is repeated from year to year. Some student who had gifts in that direction was employed to train classes in singing. In 1837 this work was committed to George N. Allen, a student who had recently entered the Junior Class from Western Reserve College. He was a young man from Boston, a pupil of Lowell Mason, and had enjoyed the best musical advantages of the time. His interest in music was intense, and his Christian character was as earnest and intense as his love of music. Indeed, his Christian earnestness seemed to require music for its best expression. The violin was his special instrument, and he claimed no skill in the use of any other; but his soul seemed to animate almost any instrument that he touched. He continued teacher of music in the college until 1841, when he was elected Professor of Sacred Music, a position which he held until 1864. In the Catalogue in which he first appears as professor of music the following statement is found : " During the past year increased attention has been paid to the study of sacred music. Systematic instruction has been given to upwards of four hundred pupils, including a large class composed

of young children of the citizens of the village."
There was a very general revival of interest in music,
and Professor Allen was the soul of it all. Yet the
work was not regarded as giving full employment to
a professor, or at least the compensation afforded
was only half a salary, even according to the Oberlin
standard. For the first two or three years the
superintendence of the Preparatory Department was
added to his duties, and after 1849, instruction in
Geology and Natural History. In the interval was
developed the germ of what has become, in these
latter days, the Oberlin Conservatory of Music.

Among the hundreds of students gathered here,
nearly half of them young women, there would inevitably be a demand for instruction in instrumental
music, especially upon the piano. For this demand
the college made no provision. Indeed the trustees
had put on record a resolution, that it was "inex-
pedient for the college to afford instruction in piano
music." This demand Professor Allen provided for,
upon his own responsibility. He saw that instruments were secured, either by purchasing them himself, or by encouraging others to purchase. He gave
lessons as far as his engagements would permit, and
provided competent teachers to meet the growing
demand. Thus the musical interest at Oberlin was
first organized.

Meantime the interests of sacred music were not
permitted to flag. For many years there was but a
single church organization, and the church choir was
enlarged to include almost all the vocal talent of the
college and the town. There was no organ, and the

satisfactory substitutes for the organ, afforded in these days, had not been invented. Professor Allen trained and organized an orchestra of six or eight performers, furnished with wind and stringed instruments; and when a double bass-viol was wanted, he persuaded a young Scotchman of the Theological Department, Alexander McKellar, to undertake its manufacture—a feat which he accomplished with entire success. When it seemed impossible to procure a sufficient number of copies of a piece of music to supply the large choir, Professor Allen procured dies, and stamped the music on blocks of cherry wood, from which he printed the required number of copies, and had the stereotype plates in reserve for future use.

With such a choir and orchestra and other appliances, Oberlin became distinguished for its music. The church services, the Commencement exercises, and the concert following, were all attractive by reason of the music. It would not be easy to find at any time a community in which music was more effective and potent. The great sermons of the Sabbath were a power, but they were powerfully sustained and enforced by the music; and Mr. Finney often paused in his impassioned appeals to give place to the winning, pleading strains of a choir, in full sympathy with the solemn truth he was urging.

In these days the little Oberlin hymn-book first saw the light, under the title " Hymns for Social Worship," compiled by Professor Allen. It embodied about three hundred of the choicest hymns, in a compact little volume, which every student could carry in his pocket without being burdened. It was first issued in 1844, before the era of hymn and tune books, and many editions followed through a period of twenty-five years, until it took the form of the little hymn and tune book which preceded our present "Manual of Praise." A slight comparison will show that the last is a growth from the first. The original book of Professor Allen was not used for Sabbath worship; and the first Oberlin hymn and tune book was not intended for such use. It was employed temporarily, while committees of the Congregational churches here were looking for a book to recommend for adoption. The little book was found so convenient that a proposal was made to enlarge it until it should contain a sufficient supply of hymns and tunes for Sabbath use, and still be manageable as a pocket hymn-book. Hence the "Manual of Praise," compiled by Professors Mead and Rice—a most satisfactory development.

Professor Allen was a composer, of some merit, both of hymns and of music. The hymn beginning "Must Jesus bear the cross alone?" which is attributed to him in many collections, was not so much his by composition as discovery. He found it in an old book, reading "Must *Simon* bear the cross alone?" and made the change which greatly elevates the hymn. As first published in his little books it contained three stanzas; but in later editions a stanza is introduced as the second, which begins "Disowned on earth, 'mid griefs and cares." This was his own composition, but the three slightly grandiloquent stanzas appended to the hymn in "Songs for the Sanctuary" and some other collections, still attributed to G. N. Allen, are not in his style, and must have some other origin. The tune "Maitland," which accompanies the hymn in various collections, and which in "Songs for the Sanctuary" is given as anonymous, is Professor Allen's composition. This tune he claimed, and not the hymn.

Out of this early church choir, built up by Professor Allen, grew the "Musical Union," which furnishes yearly the grand concert. This concert is older than the Musical Union, dating back probably to 1840. The profits of these concerts were formerly devoted to some public object. A large part of the cost of the organ, secured by the efforts of Professor Allen, for the First Church, was met in this way. The present college chapel bell was thus paid for, and several portraits of the older professors, hanging in the rooms of the societies, and in the Library of Council Hall, came by the same means. They were painted by Alonzo Pease, the earliest Oberlin artist. In later years the profits have been expended in giving some special interest to the concert, and in advancing the general interests of the Union.

Under Professor Allen's training there grew up at Oberlin musicians of various merit, four of whom at least call for special mention, as being sons of early residents, and having obtained for themselves a recognition in the world. These are Smith N. Penfield, Frederick H. Pease, John P. Morgan, and George W. Steele. Two of these, Messrs. Morgan and Steele, after Professor Allen had been obliged to relinquish musical work, on account of his health, organized in 1865 the "Oberlin Conservatory of Music," to meet the demand for musical culture. This school was in its organization independent of the college, but was operated in full harmony with it, and furnished the instruction of the choral classes made free by the college to all its students. In 1867, Mr. Morgan having withdrawn from the Conservatory to engage in musical work in New York, Mr. Steele was elected Professor of Music in the college, and the Conservatory was brought into connection with the college as one of its departments. In 1871 Mr. Steele retired, and Fenelon B. Rice was elected to the Professorship of Music, and made Director of the Conservatory. These positions he still holds.

The Conservatory has attained a high degree of prosperity, having employed the past year thirteen instructors, and having in attendance four hundred and sixty-one pupils, of whom three hundred and ten took music only. It still relies upon its own income, having no endowments, and drawing nothing from the funds of the college. So far it is a private institution. But its teachers are all appointed by the trustees of the college, and its pupils are members of the college, and under its regulations. In return for its position and opportunity, the Conservatory gives instruction to four choral classes weekly, which are open without charge to all the students, directs the singing at college prayers, and furnishes the music for Commencement and other public occasions.

It thus appears that musical culture belongs his-

torically to the educational work of Oberlin, and
there is obvious and abundant reason for its continued
prosecution.   Music is one of the great forces of
society, especially of Christian civilization.   It must
not be left wholly in the hands of the irresponsible
and the worldly, to give it such direction as may
suit their tastes or interests.   There must be Christian
schools of music, as well as of other forms of education and culture ; and such schools must exist in our
own land, because the work is here, in large measure,
that needs to be done, and because it is necessary
that our musical culture should have a natural and
spontaneous growth, in harmony with American
character and life.   It must be naturalized and
acclimated—not a mere exotic.

The spontaneous growth of this interest at Oberlin, is an indication of favorable conditions here.
These conditions belong to a large school of young
men and young women, among whom the natural
taste and gift for music may be found, and who
furnish an appreciative audience, as an inspiration.
The reaction, too, of the general educational spirit
upon the quality of the musical work will be most
helpful.   It is a mistake to suppose that music alone
can yield substantial culture or character, cr that it
is sufficient to itself.   Those who propose to work
effectively in this line need breadth and substance
of personal character—something more than mere
effervescence of sentiment.   The neighborhood of
a university of general education, and especially of
Christian education, and of co-education, is the natural
place for a school of music.   It is the desirable place

to train those who shall go out as leaders of choirs and organists in the churches, and teachers of music in its various forms. The attention given to musical culture at Oberlin is in the line of its original purpose and plan ; and present indications point to this as a part of its future work.

The trustees of the college have therefore taken action, encouraging the endowment of the Conservatory, and looking toward its permanent establishment as a department of the college. The corner lot, formerly occupied by President Mahan, and later by Professor Morgan, has been secured for the Conservatory, and the original president's house now echoes to the sound of instruments of music. There is hope that another year may witness the erection of a building adapted to the necessities of this growing college of music.

The school of music has already shown its value as an educating force, operating upon the whole body of students. It elevates their ideals, and furnishes an atmosphere of culture, of which they partake almost unconsciously. Our music is also a spiritual power which we could not spare. In the churches, and in the college chapel, at daily prayers, it lifts and inspires many souls. The service of prayers in the chapel can never become wearisome or monotonous while so many hundred voices, under a skilful director, unite in the hymn of thanksgiving or of supplication. There are few among teachers or pupils who feel that they can afford to miss the opportunity. It is a constant benediction on our college life.

CHAPTER IX.

THE FINANCIAL HISTORY AND MATERIAL DEVELOPMENT OF THE COLLEGE AND THE COLONY.

THE two founders of Oberlin, a home missionary and a returned foreign missionary, were entirely destitute of means when they undertook the work. Mr. Shipherd owned a small one-story house in Elyria, and nothing more. Mr. Stewart had nothing. No man of any means was associated with them, and they knew of no one to whom they could look. Their estimate of the funds required in such an enterprise was very moderate, and this was their encouragement. Mr. Shipherd, in a letter to his parents, in which he lays the plan before them, says that two thousand dollars would be required as an outfit for his school. The light on this subject came to them as they were able to bear it. There is a tradition that Mr. Shipherd left Elyria, on his first Eastern campaign, with three dollars in his pocket.

The first material contribution to the project was the gift of five hundred acres of land by Messrs. Street & Hughes, of New Haven, as a school farm. At the same time, Mr. Shipherd contracted with them for five thousand acres in addition, for his colony, at a dollar and a half an acre, with the privilege of selling it to colonists at an advance of a dollar, thus securing five thousand dollars in addition, pledged to the school. But this was balanced by a pledge given by Mr. Shipherd to the colonists whom he invited, that, early in the first summer, a steam saw-mill should be in operation on the ground, and, as soon as necessary, a grist-mill. Both were in place, nearly at the time appointed, and both were a source of expense to the college for years, until they were at length sold to private parties. The investment would seem unwise, but it was doubtless necessary. No one among the colonists had any surplus capital for such an investment. In general they had only means to pay for their land, to make the journey, and build small houses for their families. Beyond this they had to depend upon their own labor to clear their lands and support their families, until they could secure some returns from the soil. There was no capitalist among them. The first collections for the college came in the form of scholarships. A contribution of one hundred and fifty dollars secured the privilege of sending one student perpetually to the school, to enjoy its manual labor opportunities, and all other advantages; but he must pay for board and tuition their full cost. The scholarship payment was simply in the way of outfit, that the facilities might be furnished by which the student could work his way.

But the expenditures of the first year exhausted all these funds. The erection of the college buildings, and the clearing of the farm, and the feeding and teaching of the hundred students in return for their work, called for increased supplies, and this was the burden upon Mr. Shipherd's heart as he made his way to Cincinnati in the autumn of 1834. The financial result of that winter's campaign, which terminated in New York, was the enlistment of the interest of several leading merchants and business men of the city in the Oberlin enterprise, especially the two Tappans, Arthur and Lewis. Several of these men united in a "Professorship Association," pledging the interest of eighty thousand dollars yearly, to pay the salaries of eight professors at six hundred dollars each. There was no definite pledge to pay the principal at any particular time, but the expectation was that this would finally be paid as a permanent endowment. Besides this definite and open pledge, Arthur Tappan privately assured Mr. Finney that he should regard the entire surplus of his income as devoted to the work; and his income at the time was about a hundred thousand dollars a year. These financial arrangements seemed all that could be desired. The professors elect came on, and as their salaries were provided for, the charge for tuition in the college classes was remitted. It was retained in the other literary departments, because there was no endowment for these. The great fire in New York, in the autumn of 1835, crippled the men of the Professorship Association, so that they were not able to meet their pledges; and the financial crash a year later completed the work. The Professorship Association never came to the surface again, and all the expectations based upon it fell to the ground. But the announcement of free tuition had been published, and students had come upon the strength of the promise. The trustees did not see their way to restore the charge for tuition until 1843.

Vigorous efforts were made by the trustees to meet the emergency arising from the failure in New York, and during 1835–36 a subscription of nearly a hundred thousand dollars was raised, to be paid in five annual payments; but the financial overturning of 1837 swept it all away, so that only six thousand dollars of the subscription could be collected. During the several years of financial depression that followed, a very limited and precarious support was secured to the professors, by constant collections among the friends of the college scattered over the country. There were many such friends, generally of limited means, who stood by the work in these years of trial. It was not a rare thing that the families of the professors were in doubt as to the necessaries of life, from day to day. The colonists were in similar straits. The returns from their new farms came in very slowly, and the supplies brought on from the East were well exhausted. Thus in the college and in the colony there was a significance, not often realized, in the prayer " Give us day by day our daily bread."

But with all this straitness there was no real depression. The work grew in interest and hopefulness from year to year, and the men who had it in hand could not withdraw from the field. There were places open to them where they could have lived in comfort, but their work was here. Mr. Josiah Chapin, of Providence, sent remittances to Mr. Finney for some years, as regularly as if he were under contract to pay his salary. Mr. Willard Sears, of Boston, did the same thing; and afterward, as prosperity in the stove business came to Mr. P. P. Stewart, he provided similarly for Professor Morgan. President Mahan was wont to spend his winter vacations at the East, in preaching, and the generous gifts which he received in the work, and in view of his position here, made up his salary. Other professors were often obliged to sell their claims upon the college in the form of " Institution Orders," to provide for pressing needs. Indeed, these orders became a sort of colonial currency, passing at a discount, like much other paper, but never so much depressed as the " Greenbacks" in the war.

Thus, in spite of every effort, in 1839 the college was more than thirty thousand dollars in debt, and bankruptcy threatened. There were no able friends in this country to come to the rescue. In this crisis two of the trustees, Father Keep, and Mr. William Dawes, undertook a financial mission to England. Prominent antislavery men in this country, like Mr. Gerrit Smith, furnished them letters, and helped them to an outfit. The application was not for endowments, or money for current expenses, but for help to pay the indebtedness. They prosecuted their mission among the antislavery people of England, especially those of the Society of Friends, to whom the Oberlin enterprise commended itself on account of its antislavery character, and its forwardness in the education of women. The fact that Oberlin students were engaged in missionary work among the freedmen of Jamaica was a matter of interest to many Christians of England. There was a natural repugnance to give to an object so remote, and in a foreign country; and the work was laborious and slow. The gifts received ranged from a hundred pounds, the largest, down to a few shillings. The two men sent forth to this work held on their way, without rest or diversion, walking by St. Paul's from day to day, never taking time to enter, and scarcely to look up at the majestic dome. They let no opportunity or prospect pass. Having learned that the Common Council of the City of London held some funds in trust for charitable purposes, they went before that large body of honorable citizens and presented their cause; and what is even more surprising, they came within a vote or two of securing an appropriation.

Messrs. Keep and Dawes went out in the midsummer of 1839, and returned near the close of 1840, after an absence of about eighteen months, bringing with them, above all expenses, thirty thousand dollars in money, sufficient "to meet the most pressing liabilities of the institution, a large accession of books to the library, with good provisions for philosophical and chemical apparatus." The old compound microscope, until recently the only microscope owned by the college, costing in its day fifty guineas, and the smaller telescope, costing forty guineas, were a part of this apparatus. Mr. Hamilton Hill of London, a very genial Christian gentlemen, with his family came with Messrs. Keep and Dawes, having been invited to become secretary and treasurer of the college, a position which he held for twenty-five years.

Relieved of the pressing debt, the college held on its way the next ten years, dependent upon the yearly gifts of its friends and making no progress towards endowment. The gift of twenty thousand acres of land in Western Virginia by Gerrit Smith was a special encouragement, and this was its chief immediate value. Ten thousand acres were at once transferred to Arthur Tappan in payment of a loan of five thousand dollars, and this was a substantial benefit. The remaining ten thousand were twice sold for twenty-five cents an acre, and in each case came back upon the college. Counter claims and hostile legislation embarrassed the title, and led to years of litigation; and now, after more than forty years, there is a prospect that the college will come through with a small balance on the right side. This is but a single instance of hope deferred, of which so many have occurred in the financial experience of fifty years.

Near the close of 1850 a movement was made to secure an endowment of one hundred thousand dollars by the sale of scholarships. The scholarships were of three varieties, securing free tuition for one student at a time, for six years, eighteen years, and perpetually; and costing severally twenty-five dollars, fifty dollars, and one hundred dollars. The money was not payable and the scholarship had no force until the hundred thousand dollars were subscribed. The plan was a popular one, and in a little more than a year the amount was pledged; twenty-two thousand dollars being pledged in Oberlin, and thirty-seven thousand in the county. By this movement a fund of nearly ninety-five thousand dollars was raised and invested, of which the annual interest received was about six thousand and seven hundred dollars. This was the sole reliance for the payment of the salaries of instructors. A professor's salary was six hundred dollars.

An immediate effect of this endowment was that the number of students was doubled, advancing in a single year from five hundred and seventy to ten hundred and twenty, and the next year to thirteen hundred and five. This was encouraging generally, and would have been helpful financially but for the fact that the scholarships sold absorbed all the fees for tuition. This, of course, was not unforeseen. About fourteen hundred scholarships had been sold, and these were transferable, so that no student appeared at the office without a scholarship. The expense of instruction in the lower departments was increased by this large increase of numbers; but most of the elementary teaching was done by students from the higher classes at a small compensation. Thus the college was enabled to make ends meet for several years with this very limited income. It would be difficult to find an instance in the whole history of education in the country, where so much work has been done for so little pay.

Until after 1860 nothing occurred in the results of the scholarship system which had not been anticipated. It had been planned and administered with the greatest care, to guard against any possible mis-

understanding on the part of purchasers of scholarships, and the entire movement was a success. But
the war with its disturbance of values had not been
foreseen. A salary of six hundred dollars was
utterly insufficient, when the prices of all the necessaries of life had more than doubled. There was no
alternative : the old friends of the college must again
be asked to come to the rescue. One of these, Mr.
J. P. Williston, of Northampton, Mass., added two
hundred dollars a year, for three years, to the salary
of every professor. Wm. C. Chapin, then of Law-
rence, Mass., pledged thirty thousand dollars to the
endowment of the college, and paid the interest on
it at seven and a half per cent during the whole
period of extravagant prices. Many others responded generously, and thus the crisis was met.

The scholarships, after the first six years of their
existence, began to be cancelled according to the
regularity with which they had been used, and after
eighteen years the next class began to disappear, and
before 1880 almost all the terminable scholarships
had been exhausted. There were nearly four hundred perpetuals, and no lapse of time could annul
these. In many cases the holders of these have surrendered them to the college as a free gift; in other
cases they have reserved the right to send their own
children without a fee for tuition; in still others
they have exchanged the perpetual for terminable
scholarships, and others have transferred them to
the college at a price. Thus, after more than thirty
years, the scholarship liabilities have been essentially worked off, and only a few relics survive.

The undertaking was a formidable one, and any school may well hesitate before venturing a repetition of the experiment.   There have been disastrous failures in similar undertakings.

During all these years the endowment of the college has been slowly advancing.   In 1867 the trustees of the estate of Dr. Charles Avery, of Pittsburg, Pa., transferred to the college twenty-five thousand dollars on condition that free tuition should be furnished perpetually to fifty needy and worthy colored students who should apply for it.   In 1870 Mr. Charles H. Dickinson, of Fairport, N. Y., as almost the last act of his life, gave ten thousand dollars toward the endowment of the Theological Seminary. In 1878–81 Miss Mary Holbrook, of Holbrook, Mass. gave twenty-five thousand dollars for the endowment of the Professorship of Sacred Rhetoric and Pastoral Theology.   In 1880 the college received from Mrs. Valeria G. Stone, of Malden, Mass., fifty thousand dollars towards endowment—the largest single gift ever received.   At the reunion of the alumni of the college in 1875 a subscription was started for the endowment of the " Finney Professorship," and nearly twenty-five thousand dollars have come into the treasury in connection with the movement. Upon the retirement of Professors Morgan and Dascomb in 1880, a second subscription among the alumni was undertaken to provide a fund for their retirement, which should ultimately constitute an endowment of the Dascomb Professorship.   About fourteen thousand dollars have come in on this subscription, and a balance of fourteen thousand remains to be collected. The "Graves Professorship" of thirty thousand dollars was endowed in part by the late R. R. Graves, of Morristown, New Jersey, and has been completed by his brother and members of his family. The present invested fund of the college above all liabilities, April, 1883, amounts to two hundred and eighty thousand dollars. Outstanding pledges which should soon come in will bring the amount up to four hundred and twenty-five thousand; and if seventy-five thousand could be added the present jubilee year it would complete a half million of endowment. Compared with former straitness this would seem an ample provision ; but it will be observed that the income of this sum at six per cent., which is all that can be safely assumed, would be but thirty thousand dollars—a very small reliance for an institution carrying forward such a wide range of educational work. The expenses of the college for the last financial year were forty-eight thousand seven hundred and nine dollars, and the receipts from all sources, including donations, aside from gifts for endowment, were fifteen dollars more than the expenses. The salaries paid to regular professors are sixteen hundred and eighteen hundred dollars. They were increased about two years ago by the addition of two hundred dollars to each. A serious financial depression during the current year would decidedly darken the prospect of enlargement of the endowment which is looked for in the payment of outstanding subscriptions, and in additional subscriptions—an experience often encountered in the history of the college.

The present year a movement has been inaugurated by friends of the college and of Hon. James Monroe, late Member of Congress, to raise thirty thousand dollars for the endowment of a professorship of political science and international law. The movement has nearly reached its consummation. Mr. Monroe was a professor in the college from 1848 to 1865, and his return will be occasion of great satisfaction.

Various friends of the college have given notice of help, to come when their estates shall be settled. Others still have transferred to the college life-insurance policies, either paid up or on which they pay the premiums as they fall due—notably Mr. Wm. C. Chapin, of Providence, R. I., for more than twenty-seven thousand dollars, and Mr. Charles J. Hull of Chicago, for nearly fifty thousand, to endow the "Frederika Bremer Hull Professorship," in memory of a daughter who graduated here. Still other friends who wish finally to benefit the college, but who need the avails of their property while they live, and are willing to be free from the care of it, have placed it in the college treasury as a gift, receiving back a bond for an annuity equal to the interest of the money given. The college holds at present annuity funds invested as trust funds to the amount of forty-five thousand dollars. The method is very simple, and has proved very satisfactory, especially to those to whom the care of their property is a burden.

Little has been done in the accumulation of beneficiary funds. The aggregate of these, in the form of scholarships and other funds, amounts to somewhat more than seventeen thousand dollars. No prize funds have ever been offered to the college.

The people of Oberlin, according to their means, have shared generously in every movement to sustain the college, sometimes contributing to endowment, at other times to buildings, and again to current expenses, to forestall the contraction of a debt. In a crisis of the Theological Department, in 1868, they came to the rescue with a subscription of twenty thousand dollars for a new professorship, and Rev. Hiram Mead was called. The tenth article of the old Colonial Covenant provided for such co-operation: "We will feel that the interests of the Oberlin Institute are identified with ours, and do what we can to extend its influence to our fallen race."

COLLEGE BUILDINGS.

The first building erected for the college was known as Oberlin Hall. It was built the first summer, in 1833, by the colonists then on the ground, and was completed, ready for the school, Dec. 8. It was planned as a two-story building, thirty-five by forty feet; but before the roof-timbers were prepared, it was decided to carry up about two thirds of the width of the building into a third story called "the attic," after the fashion of a modern grain elevator. This building contained all that was known as Oberlin College, until the summer of 1835. It embraced boarding-hall, chapel, meeting-house, school-rooms, college office, professors' quarters, and private rooms for about forty students. The attic received twenty young men, with a room for every two, affording space still for a corridor four feet wide, and for a flight of stairs. The attic gave way for a full story in 1838, and the building still stands as private property on the south side of College Street, nearly opposite the historical elm. It is still useful, the lower stories being occupied for business purposes, and the upper story recently as a photograph gallery. It has endured well the ravages of time, considering the difficulties under which it was erected. The cellar walls and underpinning were originally of heavy oak timbers, squared and laid up like a block-house; but stone walls took their place when the road to the quarries in Amherst became passable. It was in the little chapel of this building that the students gathered to welcome Mr. Finney, upon his first arrival in Oberlin, in 1835.

The second building was the carpenter's shop, a two-story frame building, intended as a shop where the students who had some mechanical skill should perform their four hours of daily labor. It was erected the first autumn or early winter, and stood west of Oberlin Hall, nearly where the post-office now is. It was one of the few buildings which were painted red, according to the early vote of the colonists. Upon the great accession in 1835, when room was in such demand, the carpenters' benches were turned out and the two stories were divided up, by rough board partitions, into rooms for students, and two lecture-rooms. One of these was occupied by Dr. Dascomb as his first laboratory, and in the other

Mr. Finney began his theological lectures. It was in front of this building, toward the south, that the so-called burning of the classics took place. In 1836 the red shop was removed to the south end of the west wing of the new boarding hall, and used as a wood-house. It still exists as a dwelling-house in Carpenter's Court, South Main Street.

The new boarding-hall, known afterward as the Ladies' Hall, was begun in 1834, but not completed until the autumn of 1835. It stood still west of the red shop, on the north-east corner of the lot occupied by the Second Church. The building was a frame thirty-eight feet by eighty, and three stories high, with a wing of two stories on each end extending toward the south. The whole force of young men was turned out for three days to the raising of the building, and a great part of the work, without and within, was done by students. Stone for the foundations was still too costly, and this large building was erected upon oak pillars, six or seven feet in length, cut from the bodies of large trees, and sunk into the ground to the depth of the cellar that was to be. Afterward the earth was gradually excavated from under the building, and the walls were put in their place. The dining-room of this building accommodated, according to the early ideas of room, two hundred boarders, and there were rooms besides for about sixty students. When first completed, the upper story, and the west flights of stairs were given up to young men, and the remainder of the building, excepting certain rights in the dining-room and parlor, to the steward's family, and to young women.

FIRST LADIES' HALL.

LADIES' HALL (NEW).

In the simplicity of the first years, there was constructed, between the dining-room and the sitting-room, a set of boxes, like large post-office boxes, a hundred or more, shut in with doors on each side. Each young man had his box assigned him, and in it he deposited his bundle of linen for the laundry every Monday morning, and found it there the next Saturday evening. In the unfinished first story of this building, Mr. Finney preached, more or less, during his first summer in Oberlin. The building stood until the completion of a second new Ladies' Hall. It was then divided into parts and removed, and now exists in the form of five dwelling-houses in various parts of the town.

In May, 1835, Cincinnati Hall, already described, was erected, to receive the students from Lane. It was what might be called, in the dialect of the early immigration, a college " shanty." It was occupied two or three years, was afterward used as a carpenter's shop, and wholly disappeared about 1840.

Another three days' raising occurred in the autumn of 1835, when Colonial Hall was built. It stood still west of the Ladies' Hall, on the corner occupied by the Soldiers' Monument—eighty feet from east to west and forty feet wide, three stories in height. It was named from the fact that the colonists subscribed nearly half the cost of the building, with the privilege of using the lower story, which was to be the college chapel, for Sabbath services. The upper stories were dormitories for young men, twenty-two rooms, for two students each, with a single recitation-room on the second floor. The chapel, well packed, seated eight hundred. At first it was sufficient for the Sabbath congregation, but before the great church was built it was necessary at times in the morning to hold a subsidiary service in the Laboratory or the Music Hall. Colonial Hall stood about thirty years, but after the building of the new college chapel, in 1855, the old chapel was divided into four recitation-rooms. Colonial Hall still exists in the form of two unsightly dwelling-houses on West Lorain Street.

Tappan Hall was begun in 1835, and with its walls at about half height it stood through the winter, and was completed in 1836—a brick building, a hundred and twelve feet by forty-two, and four stories in height, containing a recitation-room in each corner of the first story, and about ninety single rooms for students in the different stories. These rooms were strikingly simple and uniform in their arrangements, being each sixteen feet by eight, with a door at one end and a window at the other. In one corner, near the door, was an open wardrobe, and in the other a narrow bedstead. In a corner by the window was the stove and, the other side of the window, the table. This was the ultimate idea, for the time, of comfort and convenience in a college dormitory, not only at Oberlin, but in the country generally. Those were the favored ones who could establish a claim upon Tappan Hall. The building was intended primarily for the students of theology, and after them for college students. The central tower was originally in two sections, giving more than twice the present height; but in the judgment of

COLLEGE CHAPEL.

some of the trustees it presented too much leverage to the strong west wind, and in Mr. Shipherd's eyes it was not according to the simplicity of " the pattern shown in the Mount." The upper section was therefore removed. The money for the building, ten thousand dollars, was given by Arthur Tappan. The building was placed in the centre of the college square, with the intention of having all other college buildings stand around the square, on different sides. The plan would not have been a bad one if the central building had been devoted wholly to public uses and not a dormitory building. Tappan Hall is now nearly fifty years old, and but for grave imperfections of constitution it might serve successive generations of students another fifty years. Many consultations have been held over it, all ending in one conclusion—that it must soon be removed.

The year 1835 marked a building era for the college. Two dwelling-houses were erected this season by the college—one for President Mahan, the other for Professor Finney, two-story brick buildings, spacious and comely, and well adapted to their uses, standing one at the south-west and the other at the north-west corner of the square, overlooking the square, but not on it. The street which separated them from the square was named Professor Street, because it was the purpose to fill up the space between these two buildings with houses for other professors. This policy was not carried out. It was soon found desirable that, in a new and growing place, the professors should build and own their own dwellings, and thus at least have homes in their

later years, if nothing more.   Such a home is more
satisfactory and enjoyable than one owned by the
college, even if inferior in its appointments.

The style and expense of these college dwellings
gave rise to some discussion.   A letter from Arthur
Tappan, received at this time, encouraged attention
to taste and comeliness in all the buildings and
grounds.   A prominent and zealous colonist addressed a communication to the trustees, criticising
the lavish and unchristian expenditure, and giving it
as his opinion that three hundred dollars had been
wasted upon the buildings, out of regard to worldly
fashion.   President Mahan occupied his house until
his retirement in 1850; President Finney his until
his death in 1875.   Mr. Finney bought his house of
the college in 1851, and Professor Morgan the
president's house a little later.

The last building to which the impulse of 1835
gave origin was Walton Hall, erected by the Presbyterian Church of Walton, N. Y.   They sent several of their young men to Oberlin, and to furnish
them quarters, they erected a two-story frame building, with twelve rooms, and placed it in charge of
one of their young men.   To students from Walton
there was no rent.   The building stood on South
Main Street, nearly opposite the site of the present
Union school-house.   After fifteen years it became
the property of the college, and ten years later it
was sold to private parties, was changed into a furniture shop, and finally was destroyed by fire.

In 1838 the building known in later times as the
"Old Laboratory" appeared—a brick building of one

MAHAN MORGAN HOUSE.

story, about thirty feet by fifty in dimensions, and containing a large lecture-room with rising seats and arched ceiling, and skylight over the lecturer's table, and all other appliances for the illustration of lectures in chemistry. It was built according to Dr. Dascomb's plans, embodying ideas which he obtained as a student under Dr. Mussey at Dartmouth and Professor Silliman at Yale. Adjoining the lecture-room was a working room for the professor, and a study. This gave to the professor of chemistry independent quarters, in which he greatly rejoiced ; and these rooms he occupied until the close of his work—more than forty years. About fifteen years ago the lecture-room was remodelled. The tiers of elevated benches were removed, the elevation was reduced, and the room was seated with chairs. The building afforded no facilities for laboratory work for students, and such work was not provided for, at that time, in any American college. Upon the appointment of Dr. Dascomb's successor, trained in the modern methods of instruction, it became necessary to remove the work in chemistry to another building. Since that time the Old Laboratory has been used as a general recitation-room.

When this laboratory was erected it occupied a very retired position, in the rear of Colonial Hall; but upon the removal of the old buildings, and the laying out of " College Place," it became quite conspicuous. It must therefore yield to the demands of progress, and in spite of all old associations, give place to a more sightly structure. As these lines are being penned it stands dismantled and ready to fall.

Those who shall gather at the jubilee, looking for the old landmarks, will scarcely recognize the place it occupied.

About this time the trustees voted to build a dwelling-house for the college farmer, and committed the responsibility of the work to the farmer himself. He proceeded to erect a somewhat spacious two-story frame house, of unpretending appearance, but larger than the trustees had intended. The farmer proposed to take the building as his own, and complete it without charge to the college. The proposition was accepted; but the original farmer's house, at the corner of Professor and Elm streets, having undergone some changes, is now the home of the college president.

The Music Hall was one of the subsidiary buildings of the early days, erected in 1842—a frame building of one story, as large as the laboratory, giving a pleasant audience-room for about two hundred persons, with two entries at the front, and between them a piano-room with elevated floor, shut off from the audience-room by sliding doors. It stood on the west side of Professor Street, in the open space south of the present Ladies' Hall.

Professor Allen secured the erection of the building, by enlisting and uniting the interests of the choir and of the college literary societies; and it was used by these different associations in common. After eight or ten years, these bodies found more desirable quarters, and the Music Hall came into the entire possession of the college. It was then divided by a partition across the building, and one part became the room for the recitations in Mathematics and Natural Philosophy, and the other a room for the young Cabinet of Natural History, of which Professor Allen had laid the foundations. After fifteen or twenty years more, better rooms were provided for the Cabinet and the Philosophical Apparatus, and the Music Hall was moved near to the Ladies' Hall, and converted into a gymnasium for the young women. Four years ago the fire went through it, and the skeleton remaining was taken down.

Twelve years elapsed after the building of the Music Hall before any further building was under taken. Then the college chapel was erected; not because the college had money to build, but because it had become an absolute necessity. Nine hundred students were present, and the old chapel could seat only six hundred comfortably. At certain seasons of the year, an overflow gathering for prayers had been held in the Music Hall.

In 1854 the walls of the chapel were put up, and the building was completed in 1855, at an entire cost of eleven thousand dollars. The dimensions of the building are fifty-six feet by ninety. It is built in two stories of twelve feet and twenty-five, the upper story being the audience-room. The first floor provided two offices, a library room, three lecture-rooms for the Theological Department, and one Literary Society room. Two broad flights of stairs in the front end led to the chapel. There was a gallery across the end, over these stairs, and the stand was next to the gallery between the doors leading from the entry to the audience-room. Students coming in must face the audience and pass the stand. There was little temptation to tardiness, or to a disorderly exit. The room was finished neatly with plain board seats, of varnished whitewood, trimmed with black walnut, arranged on a level, without any rise in the floor. This made the seats in the remote part of the room seventy-five feet from the stand undesirable for those who were interested in the services. The bell of the old chapel was at first placed in the cupola, but soon a new bell was purchased from the profits of a Commencement Concert, by the Musical Union, and the old bell went to the Union school-house.

Externally the chapel stands as it was first built; but the audience-room has been reconstructed, by removing the gallery, placing the stand at the side, and arranging the seats in elevated circular ranges, so that every student has a good view of the stand. Thus we have an admirable audience-room, of nine hundred sittings. In these changes the stairs appropriated to the young women were transferred from the front to the rear. The cost of these changes, amounting to twenty-three hundred dollars, was met by a subscription by students and Faculty. Still another change is thought of, involving about the same expense. It is desirable to have more means of exit than the two broad flights of stairs afford. A projection built upon the south side, broad enough and deep enough for an organ recess, and a flight of stairs on each side, would bring a needed relief and improvement. The organ has been purchased by the Director of the Conservatory, but the recess for it is not provided for.

For many years a site had been reserved for a new Ladies' Hall—the south-west corner at the intersection of College and Professor streets, but no practical movement had been made until the Commencement Reunion of 1860. Then, just at the close of the exercises, without previous consultation or arrangement, after a stirring address from Governor Dennison, who was present, in which he alluded to the pressing necessity, the subscription began, and at the close amounted to more than three thousand dollars. This was enough to lay the foundations. The contract for this part of the work was made as soon as plans could be formed and approved, and the material soon began to be collected. In the spring of 1861 the corner-stone was laid by Father Keep, and the building of the foundation went on. Before the work was half finished the war came, and the contractor had difficulty in holding enough of his men to complete the work. It was finished by midsummer, and stood through two winters, before any superstructure was reared upon it. The contracts for materials were made, and mostly filled before the great rise in prices came. The walls were built, and the roof added, in 1863; and the interior was so far completed at the time of Commencement, 1865, that the alumni gathered in it for their reunion dinner. The first cost of the building, including the furniture for the private rooms, was about forty thousand dollars—a small sum for a building of such extent and value, but more than all the build-

ings previously erected by the college had cost.   In
form, it is adjusted to the corner lot on which it
stands, with two similar fronts, of one hundred and
twenty-one feet each, at right angles to each
other, with a depth of fifty feet, and three stories in
height.   It is a building of pleasing aspect and satisfactory in its arrangements ; and, unless some catastrophe befalls it, it should serve its purpose for
generations to come.   In 1880, after the burning of
the gymnasium, an addition was built, projecting
from the western extremity of the hall toward the
south, and carried up two stories.   It provides a
fine gymnasium, several rooms needed for the
steward's department, and several additional rooms
for young women.   The hall, as thus enlarged, provides, in its second and third stories, rooms for
about a hundred young women ; and on the first
floor, parlors, offices, society room, assembly room,
and reading-room, besides the rooms connected with
the boarding department, including a dining-room
for about two hundred boarders, with bake-room,
laundry, etc., in the basement.

In 1874 the college purchased of the Oberlin
School Board the old Union School-house, for five
thousand five hundred dollars.   It was built on
ground rented to the district by the college, in close
proximity to the college grounds.   The building
had become inadequate to the needs, and must
either be enlarged or given up.   This building afforded six comfortable recitation-rooms, and a large
room in the third story for the Cabinet ; hence the
name Cabinet Hall.   Upon the acquisition of this

building, the old recitation-rooms in Tappan Hall were deserted, a large writing-room was constructed by joining two of them, and the others were converted into music-rooms. When a new Professor of Chemistry was appointed in 1878, the lower floor of Cabinet Hall was devoted to his uses, giving a lecture-room, a working laboratory for students, with all needed appliances, a special laboratory for the professor, with balance-room and study adjoining. The Professor of Geology and Natural History has gradually extended his domain over the entire second story of the building, securing lecture-room, microscopical laboratory, general working room and study, with his cabinets above. While the scientific departments have been thus comfortably provided for, other classes have been excluded, and the old rooms in Tappan Hall, with some changes and repairs, have been resorted to.

Before the purchase of the school-house, two buildings for recitations and similar purposes had already been erected on the college square. These are called "French Hall" and "Society Hall." They are brick, of two stories, alike in outward form, and giving six comfortable rooms in each. They were built in 1867–8. French Hall was named for the late Mr. Charles French, of Cleveland, who gave five thousand dollars toward the building, and Society Hall took its name from the literary society and library-rooms which it contains. These buildings are to-day the chief dependence of the college for general recitation-rooms. French Hall contains four lecture-rooms, a room for drawing, and rooms for

the apparatus in the department of physics. Society
Hall gives three lecture-rooms, a college society
room, and library-rooms. The libraries have outgrown the space devoted to them, and new books
can be placed on the shelves only by retiring old
ones. These two buildings are measurably convenient and satisfactory. They were planned for a
summer term instead of a winter term, and have
required some changes to adjust them to the new
order. They were built in costly times, and together involved an expenditure of nineteen thousand dollars.

The idea of Council Hall, the elegant and com-
modious building of the Department of Theology,
was first practically indulged in 1869. Plans and a
location were agreed upon, and, during 1871, about
five thousand dollars were secured for the object—
sufficient to lay the foundations. At the meeting of
the National Council of Congregational Churches,
held at Oberlin in November of that year, the corner-
stone was laid, and by vote of the Council the name
Council Hall was given for the building that was to
be. The foundation was completed in the summer
of 1872, and the walls and roof were completed
in 1873. The work went on as money could be
obtained. The generous friends at the East gave
liberally, and, to complete the interior, the larger
Congregational churches of Ohio came forward with
subscriptions varying from two hundred to two
thousand dollars each, the name of such church
being placed over the room for which its subscription provided. The building, not fully completed,

COUNCIL HALL.

was dedicated at Commencement, 1874, and was opened for use the following autumn. Its front is one hundred and one feet, and its depth seventy feet. The height is four stories, including the Mansard. Its cost, including the furniture of public and private rooms, was about sixty-eight thousand dollars. It provides two lecture-rooms, a chapel seating three hundred, and divisible by a lifting partition into two lecture-rooms, a reading-room and reference library, and private rooms for sixty students. It is devoted exclusively to the Theological School, except an occasional use of the chapel for social meetings.

To provide board at the least possible cost for those who need such provision, the building on Main Street, opposite the north-east corner of the college square, was purchased in 1880, and fitted up for a boarding-hall. It has cost, including an additional lot, five thousand dollars, and has been named "Stewart Hall," in memory of the early founder, and for the maintenance of his principles of economy. The house is furnished without rent to the matron, and she receives young women for board and room at two dollars a week, and young men, at table only, for two dollars. This goes beyond the early times in cheapness, when, with flour at two dollars and a half a barrel, beef two and a half cents a pound, and butter seven cents, students paid one dollar a week for their seat at table. The house receives sixty boarders, and is always full.

This completes the list of the buildings erected for the college. The aggregate first cost of them all, not including the dwelling-houses, is about one hundred and eighty thousand dollars. The cost of the buildings still in use was one hundred and sixty-three thousand.

The only additional building, in immediate prospect, is that for which the old laboratory yields its place. It is to furnish, in its first story, a young ladies' assembly room of three hundred and fifty sittings; and in the second, two rooms for the literary societies of the young women. It is planned to cost eleven thousand dollars, of which the societies have raised three thousand, and Miss Susan M. Sturges, of Mansfield, gives five thousand.

The pressing needs to be provided for in future buildings, are ten more recitation and lecture rooms, rooms for instruction in drawing and art, libraries and cabinets, a building for the Conservatory of Music, the beginning of an art-gallery, and probably a dormitory building for young men, which shall provide for the more advanced college students, as Council Hall for the theological.

LIBRARY, CABINET, AND APPARATUS.

The library of the college has had a slow growth. It was begun the first year by the collection of such books as could be spared from the libraries of New England ministers, and from time to time received accessions of this kind, with an occasional gift of fresher books from some publisher. The deputation to England brought back books of some value, and an occasional gift for the purpose has helped in the growth. Originally a small fee was charged for the use of the library, and a majority of students saved the fee. For the last fifteen years every student has paid about a dollar a year for the library, charged in his bill of incidentals. This arrangement has promoted both the use of the library and its growth. A fee for special or extra examinations has also been charged, and this is added to the library fund. From these funds the librarian's salary is paid, the library is kept in working order, and a few hundred dollars yearly are appropriated for new books.

The literary societies of the different departments are united in a Union Library Association, to build up a common library. Their funds come from initiation fees, from an annual tax, and from the proceeds of a course of lectures and literary entertainments. Thus they add to their library several hundred volumes a year. The college library contains eleven or twelve thousand volumes, and the societies' library five thousand, and the two are so arranged as to present the appearance of a single library.

The theological reference library in Council Hall is still small, containing about sixteen hundred volumes. No permanent fund is connected with any of the libraries, and the largest gift ever received was five hundred dollars. The present need is more books and more room for them.

The Cabinet first took form under the hands of Professor Allen. He was himself a diligent collector, and he increased his personal collections by exchanges. He imparted something of his own enthusiasm to numbers of his pupils, and as they scattered abroad they remembered the Cabinet. Missionaries in the Micronesian and Hawaiian Islands, in Western and South-eastern Africa, in India, China, and Japan, have sent collections illustrating the natural and the social history of these diverse regions. Professor Allen himself spent six months in Jamaica as a collector, and the Cabinet shows the results in almost every department. At rare intervals a special appropriation has been made from the college funds to secure some rare specimen, and at still rarer intervals gifts in money have been received. Thus the cabinet has been constantly improving until it serves very satisfactorily in the illustration of the different departments of Natural Science. More space is required for the display of the collection, and a fire-proof building for its protection.

The chemical laboratory is reasonably well provided with apparatus. Facilities are afforded for whatever work the professor or the student needs to do. The rooms themselves are by no means ideal, but they serve all essential purposes. The microscopical laboratory is a recent institution, the instruments having been furnished by a gift of a thousand dollars for the purpose, from Mr. David Whitcomb, of Worcester, Mass. The arrangements are sufficient for a class of about twenty students at a time. This laboratory work is elective in the course, and the provision is at present adequate to the demand. In the department of Natural Philosophy, especially in the direction of dynamic electrictity, valuable additions to the apparatus have been made by Professor Elisha Gray, in connection with his course of lectures. The latest results of experiment and discovery are very fully illustrated. An observatory moderately furnished has long been a need in the line of astronomical study. A refractor with seven-inch aperture was presented to the college, some years since, by Mr. Kenyon Cox, of New York; but for want of a place where it can be permanently mounted and safely kept, its use has been very limited. The time for these various improvements ought not to be far away. For several years past the manifest duty has been to seek for enlarged endowment, and these subordinate necessities have been studiously kept out of sight.

GROWTH OF THE COLONY.

The fifty years have yielded some results in the growth of the town as well as of the college. The first streets built up in the settlement were those which surround the college park; and for many years almost all the houses were on these four streets, Main and Professor Streets running north and south, and College and Lorain Streets east and west. The centre of the Oberlin tract is at the north-east corner of the college park; but the first dwelling and the first college building were placed at the south-east corner, and this naturally determined the centre of the settlement. Again the first mills were placed still farther south, where Main

Street crosses Plum Creek, and thus the settlement was directed toward the south, a tendency which was never overcome. The position of the railroad station, in later times, has increased and confirmed the tendency. Other streets which were opened and occupied in the early times were Pleasant, Morgan, and Mill Streets. All these were laid out and more or less occupied the first year or two, but were afterward much extended.

The only road which at first was vital to the convenience of the colony was the road to Elyria, and upon this efforts were first expended. Citizens and students and professors subscribed labor, and performed the work in person. This road took the direction of College Street, intersecting Lorain Street, a mile and a half east. The plan first adopted in road-building was to cover the road-bed with a cross layer of rails split from the oak and ash trees along the way, and cover these rails with a top-dressing of clay and soil, obtained by digging a ditch on each side. While the rails continued sound, the road was quite a success, but as they decayed, the fragments must be taken out, and the original clay be made the foundation. Another fifty years may possibly disclose the art of constructing, on such a foundation, roads which shall be comfortable for every season of the year.

The streets and sidewalks of the village have formed a formidable part of this road problem. The first sidewalks were constructed of white-wood plank, three inches in thickness, laid end to end, lengthwise of the walk, indicating the superabundance of timber. After a few years it was ascertained that the excessive thickness of the plank, and the contact of the ends, both tended to hasten decay. Thereafter the plank was made an inch and a half in thickness, and laid crosswise ; and most of our walks are still thus constructed—pine lumber having taken the place of the white-wood and the oak. Sandstone flagging from Berea and Amherst, since the construction of the railroad, has been extensively introduced. The first attempt at a more satisfactory roadway for the streets was a heavy oak plank covering on Main Street, from College Street to the railroad station. Like all plank roads it was a comfort at the outset, and a nuisance at the end. The next experiment was a layer of broken sandstone. It was soon ground into sand, and sunk out of sight in the clay. The latest method is a pavement of blocks of sandstone eight inches in thickness, with eight or ten square feet of surface. These blocks keep their place, and promise durability. Stone suitable for a macadamized road-bed is too distant and costly to be available. Such mention of the work of road-building will not seem out of place to those who bore the burdens of the early days.

The great solution of the road problem for Oberlin was found at length in the construction of the Toledo, Norwalk and Cleveland Railroad, in 1852. The number of students in the college had been doubled by the scholarship endowment, and it was a formidable undertaking for them to get into town at the beginning of the Spring term, and out of town at the close of the Fall term. The Cleveland and Columbus road had been built a year or two before, with a station at Wellington, nine miles from Oberlin. This was a great relief, but the road to Wellington was often intolerable. When the proposal was made of a railroad from Cleveland to Toledo, the people of Oberlin were awake to the opportunity. They sent out surveying parties east and west, to show that the road from Grafton to Norwalk could easily be made to pass through Oberlin. The township subscribed twenty thousand dollars to the stock, and the citizens of Oberlin individually as much more. Many who subscribed did it simply to promote a necessary public enterprise, never expecting to see their money again. The road was deflected from a straight line sufficiently to touch Oberlin, and even proved a success financially, so that the original stockholders received their own with usury. It is now the Southern Division of the Lake Shore and Michigan Southern. After some years the people of Elyria, on the Northern Division, secured the transfer of the section between Oberlin and Grafton, so that the intersection should be at Elyria, and thus the journey to Elyria is different from that of fifty years ago.

The Oberlin colony had no municipal or corporate existence. It was simply a settlement in the township of Russia, and could have no privileges or regulations apart from the township. In 1846, the village of Oberlin was incorporated by act of the legislature, and the Oberlin colony was no longer spoken of. The "Town Hall" was erected in 1870, at a cost of nearly twenty thousand dollars. In 1858, a

stranger came into town to establish gas works, and
the citizens subscribed the required stock. The enterprise failed financially before it had afforded any
light to the town, and Mr. Samuel Plumb, one of the
citizens, took it up and carried it forward, the subscribers having surrendered their stock to aid in the
enterprise. Thus Oberlin was provided with gas-
works some years in advance of other and older
towns in the neighborhood. The discovery of kero-
sene a year later made the gas less necessary.

The Oberlin Fire Department was organized, or
rather equipped, in 1852, by the purchase of two
hand-engines from Rochester, N. Y. These served
the necessities of the town until 1865, when a Silsby
steamer was bought for four thousand dollars.

No very disastrous or sweeping fires have occurred
in Oberlin. One of the business corners has been
twice burned out, involving considerable loss to individuals. The first burning was in 1848, when the
printing office of Jas. M. Fitch, the publisher of *The
Oberlin Evangelist*, was destroyed, and several less
important business places. The buildings which
took the place of those burned were somewhat better, but they were of wood, designed to be temporary. In 1882 this corner was again burned, with
much greater loss to various parties, but the result
has been a great improvement to the town. A very
fine business block now occupies the corner, and a
similar fire on that corner is not likely to recur.

The two-story frame hotel on the corner opposite
was burned in 1865, and thus place was made for the
better hotel and business block now occupying the

corner. The third corner, which was the first occupied, embracing Oberlin Hall, the first college building, has thus far escaped the catastrophe of fire, an immunity which cannot be expected another fifty years. Other fires have been limited to single buildings of more or less value. The most serious, perhaps, of them all was the burning of the original mills, at the corner of Main and Mill Streets, in 1846. They had been sold by the college some years before. No serious fire has ever occurred in the college buildings, but there have been many narrow escapes.

The first school for children in the colony was taught by Miss Eliza Branch, now Mrs. George Clark, of Oberlin. Her school-room was the log house built by Mr. Pease. This was the primary department of the college. The first school-house was built in 1838—a small frame house, of one story, placed on a corner of the lot occupied by the First Church. This old school-house still survives in a dwelling house on South Main Street, owned by E. M. Leonard. It was the only school-house until 1851, when a two-story brick house was built on the west side of Professor Street, over against Tappan Hall, sufficient for three departments; and the school was graded accordingly. After a few years this was found inadequate, and the building was enlarged by adding two wings and carrying up the central part to three stories. Thus seven school-rooms were provided, and the school was more fully graded. In 1874 this building was sold to the college, and a new Union school-house was built on

SCHOOL HOUSE.

the east side of Main Street, a little south of the principal business corners—a fine building containing eleven school-rooms and costing about forty thousand dollars. The school has again outgrown its quarters, and other rooms in the vicinity are occupied. The number of pupils enrolled in these schools is about seven hundred and fifty, and a superintendent and seventeen teachers are employed.

The following superintendents have been employed: Joseph H. Barnum, from 1854 to 1860; Samuel Sedgwick, from 1860 to 1869; Edward F. Moulton, from 1869 to 1876; Henry R. Chittenden, from 1876 to 1878; H. J. Clark, from 1878 to 1882; and George W. Waite, the present superintendent. The first four were graduates of Oberlin College, Mr. Clark, of Western Reserve, and Mr. Waite of Amherst.

The churches and church buildings were briefly described in a preceding chapter.

The earliest cemetery was on the south bank of Plum Creek, and west of Main Street, and the first burials were near the street, a little north of the lot occupied by the Episcopal church. After a few years the graves were removed from the lots on the street, and only the land in the rear was occupied. In 1863 grounds about three fourths of a mile southwest of the village were purchased by a Cemetery Association, and carefully laid out and adorned. Since that time the old ground, which was leased to the Oberlin Society by the college for cemetery purposes, has been surrendered to the college, and most of the graves have been removed to the new cemetery.

The first two years the mail for Oberlin came and
went by South Amherst, six miles north, and was
carried in a small hand-bag, by Harvey Gibbs, the
first post-master.   He built the first post-office,
which was on North Main Street, over against Tappan Hall.   The walk from Tappan Hall eastward
across the park was constructed by the students,
for the purpose, chiefly, of going to the post-office.

Mr. Brewster Pelton built and kept the first hotel,
a log building, on the east side of the lot occupied
by the present hotel.   No strong drink or tobacco
was furnished at his house, but after some anxiety
and discussion it was decided to be " impracticable"
to keep a hotel without furnishing tea and coffee.
In the spring of 1834 he built a large two-story
frame house on the corner, and this was the principal hotel until it was burned in 1865.   For the purpose of securing a suitable hotel, in the absence of
business sufficient to sustain it, the citizens, in 1867,
subscribed the sum of twenty-five hundred dollars,
and the college a like sum, to encourage the enterprise.   Mr. Henry Viets accepted the proposal,
received the money, giving to Oberlin College a
mortgage of five thousand dollars on the property,
the condition of which is that a suitable building
shall be provided, and a hotel kept in a satisfactory
manner, and that all intoxicating drinks and danc-
ing parties shall be excluded.   Thus the hotel, called
until recently the " Park House," was built, and on
these conditions it is carried on.

The private dwellings of the town began in a
humble way.   After the first year few, if any, log

houses were built, but the frame houses were small, and most of them were so constructed as to suggest future enlargement. They were of one story, or a story and a half, and the cornice was often lacking on one gable, suggesting a front or main part. One house, near the corner of Main and Lorain Streets, a story and a half in height, exhibited, for some years, a solitary plate of a two-story building, high in the air, a symbol of the owner's confidence in the future. In the majority of cases, the hope of enlargement was not realized. The lacking cornice was at length added, and a pleasant porch was constructed over the door. But the enlargement came with a new generation, and the work of adding a front or main part to the humble dwellings of the early day is still going on. At present the town is conspicuous for the large number of unpretentious but pleasant and homelike dwellings, with spacious yards attractive with trees and grass.

The Soldiers' Monument was built in 1870, by a contribution of four thousand dollars, in which citizens and students and alumni and friends all united. The generous contractor did not limit the expenditure to the amount placed at his disposal. The cost was about a thousand dollars more than the subscription.

The college square in 1834 was a field of stumps surrounded by a Virginia "worm" fence. In 1836, as Tappan Hall came into use, the students occupying it waged war upon the stumps, and under axe and fire they rapidly disappeared. Soon afterward, students from the East, whose life had not been a constant warfare with trees, led in the enterprise of replanting the square with young trees from the forest, and the largest trees upon the square, excepting the historical elm, are the result of that first planting. An annual tree-planting was established, and the good work was continued, Evergreens were added fifteen or twenty years later, by a special movement set on foot by Professor Peck.

The crooked rail fence had given place some years before to a stately post and rail fence, of oak timber, painted white. The expense was provided for jointly by the college and the people of the town. When this fence began to fail, a hedge of the Osage orange took its place, and when, in the advance of civilization, hedges and fences became unnecessary, the hedge which had been trained with so much care was exterminated. The grading and general improvement of 1881 cost two thousand dollars, the citizens subscribing one thousand, and the college furnishing an equal amount.

There was no early necessity for a bank in Oberlin, or rather there was no capital to provide such a convenience. The "First National Bank" was established in 1863, with Mr. Samuel Plumb as principal stockholder and president. Upon the recent expiration of its charter, it was reorganized as the "Citizens' National Bank." The other business operations of the village are such as belong to a college town, with very little in the way of manufacturing interest. A flouring-mill, saw-mill, and two planing-mills, two carriage factories and a furniture factory, give the extent of business in this form. The chief support of business is the presence of hundreds of students who must be fed and clothed, and the families that naturally gather at such a centre of education.

Book stores are among the most conspicuous of our business establishments. Besides the college some special schools have been carried on here for many years—a telegraphic school and commercial and writing schools. The outside public often connect these special schools, in their thought, with the college. The college has no connection with any of these, except a single writing school.

The town has supported no saloons, and there is a very earnest purpose among the people that no saloon shall ever flourish here. A dubious drug store has caused them some anxiety, and a single tobacco store has had a patronage beyond the benefits it has conferred.

A printing establishment was among the early business institutions of the place. The Catalogue of 1834 was printed at Elyria, of '35 and '36 at Cleveland, and of '38 at Cuyahoga Falls. The college was too busy, or too poor, to publish a Catalogue in '37. The Catalogue of 1839 was printed at Oberlin by James Steele, and the work was well done. Mr. Steele was also printing the *Evangelist* at the time, the first volume of which was issued that year. He established the office while he was a student in the Theological Seminary. The *Evangelist* was an eight page quarto, issued every two weeks for twenty-four years, at one dollar a year. In 1844 James M. Fitch,

having returned from the Jamaica Mission, became publisher of the *Evangelist*, and carried on the
printing and book business until his death, in 1867.
Besides the *Evangelist*, and from time to time a village paper, he printed on his hand-press and published several volumes, among them, in 1846–47, two
volumes of Theology, by Professor Finney, of six
hundred octavo pages each.

Since Mr. Fitch's day, two and sometimes three
printing establishments have been maintained here.
The earliest village paper that attained permanence
was the *Lorain County News*, now the *Oberlin
News*, first issued in 1860. The first editor was A.
B. Nettleton, then a student, afterward a soldier, and
now proprietor of the *Minnesota Tribune.* J. B. T.
Marsh took up the pen laid down by Mr. Nettleton,
afterwards entering the army, and returning again
to his editorial work. Later he was eight years editor of *The Advance* at Chicago, and is now treasurer of Oberlin College. The *Oberlin News*, through
many changes, has held on its way, and has attained
a permanent character and success under its present
proprietor, Mr. W. H. Pearce.

In 1868 Rev. W. C. French, rector of the Episcopal church, began the publication of *The Standard
of the Cross*, at Oberlin, and continued it five years,
when he removed his office to Cleveland. Other
papers and other volumes, of more or less importance, among them the papers published by the students, have been printed at the Oberlin offices.
Thus printing and publishing, though less conspicuous here than in some other university towns, has

been among the prominent industries of the place. The later volumes published at Oberlin by Mr. E. J. Goodrich have in general been printed in Eastern cities.

The first physician in Oberlin, after Dr. Dascomb's early service in that capacity, was Dr. Alexander Steele, who came in 1836, and continued his professional work until his death in 1872. Dr. Isaac Jennings came in 1839; then followed Dr. Otis Boise, Dr. Homer Johnson, Dr. William Bunce, Dr. Dudley Allen, and others later. Dr. Jennings was a thoroughly educated physician, holding the honorary degree of M.D. from Yale, and had had a successful practice of some years; but becoming convinced that medicine was harmful instead of helpful, he had entirely discarded it. He called his system "Orthopathy," upon the theory that nature, even in disease, was doing the best possible, and could not be assisted, except by judicious nursing. He would visit any one that called for him, and give suggestions, but no medicine, and made no charges. He published several volumes setting forth his views. He died in 1875, in the eighty-sixth year of his age.

CHAPTER X.

COLLEGE WORK AND STUDENT LIFE—THE EARLIER AND THE LATER.

THE general view of the college work set forth in the preceding pages would perhaps suggest the inquiry whether it had not involved so much of outside interests, and so many diverting influences, as seriously to interfere with its value and effectiveness in the definite work of education. Has the college been able to maintain regular and systematic and thorough scholastic work in the midst of these various movements and interests? If such an impression or doubt has been produced, let it be remembered that a record of fifty years, crowded into a few pages, necessarily involves a concentration of events which does not belong to the actual experience; events separated by years in the actual life, stand side by side in the record. Thus what appear as multiplied perturbations have in fact occurred at rare intervals—one or two perhaps in a single generation of student life.

Still another suggestion occurs. With the most careful arrangements to concentrate the thought and attention of a body of students upon their studies, diversions of some sort will occur. If they do not come from without, they will spring up from among themselves. Interest in the affairs of the community, the country and the world is often absorbing, but not more so than interest in college politics, in such profound and weighty questions as which class shall win the field in the rush, or which " nine" or which club shall bear off the honors in the matched game or regatta. There will be agitations of some kind in such a mass of active, fervid human nature. It is quite possible that the more grave and weighty the concerns which press upon such a body, the less the effervescence may be. Efforts are sometimes made to exclude national politics from college life. But the question, who shall be president of the Republic? is no more distracting than who shall be president of a college society? and it is far more worthy of interest and attention. The gravity of any matter of concern tends to give seriousness and steadiness to those who cherish it. There are concerns pertaining to the country and the world from which no one, young or old, in student life or in active life, can afford to be excluded. An important factor in all education consists in giving to such interests their proper place and thought, and strong and well-balanced character can no more be secured apart from such influences, than vigorous plant life without light and air. Those who planted Oberlin, and those who have since had responsibility in its direction, have not felt at liberty to provide for sheltering the young people from the interests and excitements of the country and the world.

There was very early a suspicion abroad that the educational work at Oberlin was to be narrow and superficial. The name " Collegiate Institute" perhaps suggested an ambitious academy instead of a modest college. Co-education was regarded as indicating the same drift, the "burning of the class- ics" fixed the impression, and the supposed ultraisms and heresies that followed rendered the investiga- tion of the facts unnecessary. Newspaper writers assumed the impression as fact, and the general public trusted the newspapers. It would perhaps be regarded as a bold statement, that there was never any foundation for the assumed fact. The first Freshman class was admitted in 1834, and the preparation of the candidates was such that they would unquestionably have been admitted at any eastern college. So persistent was the misrepresen- tation, that in 1839 an appendix to the Catalogue was published, giving a comparison of the courses at Yale and at Oberlin. In science and literature and philosophy, the two courses were almost identi- cal. In languages the Yale course gave considerably more Latin, and the Oberlin course an excess of Greek and Hebrew which more than balanced the deficiency. The facts were that a student in good standing at Oberlin found no difficulty in entering *ad eundem* any New England college. Nothing less than this was to be expected, in view of the fact that the leading professors at Oberlin were men who had graduated with honors—in two cases, the high- est honors—at Williams and Amherst and Yale. It is true the course in languages at Oberlin was modi- fied by excluding the most objectionable classic authors, especially Latin poets, and substituting New Testament Greek, and Hebrew in part. Instead of Horace, George Buchanan's Latin version of the Psalms was announced, but when the time came for its use only a few copies could be gathered up in this country and abroad. At length such editions of the poets were published that they could be introduced with propriety into classes of which young women were members, and the differences of the Oberlin course disappeared. The requirements for admission have been increased, during the progress of the college, by a full year's study, and a similar change has taken place in the colleges throughout the land.

The establishment and maintenance of a large preparatory department or academic school at Oberlin has been essential to its work. Such schools have existed in connection with all Western colleges. In the absence of academies adequate to the work, and from the fact that the high schools of later days have rarely undertaken it, the college has been compelled to prepare its own students. The work at Oberlin began in this way, and has continued until the present time. Five sixths of the present Freshman class have received the whole or a part of their preparation here. Besides being a preparatory school, this department provides for a large number of students who do not contemplate a full course, but desire preparation for business or teaching. One incidental result of gathering these persons in the school is that large numbers of them fall under the attractions of study, and within a year take up the preparation for a college course. A large proportion of those who enter the course here are drawn from this class of students.

To Oberlin this large preparatory school has probably been more essential than to any other college. By no other arrangement could large numbers of students have been gathered; and the large numbers were necessary to furnish an inviting field of labor to Mr. Finney, and others who came at the same time. The influence of the school could not have been what it has been without these numbers.

From the beginning, care has been taken not to exhaust the strength of the college professors upon the preparatory department. Only in very rare instances has a preparatory class been instructed by a college professor. The policy has been to confine each professor to his own general department, and as far as possible to his own specific work. Theological professors have very rarely been called to college classes, nor have college professors taught in the preparatory department. Thus students do not in the beginning of their course feel that they have received all that the college can do for them. Passing from one department to another they come under new instructors, almost as really as in going to a different school.

To avoid this difficulty, which besets young colleges with preparatory departments, the preparatory school, from the beginning, was carried on by placing a principal in charge, and giving him one or perhaps two permanent teachers, who should take the advanced classes in languages; while other classes were provided for by drawing their teachers from the large body of advanced students in the college and theological departments. Rarely was more than one class given to a student. It is quite probable that there were disadvantages in this arrangement. The teachers would often lack experience, and could not often acquire the force and authority of one familiar with the ground, and who carried with him the weight and momentum which years confer. This was in part counterbalanced by the presence and general influence of professors in the other departments, which was diffused throughout the institution. The whole school has been managed as one establishment, and the wisdom and influence of the Faculty as a whole has permeated the entire body, securing advantages not to be found in a moderately equipped academy or high school.

To the students employed as teachers the arrangement is specially profitable. The compensation is small, originally twelve and a half to eighteen and three fourths cents an hour, later thirty-five to sixty-five cents, but the discipline and experience are more than the compensation. It gives the student-teacher an opportunity to test his own knowledge, and is often a training for his life-work. The college has thus, to a considerable extent, brought up its own professors, and has furnished professors for many other colleges. By this means, and by teaching in vacations, the teaching impulse and faculty have been quite widely developed among Oberlin students, and to this influence, in part, their tendency to establish colleges and schools may, doubtless, be traced.

In later years the number of permanent teachers in the Preparatory Department has been much increased, but more than twenty students, young men and women, are still employed. These furnish a natural link between the Faculty and the body of students, to preclude the painful separation which sometimes occurs; and this result comes spontaneously, without any intentional effort. The pupils in the preparatory department are under the same general regulations as in the other departments. They have never been gathered in a school-room to pursue their studies under the eye of a teacher. They prepare their lessons in their private rooms, and come together for recitations only. None can be received who have not sufficient maturity and self-control to prosper under this arrangement.

The college work has been essentially like that in other American colleges, with a similar apportionment of studies. Latin and Greek and Mathematics have characterized the first part of the course, and Science and Literature and Philosophy the latter part. From the first, special prominence was given to philosophical studies and inquiries. The presence and preaching and teaching of such men as President Mahan and Professors Finney, Morgan and others, awoke an interest in this direction. Besides, it was a time of great quickening of speculative thought in the country. The New School Theology was claiming attention, and arousing the country to earnest inquiry.

The antislavery movement, too, was not simply a movement in practical action, but it was laying its foundations in great principles of ethical philosophy; and Oberlin became inevitably one of the centres of this speculative activity. President Mahan was a strong thinker in this direction, and impressed himself very decidedly upon the whole school. At his coming there was no class in college in advance of the Freshman, and he began a course of philosophy with them, and carried them through the three remaining years with such authors as Abercrombie, Cousin, Dugald Stewart and others, followed by a year's course of lectures. The whole school shared more or less in the enthusiasm, and received an impulse which it has never quite lost. In the Catalogue of 1835, no definite place in the course is given to these studies, but the statement of studies closes with the remark, "Intellectual and Moral Philosophy extensively." In the following Catalogues it is confined to the Junior and Senior years.

Mr. Finney's work in the Theological Department was equally effective; and the difference between these two prominent teachers, which was soon developed, as to the "nature and foundation of moral obligation," increased the interest. No parties were ever formed around these diverse views; but whatever may be said at this day about the feebleness of the original Graham diet, Oberlin students, in the line of intellectual nourishment, were fed on strong meat. To discuss first principles became their pastime. They rested on their hoes in the cornfield to look into the inner consciousness, and the manual labor cause suffered in the interests of philosophy.

The demand for books was quite limited. Kant, Coleridge, Cousin, Locke and similar authors were called for, but the want of libraries of history, general literature and science was not greatly felt. Possibly it was, in part, the absence of the books that prevented the existence of the want. It is true there were at that day great readers among the students, in the various lines of literature, but the tendency was not general. A student of that period, burdened with the duty of an essay, rarely went to the library for relief. His first impulse was to draw upon the resources of his own consciousness.

In these respects there is a change. Science and literature and history have come to occupy the places which belong to them, and the students are drawn toward the libraries; but we may hope the day is far distant when they shall cease to have a lively interest in the study of philosophy. The study of the ancient languages, Latin, Greek and Hebrew, has always held a prominent place, and linguistic study is quite as prominent to-day as at any time in the past. Natural Science has come into great prominence in the world during the fifty years, and it has made a much wider place for itself in our course than was originally assigned it. The modern languages, French and German, have claimed their share of attention.

It was the purpose of the founders, and of the men who joined the enterprise in 1835, that Biblical study should be a prominent feature of the course; and the early deviation from the general college course was in this direction. The Greek and Hebrew Scriptures were to take the place of some of the classic authors. This arrangement was earnestly adopted, and there was no division of feeling on the subject. It was a very common thing for the trustees at their meetings, in the earlier years, to propose to the Faculty the inquiry whether this idea had been fully and thoroughly maintained. The first difficulty encountered was, that it placed the college in misadjustment with other colleges. Oberlin graduates entering the Theological Department would have had more than a year of Hebrew, while those from other colleges had none. In going to other theological seminaries a similar difficulty was encountered. Then it was not clear that those who were not to enter the ministry could wisely devote a year or more to the study of Hebrew. Similar difficulties were felt in regard to the New Testament Greek, but they were not so pressing. The result at length was that the Hebrew was committed wholly to the Theological Department, and the New Testament Greek was limited to a term or two, and more recently has been mostly discontinued.

Through all the fifty years there has been persistent and careful attention to the study of the Scriptures. Every class, in all the literary departments, has its hour a week for this study; and it is not introduced as an extra, but takes the place, for the day, of one of the regular studies. The Bible course is so arranged as to secure on the part of the pupils some intelligent apprehension of the contents of the Scriptures, the last year being devoted to a consideration of the leading facts and doctrines of the

Christian faith, with a free and open discussion of doubts and difficulties. The study of Christian evidences has held its usual place in the course.

The requirements upon the student in the way of attendance upon religious services have always been two church services on the Sabbath, and daily evening prayers at the chapel. As in New England colleges, six o'clock morning prayers were originally held for the young men, but attendance upon family prayers at their various boarding places was at length substituted. Students select for themselves the church which they will attend, but the attendance must continue for a term. No college church exists, nor is any regular Sunday service held for students. A special voluntary gathering is sometimes called.

In 1835 the "Thursday Lecture" was established, which students were required to attend. It was a religious lecture, not specially a college arrangement, but an appointment of the church, held at a late hour of the afternoon. As students were required to attend, and the lecture was given by Professor Finney, or by some other professor, it came at length to be regarded as a college appointment, and as such it has been continued to the present time. Within the last ten years it has ceased to be a distinctively religious lecture. Each professor, in his turn, takes his own topic, literary, scientific, historical or practical; and the hour is regarded by the students as an occasion of interest and profit. A lecturer is frequently invited from abroad.

A weekly prayer meeting is appointed for each

class, in all departments, led by a professor or other teacher. Attendance upon this is voluntary. Occasionally, in seasons of special interest, a class arranges for itself a daily half hour meeting. No meeting continues beyond an hour. The "Young People's Meeting" is an appointment of long standing—not strictly a college arrangement nor the appointment of any church. It is a meeting held on Monday evening immediately after the supper hour, to which all the young people of the place are invited, with a permanent leader, usually one of the younger professors. The meeting generally gathers some hundreds, mostly students. The chapel of Council Hall is the regular place of meeting. When this becomes too strait the college chapel is resorted to.

It is a peculiarity of college arrangements at Oberlin that every recitation or lecture is opened, after the roll call, by a brief prayer, in which the teacher leads, scarcely longer than an ordinary blessing at table, or by the singing of a verse or two, in which the class chorister leads. The general cultivation of music, and the pocket hymn-book, make the singing possible and pleasant. This practice came in with Mr. Finney, in 1835—not by any ordinance, but by spontaneous adoption, and the custom has made the law.

At Oberlin, as everywhere, many features of the college life are determined by the students themselves, within certain limitations. They organize and conduct their own literary societies, with the provision that there shall be no secret organization or fraternity, that no society shall embrace both young men and young women, and that the meetings shall not be continued after ten o'clock in the evening. Of the permanent societies, of long standing, there are three among the young men of the college classes, and two among the young women. These are devoted exclusively to literary exercises, and are conducted with great vigor and decorum and success. In some of these, failures to meet appointments are so rare that they are said not to occur at all. Offensive rivalries among the societies have been almost unknown.

The three societies of young men unite in fitting up and occupying a single room, as do the two societies of young women. More rooms are desirable, and will probably soon be attained. The five societies are again united in building up a single library, under the charge of the "Union Library Association."

The "Oratorical Association" is an organization of the college classes to elect speakers for a yearly "Home Contest." The successful speaker appears again in a "State Contest" in which several colleges of the State are represented, and the fortunate competitor finally represents the State in an "Inter-State Contest," where several Western States are represented. This Association has existed for several years past, but whether the benefits equal the outlay does not seem to be determined in the judgment of either students or Faculty.

The history of college journalism at Oberlin is brief. The *Oberlin Student's Monthly*, a magazine of thirty-two pages, was published by the literary societies for two and a half years, beginning with November, 1858. The war made such drafts upon editors and subscribers that it was discontinued in 1861. The *Oberlin Review*, a quarto of sixteen pages, was begun in 1873. It is published by the "Union" of the literary societies, each of the five societies appointing an editor, and the Union an editor-in-chief. The paper has been conducted, in general, with ability and dignity, and in harmony with the interests and honor of the college, and has been financially successful.

The social opportunities of Oberlin students are naturally provided for in the organization of the college. It is one of the advantages of the system that it secures a good degree of social culture and enjoyment without any expenditure of time or thought or effort. The student who holds on his way, passing his fellow-students on the sidewalk, meeting them in the recitation room and the chapel, will receive the essential benefit of cultivated society, even if he should attend no social gatherings, nor make any personal calls. Like the sunlight and the atmosphere it is diffused around him, without his responsibility. He will not grow into a recluse, nor find himself disqualified for general society, whenever the time shall come. But every student who becomes identified with a class will find further social opportunities opening to him—an annual or semi-annual class gathering, an invitation with his class to the home of his professor for an evening, or an hour or two at a "social" in the church parlors. One wholesome social habit established in the early times has come down to us. Only the early hours are devoted to social entertainment. Even in general gatherings with which college arrangements have nothing to do, the hour of ten seems to be regarded as the natural limit.

In the matter of recreations and sports, the students, with reasonable limitations and suggestions, arrange for themselves. There is an Athletic Association having in charge a ball ground, and with the large number of students games are arranged between different classes and groups which have sufficient interest, so that it is not necessary to visit other colleges in the pursuit of sport. The Association has sometimes received and entertained another college club, on its travels, but its champion " nine" does not go abroad in term time. There are no boating facilities within reach at Oberlin; thus all the questions which elsewhere arise, in connection with such privileges, are easily disposed of.

The gymnasium made its way slowly at Oberlin, because it seemed to be inconsistent with the manual labor idea; but after various attempts, an unpretending establishment with moderate equipments is open to young men, and a better one for young women. The exercise is at present voluntary, but classes are organized under competent teachers, and all who desire can have the benefit without charge.

Sedentary games of chance and skill were formerly prohibited at Oberlin, but the restriction has been removed except in the case of cards. To visit a billiard saloon is still reckoned a misdemeanor.

The general discipline of the college was at the beginning conformed to the parental idea, and it has not been materially changed. The idea has been accepted that the college is a place where character and habits are to be formed, as well as instruction imparted. No strict personal surveillance was ever undertaken. The student has been thrown greatly upon his own responsibility, with the understanding that his continued enjoyment of the privileges of the school must depend upon his satisfactory deportment. No study hours have ever been prescribed, except as limiting the time of ball-playing and other sports upon the college grounds, and of social calls upon the young women of the college. Each student studies when and where he pleases, provided he reports himself, with due preparation, at the appointed hour. The regulations are few and obvious, such as are necessary to the comfortable association of such a body of students. There is a special requirement, which was once peculiar to Oberlin College, but is not now, to abstain from the use of tobacco. The rule is coeval with the college, and the time has never come when it seemed advisable to dispense with it. The Faculty are a unit in support of the rule, and have always been. At the beginning, the maintenance of the rule was not difficult ; very few young men came who had formed the habit. The use of tobacco has been greatly extended in the country within the last twenty-five years, and many young men come with the habit fastened upon them. They come with a full understanding of the requirement, and often for the purpose, on their own part or that of parents and guardians, of recovery from the habit. Frankness is encouraged. No disgrace is visited upon the one who fails. If without deceit, or attempts at imposition, he avows his failure, he receives an honorable dismission and can go where he will encounter no prohibition of the kind. Every year brings more or less of such failure; and it is too much to hope that there are no cases which escape observation. But the rule has been maintained with a good degree of success; and since the principle has been adopted in government schools, in this country and abroad, as well as in some others, we may hold on our way with even more courage. It would seem that every school open to young women might insist upon the principle as a matter of essential decency.

Undoubtedly, the general reputation of Oberlin tended at first to bring to the school those of serious character and aims. But for many years past it is not probable that those who have come have differed essentially from the students gathered from the same regions in other schools. The influence of wholesome traditions has been helpful. The moral atmosphere has been measurably clear and a healthful condition has been maintained. There have been anxieties and disappointments, but on the whole those upon whom the responsibility of direction has rested have had occasion to rejoice in the results. The exceptions to good order and earnest work have been comparatively few, and the product in genuine character and purpose has been most gratifying. There has never been a time when the

overwhelming sentiment of the school was not on
the side of good order and wholesome discipline, and
this has to a great extent made the manifestation of
authority unnecessary. Nothing has occurred in
the fifty years that could take the name of a college
rebellion. There has been no organized resistance
to authority. Only twice in the fifty years has anything occurred to which the term "hazing" could be
applied. The first case took place more than forty
years ago, when several prominent young men in
college entrapped and punished with stripes a vile
youth who had sent anonymously most disgraceful
and infamous missives to worthy young women in
the school. They were reputable and conscientious
young men, but their indignation carried them away.
When they had time for consideration, although they
were entirely unknown, five of them came before
the church of which they were members, and con-
fessed their own part in the transaction. As they
apprehended, the confession cost them dear. In a
criminal prosecution which followed they were fined
a hundred dollars each, and costs, and in a civil
prosecution, damages were laid upon them to the
amount of three hundred dollars each. This case
has been quoted within the past few years as having
a bearing against co-education. What, exactly, the
argument is, does not appear. The second case
occurred five years ago, too recently to need to be
recalled. It was a painful one, and the treatment of
it was decisive and effectual. One such case in fifty
years ought to be enough. The earnest life which
came in with the founding, and which has in a good

degree continued to the present hour, has proved a safeguard against many of the follies which tend to spring up in college life, and the aim of the administration, which has been measurably successful, has been to retain the convictions and sympathies of the students on the side of the order of the school.

No monitorial system has ever been adopted: each young man reports weekly, in writing, to the professor in charge, his success or failure in attendance upon prescribed duties. The young women report to the lady principal. This method might not be always wisest, but it has served the purpose so well that it has continued until the present time. Each student is marked for his performance in recitations and examinations, and a record is kept, but this record is not made the basis of any grading of the class, or of a distribution of honors. Nor is any announcement of standing made at any time. The record is for the private information of teachers and pupils and guardians. A certain standard must be attained as a condition of advancement; beyond this the record has no formal bearing.

The college has no special honors to distribute, and no prizes. The commencement programme is arranged alphabetically, and position has no significance. With the exception of one or two years, the entire classes have appeared at commencement with their orations or essays. As classes enlarge, this will be impracticable, and some selection must be made. Thus far the number has in no case exceeded forty, and four or five minutes is the time allowed to each. There is no question that to a Commencement audience this arrangement is more interesting than to have a few speakers, and twelve or fifteen minutes for each. They come to see the young performers and hear their voices, not so much to be instructed. Yet there is a certain special interest in seeing how much can be said in five minutes, and the discipline is good. Commencement at Oberlin has always brought an audience—not many visitors from great distances, but the friends of the graduates, and the people from the immediate neighborhood. In the earliest days the great tent, which would shelter three thousand, was filled, and afterward the church, and often there were almost as many without as within. The novelty has passed away but there is still a sufficient audience.

The college confers the usual degrees, but has done little in the way of honorary degrees. There has been no positive action by trustees or Faculty in opposition to such degrees, only a traditional repugnance. Even the common degrees, in course, have been sometimes held in disrepute among the students. Half of the class of 1838, which numbered twenty, declined to receive the degree, and the President announced, at the commencement, that those who desired the degree could receive their diplomas at the college office. No other instance of such scrupulousness has appeared. The degrees have always been conferred in the simplest manner, without any attempt at Latin discourse. The earlier diplomas were in English, and written by hand, but when plates were procured a Latin text appeared.

The honorary degrees thus far conferred by the

college are of two kinds, the honorary A.M., given to such students of the college as make good progress in their course but failed to graduate, and afterward secured a good standing for themselves in literary or professional work; and the same degree granted to those holding the diploma of the " Literary Course" who have attained a similar standing. The Literary Course at present carries with it no degree. No doctorate, in any line, has ever been conferred by the college. Neighboring institutions have sometimes shown their good-will in this way towards Oberlin men, but thus far without any reciprocity.

The *student's expenses* have always been moderate at Oberlin. It was a prominent idea with the founders to provide a school where young men, at least, without money, but with courage and industry and economy, could make their own way and come out without a load of debt. In the earlier history of the college this was to a great extent realized. Probably a majority of the graduates of the first twenty-five years thus made their own way. The facilities for manual labor and for school teaching gave them the opportunity. During the last twenty-five years many have done the same. The scholarship system has made tuition merely nominal, and the college has arranged to keep other expenses at the lowest point. The boarding halls under the direction of the college have served in a measure to regulate prices in the town. A seat at the table in the most desirable families has rarely been more than three dollars a week. While the winter vacation continued, and winter schools called for teachers, an enterprising young man could often make ends meet without any, or very little, loss of time from the college term. The general disappearance of winter schools, and the consequent, or subsequent, change of vacation to the summer, has made entire self-support more difficult. The student who undertakes it now may be obliged to lose a year, or to come through with a debt. But the necessity of self-support is not as great as it was fifty, or even thirty, years ago. The families of what was then the "New West," that made the constituency of the college, are able now to aid their sons and their daughters towards an education, while then they could only spare them. The daughters were the first to receive aid, and the sons afterward. The present estimate of a student's necessary expenses, including term bills, board, room rent, fuel, lights, washing, books and stationery, for the school year of thirty-eight weeks, as published in the annual announcement, is one hundred and twenty to two hundred and twenty-five dollars, according to the arrangements he chooses to make. This, of course, includes no extras, in the way of music or art, nor does it provide for clothing or travelling expenses, nor various incidentals which attach to student life. The statistics of the Class of 1881, the latest at hand, give nine hundred and ninety dollars as the average expenses of the class for the entire four years, or a little less than two hundred and fifty dollars a year; and about one fourth of the young men of the class made their own way.

The uncertain part of the student's expense for

education, here and elsewhere, is that which he makes for himself, or rather that which the students make for themselves. This, too, is the part most difficult to regulate. Class expenses, society or club expenses often outgrow all the college charges, and they seem to be beyond the reach of college arrangement or authority. The most that can be done is to guard the door, with great vigilance, against their intrusion. Thus far, little progress has been made in the way of such extravagances at Oberlin. Some weaknesses have occasionally appeared, in the direction of costly programmes, or unnecessary music, or flowers, and in a few instances a class or society has indulged in an unnecessary entertainment, but a wholesome reaction soon appears, and the tendency is counteracted. The aim at Oberlin has been, and it is to be hoped will continue to be, to make it possible for one with limited means, or with determination and industry and tact, without means, to receive all the essential benefits of the course. To the inefficient this must be impossible. For one who has never earned his way at home, to come with the expectation of doing full work as a student and earning two hundred dollars a year besides, is absurd. There are successful students, without any practical gift whatever, who can never do anything towards their own support, in a course of study. But a young man of practical gifts, and some experience in self-support, should never be deterred by want of means from making his way through a course of liberal education.

The education which students receive in their college course they obtain in large part from each other. An instructor and books are not sufficient. The student needs contact with those of his own age, who have impulses and ideals somewhat like his own ; and to save him from narrowness he needs to have contact with a reasonable variety of life and character. In this respect the student at Oberlin has had more than ordinary advantages. The college has always been national rather than local in its character. During the earliest years more than half of the students were from outside the State, mostly from New England and New York, and through all its history students have been gathered here from many different States and from foreign lands. At present sixty per cent of the students are from Ohio, and the remainder from forty-nine different States and territories and foreign countries. All the States of the Union are represented except Delaware, Maryland, Florida, Nevada and Oregon. At the same time the Faculty of the college represent, in their places of education, more than a dozen colleges, universities, and professional schools. The arrangements are adapted to give the student a Christian education which shall not be narrow or provincial.

CHAPTER XI.

PERSONS WHO HAVE SHARED IN THE WORK.

THE Oberlin enterprise, from its beginning, has filled many hearts and many hands. Many lives have been concentrated in it, and none of these could have been spared. Some have had more to do than others, but human judgment cannot determine who have been most useful. Those who have held conspicuous positions attract our notice, but it is possible that persons out of sight, in the quiet of the household, providing, through many years, a Christian home for the youth who needed it, have contributed as much as any others to the general cause. It seems necessary that some mention should be made in these pages of those who have occupied public positions, and have helped to give direction to the movement. But such mention will, in general, be limited to those who have passed away, or who have retired from the field. Of the founders themselves little more needs to be said than has already appeared, or will appear in their letters found in the Appendix.

MR. SHIPHERD, in 1844, removed his family to Olivet, with the purpose burning in his soul to build another Oberlin, and even a better, but in a few months he lay down in his last rest. His grave was made in the new colony, and his memory is still cherished there. He was only forty-two years of age at his death, and only thirty when he commenced the work at Oberlin; yet such was his appearance and bearing and the weight of thought and care that seemed to rest upon him that he was called "Father Shipherd" by all the young people of the colony and the school. No published writings of his remain. Such letters as are found in the Appendix are all that can now be gathered up. The photographic art had not become diffused through the country at the time of his death, and not even any outline of his features was left.

Mrs. Esther Raymond Shipherd returned to Oberlin with her fatherless boys, and by the help of the people here her former home was secured to her. After some years these sons came forward to their mother's aid and provided her a home in Cleveland, where several of them were settled in business, finally relieving her of all care and making her declining years full of quiet usefulness and peace and rest. She died Dec. 7th, 1879, at the age of eighty-two. A memorial window in the Plymouth Church at Cleveland symbolizes the self-forgetful usefulness and beauty of her life. A simple tablet in the Ladies' Hall is all that bears the Shipherd name at Oberlin. Oberlin itself is their monument.

Mr. and Mrs. Stewart, having no children, had pledged themselves to the service of the Oberlin Institute for five years, with no other compensation than the mere cost of living. When the school was opened, in 1833, Mr. and Mrs. Stewart took charge of the boarding hall, and continued in this capacity of father and mother to the young people until 1836. The first year he was also general manager in the absence of Mr. Shipherd, and treasurer of the college. His views and practice of frugality, and plainness of diet were somewhat too rigid for general acceptance with the students, and in 1836 he resigned the stewardship of the " Hall," and with some sense of disappointment Mr. and Mrs. Stewart made their way eastward to Vermont, and finally to New York, to work out the stove problem which for two or three years had been held in suspense. In this enterprise Mr. Stewart attained the fullest success; not so much in the acquisition of wealth for himself, which was not his aim, as in bringing economy and convenience and comfort into thousands of the homes of the land. He was a philanthropist in his stove work, as in his work among the Indians and at Oberlin. He established his home at Troy, N. Y., in the neighborhood of the manufacturers who worked out his inventions. Mr. and Mrs. Stewart maintained through the years of their prosperity the same habits of simplicity and frugality which had characterized them in earlier life, and all their surplus means went to some good cause. Oberlin shared in their prosperity, although their ideal of a college and Christian community had not been fully realized.

Mr. Stewart died December 13th, 1868, worn out with the cares and perplexities of his business, at the age of seventy years. Mrs. Stewart still remains at her home in Troy, and hopes to visit Oberlin on its jubilee anniversary, the only survivor of the group that in the parsonage at Elyria, in prayer and consecration, devoted themselves to the work of building up in the wilderness a Christian college and Christian community.

REV. SETH H. WALDO was the first permanent teacher that reached the place. He had arranged to be present at the opening of the school, December 3d, 1833, but was prevented by serious illness. He came about the first of May, 1834, a week before the opening of the summer term. He was a graduate of Amherst and Andover, and was about thirty years of age at his coming. The arrangement with him was that he should have the charge of the school until the appointment of a president, and should then take the professorship of languages. He entered upon the work with enthusiasm and success, but the discussion upon the study of the classics, which followed the coming of President Mahan, led to the apprehension that his ideal of education could never be realized at Oberlin, and he resigned. He was afterward connected for several years with the Grand River Institute at Austinburg, and for many years past has maintained a classical school at Geneseo, Ill., still full of energy, though full of years.

Three days after the opening of the term in 1834, DR. JAMES DASCOMB, with his wife, reached Oberlin. He had been elected professor of chemistry, botany and physiology, and was also expected to have the responsibilities of physician to the new settlement. He was a native of New Hampshire, and was

twenty-six years of age at the time of his coming
to Oberlin. He had received his professional education at Dartmouth, under the instruction of Dr.
Mussey. In temperament he was naturally cautious
and conservative. Novelties had no attraction for
him, and no enthusiasm ever took him off his feet.
The truth was what he wanted, and nothing else had
any value in his eyes. The radicalisms which were
soon developed at Oberlin he at first regarded with
some apprehension, and there were times in the
early years when he felt a little inclined to retire
from the position. He did not lift his voice against
the new movement, but quietly held on his way,
taking time to test the new idea or the new doctrine. The value of such a conservative force in
the midst of the fervid and plastic mass at Oberlin
was unquestionable. His influence extended beyond his own department in this respect, and tended
everywhere to thoroughness.

Through all the changes Dr. Dascomb held the
same position, without any change in his prescribed
duties, from 1834 till 1878, forty-four years, a conscientious, thorough, successful instructor. In 1878,
at the age of seventy, his strength failed him, and
he retired from his work. Two years later, in April,
1880, he died, forty-six years after his coming to
Oberlin.

MRS. MARIANNE PARKER DASCOMB was also a
native of New Hampshire, trained in the schools and
the academy near her home in Dunbarton, and
finally in the Young Ladies' Seminary at Ipswich,
Mass., under Miss Grant. After a year of teaching

she was married to Dr. Dascomb, April 14th, 1834, and left at once for her new home in the wilderness. The first year she was a teacher in the school, and the second year she was elected principal of the Ladies' Department. The following year, at her own request, she was released from these duties, but was at the same time made a member of the " Ladies' Board," then first organized. In 1852, under earnest pressure, she again consented to take the principalship, which she held until 1870, eighteen years, being then sixty years of age. The remaining years of her life she continued a member of the Ladies' Board, and a most helpful counsellor of her successor. She died on the 4th of April, 1879, just a year before her husband.

Mrs. Dascomb was wonderfully fitted for the work she had to do, strong in the simplicity and transparency and integrity of her character, and in the unconscious influence which constantly attended her. Her power as an instructor and guide did not lie in any special theories of education which she consciously held and applied, but in her rare good sense, in her ready adjustment to every emergency, and in her cheerful and hopeful temper, which no cloud could darken. Such a character was an essential factor in the forces which gave form and vitality to early Oberlin.

REV. ASA MAHAN reached Oberlin in May, 1835, having been elected to the presidency of the college, and entered directly upon his duties. He was then thirty-six years of age, a native of Western New York, educated at Hamilton College and Andover

Seminary. He came from the charge of the Sixth Presbyterian Church of Cincinnati, and his earnest and vigorous preaching made at once a strong impression upon the people of Oberlin. He was a bold and aggressive advocate of all the Oberlin ideas and doctrines, and was always ready, at home or abroad, to give a reason for the faith that was in him with earnestness and full conviction. He was an enthusiastic teacher in his own department, that of philosophy, and gave an impulse to the study at Oberlin which it has never lost. His administration of the college was, in general, successful, and he gave his heart and strength to its prosperity without any reservation. An infelicity which often attends great strength of purpose and of character was sometimes suspected in him, namely, a greater facility in conviction than in conciliation. While he had many ardent friends, there would be another class who were as distinctly not his friends. Some of his colleagues felt at times that his strong aggressiveness awakened unnecessary hostility against the college; and in 1850, some of his friends having planned a new University at Cleveland, and invited him to take the direction of it, he resigned at Oberlin, having held the presidency of the college fifteen years. With President Mahan, Oberlin lost somewhat of its positiveness and aggressiveness.

The enterprise at Cleveland was not a success, and Mr. Mahan was called to a professorship in Adrian College, Mich., and at length to the presidency of the college. The last ten years he has spent in England, in abundant labors in the special

PRES. ASA MAHAN.

work of promoting the "higher" Christian experience, and now, at the age of eighty-three, he is preaching to large congregations, editing a magazine called *Divine Life*, and issuing one volume after another, such as "The Baptism of the Holy Ghost," "Out of Darkness into Light," and "Autobiography, Intellectual, Moral and Spiritual." While at Oberlin he published works on "The Will," "Intellectual Philosophy," and "Moral Philosophy." Other works, since published, are on Logic, Spiritualism, Natural Theology, and a Criticism of the Conduct of the War.

REV. CHARLES G. FINNEY came in June, 1835, about a month after Mr. Mahan. He was then nearly forty-two years of age, with health somewhat broken by the exhausting evangelistic labors of the preceding ten years. He found a theological department of thirty-five students, and entered at once upon his work, as professor of systematic theology. His habit was to preach once on the Sabbath, not often twice; and the year following he was called to the pastorship of the church. For many years he gave the long winter vacation to preaching as an evangelist, for the most part with some church at the East. In 1849 he went to England, and spent a year and a half in similar labors in London and other cities of England and Scotland. Ten years later he went again in the same work for about the same length of time. In 1851 he was elected President of the college, and held the position until 1865, with the arrangement that he was not to give attention to the details of the position, but only to the more public duties. His work as an instructor was not changed except that he took the Senior college class for some years in moral philosophy. In 1865 he resigned the presidency, being then seventy-three years of age. He had already, in 1858, surrendered the work in systematic theology, retaining the pastoral theology and his work as a pastor. In 1872 he laid down the pastoral work, but continued his pastoral lectures until the year of his death, 1875, having completed, lacking a few days, his eighty-third year. No brief mention can characterize him or set forth his work; nor is it necessary. He belongs to the world, and not to Oberlin alone. His "Sermons on Important Subjects" and "Revival Lectures" were published before his coming to Oberlin. His "Lectures to Christians" appeared a year or more afterward, and his two volumes on "Systematic Theology" in 1846 and 1847. These were numbered as volumes second and third, his purpose being to prepare a volume on "Natural Theology" to precede them. This volume was never written. While he was in England in 1850, he prepared and published an edition of his Theology in one volume, involving the substance of the two preceding volumes. His latest works were a volume on "Masonry," published in 1869, and his "Memoirs," written by himself, and published after his death. Upon the publication of his Theology very diverse opinions were expressed in regard to it, according to the standpoint.

Rev. Wm. H. Burleigh closed a notice of the

C. G. Finney.

ÆT. 80

work in the *Charter Oak*, Hartford, Conn., 1846, with the following paragraph:

"We will venture the prediction that fifty years hence this volume will rank among the standard works on theology, and the name of Finney be mentioned with those of Edwards, Dwight and Emmons. Sooner than that we fear he will not be generally appreciated. The time will come when Finney will have justice done to his exalted talents, and when the host of his revilers—men not possessing, in the aggregate, half his mental grasp, will be lost in oblivion unless he should preserve their names from utter extinction by an incidental allusion in his works."

Dr. Charles Hodge, in the *Biblical Repository*, 1847, wrote as follows:

"The work is therefore in a high degree logical. It is as hard to read as Euclid. Nothing can be omitted; nothing passed over slightly. The unhappy reader once committed to a perusal, is obliged to go on, sentence by sentence, through the long concatenation. There is not one resting-place, not one lapse into amplification or declamation, from the beginning to the close. It is like one of those spiral staircases, which lead to the top of some high tower, without a landing from the base to the summit; which, if a man has once ascended, he resolves never to do the like again. The author begins with certain postulates, or what he calls first truths of reason, and these he traces out with singular clearness and strength to their legitimate conclusions. We do not see that there is a break or a defective link in the whole chain. If you grant his principles, you have already granted his conclusions. . . . We propose to rely on the *reductio ad absurdum*, and make his doctrines the refutation of his principles. . . . We consider this a fair refutation. If the principle that obligation is limited by ability, leads to the conclusion that moral character is confined to intention, and that again to the conclusion that when the intention is right nothing can be morally wrong, then the principle is false. Even if we could not detect its fallacy, we should know it could not be true."

Dr. George Redford, of Worcester, England, in the preface to the London edition, which he edited, 1851. writes: "As a contribution to theological science, in an age when vague speculation and philosophical theories are bewildering all denominations of Christians, this work will be considered by all competent judges to be both valuable and seasonable. Upon several important and difficult subjects the author has thrown a clear and valuable light which will guide many a student through perplexities and difficulties which he had long sought unsuccessfully to explain. The editor frankly confesses that when a student he would gladly have bartered half the books in his library to have gained a single perusal of these lectures; and he cannot refrain from expressing the belief that no young student of theology will ever regret the purchase or perusal of Mr. Finney's lectures."

REV. JOHN MORGAN arrived at Oberlin in company with Mr. Finney, in 1835. He was then thirty-two years of age, a native of Ireland, having been

DR. JOHN MORGAN.

brought to this country at the age of ten, trained as a printer in eastern cities, prepared for college at Stockbridge, Mass., and graduated at Williams, as valedictorian, in 1826. He had taken no seminary course, but studied theology some years in New York. He was an instructor in the literary or preparatory department of Lane Seminary, at the time of the antislavery excitement there, and was in entire sympathy with the students in their withdrawal. His first appointment to Oberlin was as professor of mathematics, but the call which he accepted was to the chair of the literature and exegesis of the New Testament. This work he entered upon at once, but his broad and thorough scholarship enabled him to fill many a gap, upon emergency, in the new college. There was not a study in the entire curriculum in which he could not give instruction at an hour's warning, as successfully as if it were his own specialty. But the New Testament was his chosen field, and for this field his linguistic, historical and philosophical gifts and attainments abundantly qualified him. He was no mere mechanical or technical interpreter, but reached at once the soul of the matter, where language and philosophy both harmonize.

The influence of Professor Morgan in the enterprise was conservative in the best sense, not by reason of any inertia or immobility of nature. His enthusiasm, in any well-considered movement, was always prompt, but his breadth of nature and thought and knowledge gave him a view of all sides of every question, and he could not hold an extreme position, or enjoy any extreme action. He could patiently tolerate the extravagances of others, because of his kindliness and his hopefulness. Probably no one among the many instructors who have been at Oberlin has held a larger place in the hearts of all. For many years he was associated with Mr. Finney in the pastorship of the church, preaching once on the Sabbath, and more in Mr. Finney's absence or ill health. Two years ago, at the age of seventy-eight, he retired entirely from his work, and since that time has been residing with a son and a daughter in Cleveland. By all right he belongs to Oberlin, and the benediction of his presence in these latest years ought to rest upon us. He expended his interest and his labor upon his classes, and rarely felt that he was ready to commit his thoughts to writing. Thus far he has given us no books. A few valuable essays are all that we have from him in this form. The "Baptism of the Holy Spirit" and "Acceptable Holiness" were published in the *Oberlin Review*, and an article on the "Atonement," in two parts, can be found in the Bibliotheca Sacra for 1877–8.

REV. HENRY COWLES was called to the professorship of languages at Oberlin, upon the resignation of Mr. Waldo, and came in September, 1835. He was born in Norfolk, Conn., in 1803, and was thirty-two years of age when he came. He had graduated at Yale, and taken his theological course there. He completed the course in 1828, was ordained at Hartford the same year, and came at once to Northern Ohio under appointment from the Connecticut

Home Missionary Society. He preached in Ash-
tabula and Sandusky, and after two years, having
received a call from the church in Austinburg, he
returned to his home in Connecticut, was married,
and commenced his work in Austinburg. From a
most successful pastorate of five years he came to
Oberlin, and found himself in full sympathy with all
the leading objects and aims of the work; and from
the first day until the day of his death—a period of
forty-six years—he gave himself, without reserve, to
these objects. There seemed to be no thought of
himself or his personal interests; no anxiety in
reference to position. His heart was in the work,
and all he asked was a place to lay out his strength.
In 1838 he took the chair of Church History in the
seminary, and of Hebrew and Old Testament Literature in 1840. In 1848, in consequence of straitened means on the part of the college, and the
necessity of reducing expenses, he resigned his work
in the seminary, and took the editorship of the
Oberlin Evangelist, a work which he had shared
with others for some years preceding. From this
time until the close of 1862 he gave his thought and
heart to the *Evangelist*, and made it greatly what
it was, a treasury of religious thought and experience, and of practical life. The twenty-four volumes
of the *Oberlin Evangelist*, with which Professor
Cowles had more to do than any other man, give a
better exhibition of Oberlin thought and character
and work during those years than any definite
attempt to set them forth can possibly do.

When the *Evangelist* was closed up Professor

Cowles was about sixty years of age, and might naturally feel that the chief work of his life was done; and it would have been a satisfactory work. But the habit of communicating his thoughts to others by writing was strong upon him, and by what seemed a divine leading he entered upon the work of writing commentaries upon the Scriptures. He commenced with the parts of the Old Testament to which he had given more particular attention as an instructor, and went on, year after year, adding volume to volume, devoting to it all his energies and all his resources, through a period of seventeen years. In 1881 he issued the last volume, and then felt that the Lord permitted him to depart in peace. His work was done; the result remains with us—a commentary on the entire Scriptures, full of practical wisdom and the ripe fruits of scholarship. He died in September of the same year. The interests of the college through all these years filled his heart and hands. He was a member of the "Prudential Committee" and a trustee, in constant attendance upon these duties, and often went out upon financial missions in behalf of the college. His last public duty was to attend the meeting of the trustees in 1881.

It would be much more satisfactory to give the family life of these men, to look into their homes and observe there the results of Christian character and fidelity. By the side of each one of these men there stood a woman of like spirit and faith, whose life in the community was no less valuable; and children were gathered about them whose work and life it

DR. HENRY COWLES.

would be pleasant to follow, but this opens too wide a field.

REV. JOHN P. COWLES, brother of Henry, was called to Oberlin, in 1836, as Professor of Hebrew and Old Testament Literature. He was a member of the same class with his brother at Yale, and graduated as valedictorian. He took up the work with great heartiness and energy, and was in essential sympathy with the Oberlin life and aims. Some of the peculiarities which appeared did not command his respect. The diet, and now and then a doctrine, suffered from his sharp and sometimes sarcastic criticism, and after two or three years he was asked to retire. A little more gentleness on one side, and more patience and tolerance on the other, would have saved to the school an instructor of the ripest scholarship and the highest ability, who was in harmony with all that was essential at Oberlin. For many years he and his wife have been at the head of the school for young women at Ipswich, Mass.

Another member of the same class, of 1826, at Yale was ELIJAH P. BARROWS. He was elected professor of Hebrew at Oberlin in 1835, but did not accept the appointment. After filling the same chair at Western Reserve College, and again at Andover Seminary, in 1871 he took up the work at Oberlin tendered him so long before, and carried it forward with great acceptance nearly ten years, until failing strength demanded rest. Dr. Barrows is still among us, bearing the honors of a useful life and of a cheerful old age.

TIMOTHY B. HUDSON came to Oberlin as a student, in 1835, and entered the Sophomore class, having been before in attendance at Western Reserve College. He was at the time about twenty years of age, an earnest and ambitious scholar, and of pronounced personal influence and character. The growing school soon enlisted his services as a teacher, and his relations as a pupil were interrupted. In 1838 he was elected Professor of the Latin and Greek Languages, and performed the work until 1841 ; then a more active life seemed necessary for his health, and he resigned, and entered the service of the Ohio Antislavery Society as a lecturer. After several years of this service, holding conventions and lecturing throughout the State, he accepted in 1847 an invitation to his former position at Oberlin, and continued as Professor of Languages until his death in 1858. He was a vigorous and impressive teacher and disciplinarian, and a speaker of unusual power. In the antislavery work he was very effective, and especially he was helpful in the establishment of the *National Era* at Washington, which was so ably conducted for many years by Dr. Bailey. In the college work every department and every interest felt his influence. His vacations were often devoted to financial work in behalf of the college, contributing materially to its support. Although his regular course as a student was interrupted, he never ceased to be a student, and in 1847 he took his degree and was formally numbered among the alumni of the college. So far as his attainments were concerned he might have had the degree ten years before, but had not cared to ask it.

His death was tragic, and never fully explained. He left Oberlin by the train, to go to Strongsville, expecting to find conveyance from one of the stations nearest to Strongsville. At Olmstead station, in attempting either to leave the train or to return to it while it was moving, he was drawn along by the side of the track and at length thrown under the wheels. It was late in the evening and no one observed him, until the engineer of a train ten minutes later saw him lying on the track, but not in time to arrest his train. It was a sad day at Oberlin when the mangled remains were brought back to be buried here. He was forty-three years of age at his death.

GEORGE WHIPPLE came with others from Lane Seminary, in 1835, already a man of mature character and judgment, and sound scholarship. At the completion of his theological course, in 1836, he was elected principal of the preparatory department, and in 1838 Professor of Mathematics, resigning in 1847, to become Corresponding Secretary of the American Missionary Association, organized the year before. At Oberlin he rendered very valuable service, not only as an instructor, but as a standing member of the " Prudential Committee" having in charge the business affairs of the college. For such responsibilities his even, well-balanced judgment admirably fitted him. The same clear judgment became afterward the strength of the Association to which he devoted his life. The incessant work and care at length broke down his strong constitution, and he died in 1876, at the age of seventy-one, having seen the Association advance from small beginnings to a condition of great usefulness and prosperity.

JAMES A. THOME was a member of the same class in Lane, and came to Oberlin in 1835. He was born in Augusta, Ky., the son of a slaveholder, of Scotch Presbyterian ancestry. At the completion of his course, in 1836, at the age of twenty-three, he was commissioned with another gentleman, by the American Antislavery Society, to visit the West India Islands, and observe and report the results of emancipation there. This mission he discharged with great acceptance, and wrote a very interesting volume, which was published in 1838, and greatly aided in the antislavery work in this country. The same year, 1838, he was elected Professor of Rhetoric and Belles Lettres at Oberlin, and held the chair with acceptance and success until 1848, when he was called to the pastorate of the First Congregational Church of Cleveland. This position he held, in abundant and successful labors, for twenty-three years, retiring in 1871, to engage in a new church enterprise at Chattanooga, Tenn. After two years, in the midst of these labors, he was struck down with sudden disease, and died in March, 1873, at the age of sixty years. In 1851, soon after leaving Oberlin, he was elected a trustee of the college, and often visited us to give a course of rhetorical instruction to the college classes, or of pastoral lectures to the students of the seminary, or to favor us with some public address or discourse—services always most welcome and profitable. He was a man eloquent in speech, pleasing and impressive in personal presence, fearless as a soldier in duty, gentle and sensitive as a woman in his respect for the feelings of others—a true Christian man.

MR. AMASA WALKER, of North Brookfield, Mass., accepted, in 1842, an appointment to the professorship of Political Economy; not as a resident professor, but to come every year and give a course of lectures continuing through several weeks. The same salary was credited to him as to other professors, but there was never any less in the treasury for his coming. Mr. Walker was trained as a business man, in New England, and did not get his theories from the schools; but he was as radical in his advocacy of free trade and solid currency as the most theoretical modern professor; and he drew his illustrations of his principles from his own wide experience and observation as a business man.

In one respect he went beyond even Oberlin radicalism in his principles of reform. He was a " peace man;" not an ultra " non-resistant," but he regarded war, under all conditions, as sinful. His coming was the occasion of earnest but friendly discussion of the rightfulness of defensive war. It is interesting to know that when the test came, in 1861, his three sons entered the army and did valiant service, with his full approval—not, as he afterward explained in a pamphlet, to engage in war, but to sustain the government in the use of its police force to execute the laws of the land. How often words instead of principles separate those who seem to differ. Mr. Walker published various pamphlets and a text-book on Political Economy. He died recently at his home in North Brookfield.

Two other names that have appeared in these pages belong to this early period of Oberlin history, those of Father Keep and Mr. Dawes.

Rev. John Keep was born in Long Meadow, Mass., in 1781, graduated at Yale in 1802, was pastor in Blandford, Mass., and in Homer, N. Y., from 1805 till 1833, when he came to Cleveland and became pastor of a new church on the West Side. While he was at Homer he had been a trustee of Hamilton College and of Auburn Theological Seminary, and was naturally interested in any educational enterprise in the neighborhood. In 1834 he was elected a trustee at Oberlin, and held the position until his death in 1870. By reason of his years and experience he was made president of the Board, and had the responsibility of the casting vote on the question of receiving colored students, in 1835. From that day he took Oberlin on his heart, and never laid it off unless when he laid off the earthly life. His last words pertained to a letter he had planned to write in the interest of the college. He traversed the land to gather means to sustain it, and crossed the ocean to save it in a crisis. In 1850, then seventy years of age, he removed to Oberlin, and from that time his home was here. At every meeting of the trustees he was present, and encouraged all by his hope and his faith. When others were depressed he sustained and bore them on by his cheerful courage, and thus he held on to the end of his days. When more than fourscore years old he would often come out at evening, with his lantern, to find some one burdened with responsibility and care, and cheer him up with a word of encouragement. His sleep was sweeter after such a service. He died in his eighty-ninth year, not from disease, but because life was completed.

MR. WM. DAWES became a trustee of the college in 1838, and at the same time made his home in Oberlin. He had been a successful business man, and upon visiting Oberlin he was greatly pleased with the spirit of enterprise and work, on the part of students and professors, which he witnessed on every hand. He at once cast in his lot with them, and through a period of twelve years he greatly aided in sustaining the work by his financial ability and personal influence. The mission to England was a success, to a great extent through his strength of purpose and personal force, his power to impress others with his own convictions. His courage at times seemed to amount almost to presumption, but he rarely failed to estimate properly his opportunity. Others were not always able to work up to his standard of faith. To keep the college from debt he proposed that the salaries of the professors should not constitute a legal claim, but that whatever came should be divided, and if there were anything lacking it should not be a debt on the part of the college. This was his view of the relations which Christian workers should sustain to any benevolent enterprise which they were carrying forward. It is the principle applied in what is known in these days as the " Faith Mission." The principle did not commend itself generally to the parties concerned, and the plan was not adopted. Mr. Dawes had set his heart upon this idea as the true Christian conception, and he at length retired from further responsibility. He is passing a quiet old age, in full possession of his faculties, at Fox Lake, Wis.

In this circle of devoted and consecrated men, one was found who proved false, the only one during the fifty years who has betrayed his trust or brought scandal upon the cause. It is not necessary to name him. He came in 1836, a graduate of Western Reserve College, and took his theological course at Oberlin, a young man of ability and promise and marked influence. When the *Evangelist* was established he was made office editor, and was appointed to other posts of responsibility. It was a dark day in the winter of 1843 when his hypocrisy and villainy and vileness were disclosed. Imprisonment and other penalties which followed did not change his character. He became an exile, and lived for many years and died in the remote south-western part of the country, with no sign of essential reformation.

George N. Allen, whose work has been already mentioned, was elected Professor of Music in 1841, and of Natural History in 1847. He continued his work until 1870. After retiring, he removed with his family to Cincinnati, and died there in 1877, at the age of sixty-five. He was buried in the Oberlin Cemetery.

William Cochran came to Oberlin as a student, in 1835, from Fredericktown, Ohio. He graduated in 1839, and took the theological course, completing it in 1842. The same year he was appointed Professor of Logic and Associate Professor of Intellectual and Moral Philosophy. He had unusual powers in the direction of philosophical inquiry and thought, and was a very impressive preacher. A series of articles in the *Oberlin Quarterly Review*, of which he was an editor, on the simplicity of moral action, gives an example of his analytical powers, and is still worthy of careful study. Professor Cochran resigned in 1846, with the thought of entering the profession of law. He died at Fredericktown in 1847, at the age of thirty-three, and was buried in the Oberlin Cemetery.

The prosperity of the college through all the fifty years has depended upon the faithful and unpaid services of its trustees, resident and non-resident, some of whom have stood at their posts almost for a lifetime, devising ways and means, and often meeting a necessity from their own personal resources. The only survivor of the nine original corporators is Jabez L. Burrell of Oberlin. The only other survivors of those elected during the first ten years are Wm. Dawes, already mentioned, and F. D. Parish of Sandusky, who was elected in 1839, and attended every meeting, except one, when he was in Western Virginia looking after the lands of the college, until his resignation in 1878. He is now, at the age of eighty-six, a resident of Oberlin. Among the non-resident trustees who stood by the college through evil report and good, was William Sears of Boston, who before the railroad came west of Buffalo often made the long journey to attend the meetings, and

Samuel D. Porter, of Rochester, who was present in every emergency with his wise and considerate counsel. Of the resident trustees, Uriah Thompson and Jabez W. Merrill have rendered the college faithful service for many years, and still live to look after its interests. Brewster Pelton removed to Cleveland in 1851, but retained his life-long interest in Oberlin, and at his death, in 1872, left a bequest to the college of twenty-five thousand dollars.

Of the earliest inhabitants—the" Colonists"—few remain. Several of the families, after a few years, moved on to the farther West, some in the way of general emigration, others to new colonies, as to Olivet, Mich., and Tabor, Iowa. Peter P. Pease, the first colonist, remained to the end, and died in 1861. Josiah B. Hall performed a home missionary work, for years, in the neighborhoods between Oberlin and Elyria, established a settlement, a mile and a half north-east, still called " New Oberlin," with the thought of having there a subsidiary preparatory school, and at length led the new colony to Tabor, in 1851. Wm. Hosford went to Olivet, in a similar way, in 1845. Samuel Daniels, Isaac Cummings, Philip James, Daniel Marsh and several others removed early to other places in the vicinity, or to the far West. Of all these, Philip James of Nebraska is the only known survivor. Of the families that came early and remained until the later years, the following names will be recalled : Hamilton, Safford, Stevens, Penfield, Ellis, Pease, Wack, Jones, McWade, Evans and Leonard, on South Main Street; Turner, Steele, Jennings, Taylor, Gaston, Wheat, Ryder, Little, Holtslander, Keep, Campbell, Campton, Leonard, Page, Platt and Bailey, on North Main Street; Ingersoll, Johnson, Gerrish, Beckwith, Gaston, Cox, Burrell, Clark, Kenaston and Crosby, on East College Street; Parish, Rawson, Smith and Hawley, on West College Street; Pelton, Hill, Elmore, Watson, Bardwell and Lamberton, on East Lorain Street; Jewell, Cox, Hopkins, Hull, Kinney, Rossiter, Shepard and Matthews, on West Lorain Street; Weed, Hovey, Ells and Bartholomew, on Pleasant Street; Kinney, Wright, Butler, Dutton and Fitch, on South Professor Street; Lincoln, Hall, Andrews and Pease, on North Professor Street; Evans, Scott, Munson and Strauss, on Mill Street; Dodge and Copeland, on Morgan Street; and Dawes, Thompson, Cole, Bailey and Spees, in New Oberlin. Other families within the limits mentioned will doubtless be recalled; but these suggest a volume of unwritten history, which it would be interesting to linger upon.

Among other memories of the past, former students will recall those with whom the term bills were settled—the Treasurers of the college—Levi Burnell from 1835 to 1841, Hamilton Hill from 1841 to 1865; and the Book-keeper of that period and of later times, George P. Wyett; and George Kinney, Treasurer from 1865 to 1875.

Nor will they forget those who spread their table at the Ladies' Hall, the Stewards and Matrons—after Mr. and Mrs. Stewart, Mr. and Mrs. David Campbell, of Boston, in the days of Grahamism; Mr. and Mrs. G. Fairchild of Brownhelm; Mr. and Mrs. W. W. Wright; Mr. and Mrs. Henry Viets; Mr. and Mrs. L. Herrick:

all in the old hall; and in the new, Mr. and Mrs. E. Follett; Mr. and Mrs. George Kinney; and Mr. and Mrs. M. Day, down to the present occupants. Thus far no one has held the Stewardship longer than eight years, but the limit is only traditional, not constitutional.

The principals of the Ladies' Department are naturally associated with the Ladies' Hall, having had their office there, and usually their personal apartments. Besides Mrs. Dascomb, already spoken of, Mrs. Alice W. Cowles, wife of Prof. Henry Cowles, held the position from 1836 to 1840, Miss Mary Ann Adams as assistant and as principal from 1839 to 1849, and Mrs. Mary C. Hopkins from 1850 to 1852. Of these Mrs. Hopkins, now living at Rochester, N. Y., is the only survivor.

The limits of this volume will not permit any personal reference to the twenty thousand students who, for a longer or shorter period, have enjoyed the benefits of the school; nor can any satisfactory record be made of the alumni proper, those who have completed a course of study here. Of these, three hundred and ninety-three have completed the theological course, ten hundred and eleven the classical course, and seven hundred and twenty-three the literary course. Some of these have become distinguished, and many of them have been useful.

It remains to mention a few that have been instructors in the college in later times, and have finished their work.

HENRY E. PECK, of Rochester, N. Y., a graduate of Bowdoin College, completed his theological course at Oberlin, in 1845. After pastoral work in Rochester until 1852, he was called to Oberlin as Professor of Sacred Rhetoric and Associate in Mental and Moral Philosophy. He held the position until 1865, when, receiving an appointment from the Government as Minister to Hayti, he accepted and went to Port au Prince. In the second year of his residence there, he died of the yellow fever. His remains were afterwards brought to Oberlin for burial. Professor Peck was not only interested in his college work, which he performed with much acceptance, but all the interests of the community, personal, social, municipal, and political, commanded his attention. Many town improvements received their first impulse from him. Many a struggling student or citizen received from him a timely suggestion or needed help; and when the young men went to the war, he saw them on their way, and visited them on many a field. He had the rare faculty of doing many things, and doing them well. Restless activity was essential to his life.

CHARLES H. PENFIELD graduated at Oberlin in 1847. He was an Oberlin boy, brought up here from his early childhood. In 1848 he was appointed tutor in Latin and Greek in college; in 1855, Professor of Latin, and in 1866, Professor of Greek, resigning in 1870. For several years past he has been Professor of Greek in the Central High School of Cleveland.

REV. HIRAM MEAD, a native of Vermont, educated at Middlebury and at Andover, pastor nine years at South Hadley, Mass., and two years at Manchester, N. H., was called to Oberlin, in 1869, as Professor of Sacred Rhetoric and Pastoral The-

ology. He entered upon the work with all his
heart, and was very helpful in bringing up the
seminary from the depression which it had suffered
after the war. Council Hall grew up under his energetic and persistent and successful work. His presence here attracted the endowment of the Holbrook
professorship. The beautiful hymn and tune book
in which we rejoice, derived much of its excellence
from his taste and experience and labor. The
disease from which he died appeared to result from
a fall upon the sidewalk one winter morning. An
internal tumor was developed, and he died in May,
1881, at the age of fifty-four.

REV. JOHN B. PERRY was called to the professorship of Natural Science in 1871. He was a graduate of the Vermont University, and had taken a
theological course at Andover. After several years
in the pastoral work, he was appointed assistant
of Professor Agassiz, in the Museum of Comparative
Zoology, at Cambridge. He accepted the appointment at Oberlin, contemplating a five months' course
of lectures each year, while still retaining his connection with the Museum, and having his home at
Cambridge. He gave his course at Oberlin in the
spring and summer of 1872, and died at his home in
Cambridge, in October of the same year, at the age
of forty-six.

WILLIAM H. RYDER succeeded Professor Penfield
in the Chair of Greek, in 1870. He was brought up
at Oberlin from a child, and graduated at the college,
completing his theological course at Andover. He
had been preaching some years in Wisconsin, when he

was called to Oberlin. He filled the position with great success for seven years, when he resigned to accept a call from the Congregational Church at Ann Arbor, Mich., where he still remains.

WILLIAM K. KEDZIE was elected, in 1878, as the successor of Dr. Dascomb in the department of Chemistry. He was the son of Robert C. Kedzie, of the class of 1847, Professor of Chemistry in the Agricultural College of Michigan. Having been his father's pupil and assistant in the laboratory from a child, he graduated at the Agricultural College, and afterward pursued chemistry in the Sheffield Scientific School. He had been several years Professor of Chemistry in the Kansas Agricultural College when he accepted the call to Oberlin. Under his superintendence the new laboratory was fitted up, and the new methods of instruction introduced. He died after two years of enthusiastic and successful work, at the age of twenty-eight.

REV. SAMUEL H. LEE, in 1878, accepted a financial secretaryship in behalf of the college, with the professorship of Political Economy, coming from the pastorate of the First Congregational Church of Cleveland. After three years of faithful and successful service he resigned to resume the pastoral work.

Those who have been principals of the preparatory department since 1845 are all still living. HENRY E. WHIPPLE, appointed in 1846, was called in 1853 to a professorship at Hillsdale College, Mich., and is now living at Mendocino, Cal.

EDWARD H. FAIRCHILD graduated at Oberlin in 1838; took the theological course here, and continued in the pastoral work until his call to Oberlin in 1853. He held the position of principal until 1869, when he resigned to accept the presidency of Berea College, Ky. Two or three years of this time he was engaged in the financial work of the college.

ROSELLE T. CROSS graduated at Oberlin in 1867, held the principalship from 1869 to 1874, and resigned to take up pastoral work. He is now preaching in Denver, Col. REV. JAMES H. LAIRD, of the college class of 1860 and Theological class of 1864, succeeded Mr. Cross in 1874, and resigned in 1877 to resume the pastoral work. He has been pastor in Andover, Mass., the last five years. Of the many tutors in this department, no student of the years 1842–53 will forgot Nelson W. Hodge, who was the presiding genius of the Latin and Greek recitation rooms during that period. He was a graduate of 1838, and resigned in 1853 to take up farming at the West. He is living at Ripon, Wis.

Those who are now living and actively engaged in the work do not naturally appear in these records. Of the whole number of instructors during the fifty years, only four have died while in active connection with the college.

That such a body of able men, of varied gifts and attainments, preachers, teachers, writers and business men, should have been gathered and held in connection with the enterprise, under such disadvantages, according to the ordinary apprehension of the case, is to be explained in part by a divine overruling which brought them, and by the strong attraction of the work itself, which retained them. It has been no unusual thing that men have left larger salaries in coming to Oberlin, and have remained against the offer of larger salaries.

The importance and magnitude of the work have also had much to do in making it possible for men of such diverse education and habits of thought— gathered from so many different schools, with widely diverging views, engaged in an enterprise involving so many new and untried features, with little experience and few traditions to guide them—to work together in essential harmony during the fifty years. There have been earnest discussions and pronounced differences, but no quarrels, no factions, no alienations. The momentum of the work itself has seemed to overrule minor perturbations. But above all a divine ordering has been conspicuous, from the small beginning in 1833, to this our Jubilee Year. "Except the Lord build the house, they labor in vain that build it."

APPENDIX.

EARLY LETTERS.

P. P. STEWART TO J. J. SHIPHERD.

ELYRIA, Feb. 4, 1833.

VERY DEAR BROTHER:

Your letter of the twenty-sixth ult. to Mrs. Shipherd, which came to hand on the second inst., greatly comforted us concerning your continued health and other favorable circumstances. We have been waiting with much solicitude to know how you would succeed in your agency in that part of the country where you now are. We have supposed that something could be determined as to the final result of your efforts in behalf of the seminary, from a few weeks' labor in that vicinity. From your letter we are led to conclude that since you left Rochester you have increased your subscription but one hundred dollars. From your success previously we had expected more from these places you have since visited. But in looking at the indications of Providence we must regard them as a whole, and then inquire what our duty is concerning them. We have now fairly put our hand to the plough, and must not look back, that is if we have done it understandingly and

in the fear of God.   The objects contemplated in the
establishment of the institution appear to me as
much in accordance with the genius of the Gospel
as heretofore.   For these very objects Christians are
continually praying.   Then the question arises, will
God hear and answer our prayers if they be not accompanied with our labors and charities?

Previous to receiving your letter from Rochester,
which contained an order for one hundred and sixty-
six dollars, I had obtained a renewal of the note
at the bank by paying fifty dollars.   My own health
is better than when I wrote you last.   Mrs. Stewart's
is not as good.   You doubtless feel anxious to know
what is likely to result from the machine.   You will
probably be surprised to know that I have done very
little about it since you left.   I may have acted in-
judiciously, but have done what seemed to be duty.
The way did not seem prepared to apply horse
power to the machine during the winter.   Under
these circumstances it seemed necessary that I
should do what I could to curtail the expenses of
the family. . . .

The circumstances of my turning my attention
from the planing machine to the making of stoves
may have the appearance of fickle-mindedness, and I
will not pretend that my character stands entirely
free from such a blemish.   But there is an overlooking Providence, which often guides us very differently from our own intentions, or wishes.   I regarded
it as a very undesirable circumstance that I was
obliged to occupy my time in procuring a stove, and
if I had had the funds at command I should have pur-

chased one at once; but as it has turned out I cannot but hope that great benefit will result to the community, especially to that part in moderate circumstances.

I am still of the opinion that the machine will be valuable if it can be got into operation, but it seems necessary that my time should be occupied about the stove, for a while at least. Several families in this village are wishing to purchase a cooking-stove, and are anxious that this should be perfected and tested before they buy. Among these are the three families of the Iron Company. There is a prospect now of its having the preference at this furnace. The making of patterns is a new business to me. I make but slow progress, but there are no pattern makers in the place that I know of, and if there were I have no money to pay them. . . .

I find that the circumstance of our inducing so many Christian families to locate together is made use of by those not very friendly to the object, as an objection to the plan. I would suggest for your consideration the question whether it would not do to dispose of some of the colonial lands to persons of a certain character who are not pious. The by-laws might be of such a character as to secure the interests of the institution. This might be better than to have the colony very small, and surrounded by a corrupt and irreligious population. Perhaps we ought not to depend to any considerable extent upon the colonists to sustain the institution, because we should want to secure for it the sympathies and fostering care of all the churches in this

region.　It might be well for you to ascertain
whether Street and Hughes would have any objection to persons paying to the Institution a certain
percentage on the land which they shall respectively
take up.　I have no doubt there will be much prejudice excited against the enterprise by the hasty and
injudicious remarks of professed friends of the cause,
and this will probably be done to some extent by
those who are the real disciples of Christ.　A circumstance apparently of a very unfavorable character has recently occurred in this place.　Mr. C.,
the agent of the Western Reserve College, came
here to solicit funds for that institution.　In three
prominent instances he failed of obtaining subscriptions on account of the colony.　The persons
were Capt. R., Mr. T., and Mr. J.　They were
pressed very hard, but maintained firmly their
ground, saying that they believed the money they
had to give, under existing circumstances, could do
more in the Oberlin Institute than otherwise.　What
Mr. C. knew about the plan of the colony I know
not, or from what source he obtained his information.　He did not, however, hesitate to express his
most decided disapprobation of the plan.　The circumstance of congregating a large number of Christian families in one neighborhood, he urged as a
most objectionable feature.　This man travelling
from place to place will probably occasion many prepossessions unfavorable to the enterprise.　You remarked in one of your letters that Oberlin would rise
by the hardest labor.　This may be true; probably is.
But if it is the work of the Lord, it matters not how

much labor is required. If it is a privilege to labor for the Lord, and we are to depend on him for direction, the question how much labor we shall perform about one thing is of very little importance. The discountenance that some may give to our manner of laboring, or the virulent opposition of others, should never discourage us, or turn us aside from the course which the word of God and the indications of his providence point out. In regard to the manner of raising funds I think it is greatly to be desired that they should come from the Christian community; that is, for the most part. After obtaining what we can from this source, and the Lord should succeed some of our other plans, we shall still find use for all, or if the Lord bring in something soon from some of our own devices, we should not, of course, reject it; but what I have more particularly in view is the importance of securing a deep interest in the hearts of Christians. If many give, and give as they ought, many prayers will be secured for the institution and the colony. This is impressed on my mind as a point of very great importance. . . .

Yours truly and affectionately,

P. P. STEWART.

P. P. STEWART TO FAYETTE SHIPHERD, TROY, N. Y.

ELYRIA, O., May 21, 1833.

VERY DEAR BROTHER:

. . . Brother John J. will be anxious to hear from us, especially since his children have fallen under our care.

Ere this we conclude sister Shipherd is in Ballston. She started the last of April, but was delayed a little in Cleveland.

The children appear perfectly contented under Mrs. Stewart's care, and on the whole we think they are doing very well.

As to Oberlin matters, they are progressing slowly. There are some things I have to say, which will probably meet you with some surprise. The steam-engine is not on the ground, as some colonists who have recently arrived supposed it would be. It is not expected to be there before the first of October.

The Board of Trust have concluded to purchase one of Mr. Andrews, of Cleveland. If the Board had concluded to make a contract for an engine immediately after their first meeting, it might probably have been obtained a little sooner. But the requisite funds were not provided, and even now we have not the amount which Mr. Andrews requires at the time he commences the work, viz., three hundred dollars. Your place could not be sold for ready money, and I shall be obliged to borrow something more from the Institute to pay Mr. Guthrie.

Brethren Ayers, Hall, Gibbs, Morgan and Safford have arrived. They are considerably disappointed in regard to the saw-mill. They say you encouraged them to expect to see the engine on the ground, at the time they should arrive there. You will recollect that to lay a plan is not the same thing as to carry it into execution. Brother Pease has been on the ground about four weeks. He has four hands at work; has chopped over about five acres. It is thought best to put up a part of the boarding-house, and transport the lumber from Captain Redington's mill. With our best efforts, I am confident the work will not go on as fast as you have calculated, and it seems to me that we ought studiously to avoid raising expectations which cannot be realized. A few instances of this kind will do much to destroy the confidence of the community in the men and in the enterprise. Colonists who have come on say that Brother J. J. S. has given the pledge that young men who come on from the East shall receive as good an education for a minister, as if they had been at college. The constitution says that the pupils of the Oberlin Institute shall receive a thorough academic course. This is all I have expected they would receive, and all I think that we ought to promise. After they shall have been at the Institute a suitable length of time to prepare for college, I have supposed they would go to Hudson, or to some other institution where they can enjoy the privileges of the manual labor system. Let students come to this institution with the expectation of obtaining a collegiate education, or what is equivalent to it, and find the advantages far inferior to those which are to be enjoyed at other institutions, and the result would be disappointment and probably dissatisfaction.

All who shall have been at this institution will be criticised with great severity, and if their education shall fall short of the pledge that was given, bad consequences must follow. If we have in addition

to a common manual labor school, a female seminary, and a system of labor connected with that
also, I think this is all that we ought to attempt
at present. By attempting too much, the whole
work will be likely to come to nothing. We are
still in Elyria. I have hired the red blacksmith shop
and the house that belongs to it.

This I have done to perfect the stove, iron stoves,
etc. We seem to be needed on the ground; but it
seems also very important that we remain here the
present summer at least. Individuals in different
places have offered to exert themselves to bring the
stove into notice, if we will send them one for inspec-
tion. I have had the greater part of four stoves
cast, and find that iron patterns must be obtained
before much can be done, or those which are made
of wood must be ironed in such a manner that they
will not warp and spring, when put into warm damp
sand. To prepare patterns for a cooking stove is a
slow and difficult work. But I think, and others
think, that the plan of the stove is superior to any
one in this part of the country. The first impression on the part of those who examine it is uniformly favorable.

This is a very encouraging circumstance. If there
were not reason to fear that we should fall short in
regard to funds, I should think differently about
our going immediately on to the colony grounds.
But the stoves cannot be made a source of profit to
the Institution, without employing considerable
time in preparing the patterns. And if the stoves
should succeed, that is, if they should be approved

by those who first use them, the sale of twenty the present year will probably prepare the way for the sale of double and triple that number the next year. Perhaps I am criminally defective in confidence in regard to the collection of funds. I have very much feared, and do still, that we shall be straitened for the means to carry into execution the work which we have undertaken. If the work is the Lord's, he will doubtless provide the means of carrying it on. But our own skill and sagacity must be employed. . . .

Yours truly and affectionately,

P. P. STEWART.

FROM J. J. SHIPHERD.

BALLSTON, N. Y., May 28, 1833.

To the Trustees of the Oberlin Institute.

BELOVED BRETHREN:

Evidence is daily increasing that God designs to do great things for the Mississippi Valley, through our seminary. We ought therefore to feel that a vast trust is committed to our hands, and exert ourselves to the uttermost, to accomplish the Lord's great work in the speediest and most effectual manner. That we should be of one mind is of first importance, and of the same mind which was also in Christ Jesus. Let us constantly wait at his feet for instruction, and show ourselves one in him, and with him in wisdom, sanctification, and redemption. Of all our weighty responsibilities, the heaviest obvi-

ously is the appointment of teachers. Upon me, as
your agent, of course, depends the peculiar responsibility of recommending them. Feeling the weight
of this responsibility, I have looked to the Searcher
of hearts for direction in my choice, and have advised
with the best counsellors among the thousands
whom I have met in my journeyings. At length,
having travelled some two thousand miles, visited
various seminaries, and maturely settled my mind,
I recommend the following appointments: 1. I recommend that you invite the Rev. Samuel R. Hall,
Principal of the Teachers' Seminary, of Andover,
Mass., to become the President of the Oberlin Institute. You probably already know something of his
reputation, although he has been publicly known
but a little time. He was a pastor in Concord, Vt.,
for about nine years, and during most of the time
the principal of an academy, which he there founded
and rendered unusually flourishing and useful. He
there wrote his lectures on School Keeping, since
published at Boston, and widely circulated as the
best work on education extant. The Legislature of
New York have obtained of him ten thousand copies
for gratuitous distribution.

He has recently published another volume of lectures on Female Teachers, etc., and several other
popular works, mostly school-books.

His present station indicates the estimate placed
upon him by the trustees of the Teachers' Seminary, Andover, Mass., among whom are men best
qualified to judge. Many applied for the superintendence of that seminary, but were all rejected in

favor of Mr. Hall, who did not ask the station, but
when invited to it, declined; afterward, however,
yielding to repeated solicitations. At the head of
that seminary, he has been constantly rising for two
and a half years, and raising the institution till it
now numbers about one hundred and fifty students.
I spent a few days with him, in his school and out,
and confidently recommend him as better qualified
to superintend our institution than any man I have
met, or heard of who can be obtained; and indeed I
know of no one, could we obtain him, in whom
there is more of what we want, than in Mr. Hall,
for, 1. His piety is more like the Divine Teacher's
than usual. He labors with his might to do good
in school and out. 2. He is better acquainted with
the art of teaching than any one I can find, having
studied it diligently for many years. 3. His education, although not collegiate, is sufficiently extensive,
much more profound than is usual with graduates
from our best colleges. 4. He is a manual labor
man. 5. He is of suitable age, thirty-eight years.
6. He is a practical teacher, makes everything a student learns useful to him. 7. He does not teach
for money, but to do good. 8. He is deeply interested in the West. 9. His government excels any
I am acquainted with. He teaches his pupils to
govern themselves; and, 10. I think he would, to increase his usefulness, accept your invitation. Mr.
Hall could not consistently leave Andover for Ohio
till the Fall of 1834, but should be elected as soon
as consistent, and aid in all our plans for buildings,
teachers, apparatus, etc. The architect should di·

rect in laying the corner-stone, and should you elect him, he says he wishes at least six months, after resigning his charge at Andover, to visit the best literary institutions of our land, and otherwise qualify himself for his responsible station. His salary is now about twelve hundred dollars annually, but I advise that you offer him four hundred dollars, with the use of a dwelling house and a few acres of land, his pasturage, hay for his horse and two cows, and his wood, and that we defray the expense of his removal with his family to Ohio, which will probably be about one hundred to one hundred and twenty-five dollars. This will be about as good as one thousand dollars at Andover, and I think he is willing to act upon Oberlin principles. In the second place, I recommend that you elect Mr. James K. Shipherd, Principal of Thetford Academy, Vt., Professor of Languages in the Oberlin Institute, and commit to him the superintendence of the seminary till Mr. Hall arrive and enter upon the duties of his office. I cannot speak as freely of this gentleman as the former, for he is my brother. However, I can say, I do not recommend him because he is my brother, but because I think him better qualified than any other one we can obtain for the place. He was in good standing in college (Middlebury, Vt.), unusually successful in common-school teaching, and is now highly esteemed as Principal of Thetford Academy, Vt. He took charge of that academy when it was in a low state, and has caused it, in a scientific and moral sense, to flourish more than for many years before. The trustees of that seminary desire him to engage with them for ten years, and are extremely unwilling to part with him. Several of his scholars expect to enter our Institute the first of December next, and expressed to me the desire that he should be elected, as I now propose. He is young, twenty-two and one half years of age, decidedly pious, studious, particularly in the science of teaching, loves to teach, practical in teaching, very successful in government, a manual labor man, and although well pleased with his present location, would, I think, accept the appointment I propose, should you think it best to make it. I advise that you offer him three hundred dollars salary, with his board, till he shall marry, and then a house, etc., like the President's.

In the third place, I advise that you invite Miss Louisa Gifford, assistant in the Geneva Female Seminary, N. Y., to become teacher of the female department. Last winter I requested Mrs. Ricord, the Principal of that seminary, to recommend a teacher for our manual labor female school. I had previously learned that her school was scarcely, if at all, excelled, and fully acquainted her with our plans and circumstances. She, evidently feeling her responsibility, and acting understandingly, recommended the Miss Gifford whom I now propose. I have not time to describe her definitely, but believe we shall be safe in taking her at Mrs. Ricord's recommendation. Besides I saw her considerably, and think her best qualified for the place of any lady whom we can obtain. So think the best of judges at Geneva.

As our female school will be small for a season, I

propose that we offer her one hundred dollars a year
and her board.

In the fourth place, I recommend that you elect
Dr. James Dascomb, of Boscawen, N. H., lecturer,
and professor of chemistry, botany, physical education or anatomy, and natural philosophy. Dr. Dascomb is a young physician of promise, a pupil of
Dr. Mussey of Dartmouth College, said by him to
be decidedly the best scholar in his class of fifty
members. He is highly recommended by Mr. Hall,
whom I nominate as President, as a Christian, a physician and lecturer. Brother Hall and I think that
the physician of the colony should be a lecturer in
the seminary, because we can't afford a full salary to
such a lecturer, or full employment to a physician.

I propose that we offer him two hundred and fifty
dollars salary. His practice as physician and duties
as a lecturer will no more interfere with each other
than those of Dr. Mussey and others who not unfre-
quently practise as physicians, and serve as professors
in colleges.

I desire a decision upon Dr. Dascomb's case soon,
because I wish to secure a physician to our colony
and seminary, and he will need considerable time to
prepare for the duties of his professorship. Besides,
he will, if not invited, soon be so settled that he
will not accept our invitation. He will not, if
elected, probably enter upon his professorship till
Brother Hall does upon his presidency, say September, 1834. My brother and Miss Gifford should be,
if invited at all, requested to enter upon their duties
by the first of December next, and they may sustain

the school till Brothers Hall and Dascomb join them. This may (and yet I hope it will not) seem premature. I believe it is safe and best, and for the following reasons: We can obtain the requisite funds. For evidence of this see my previous communications, and add to the evidence they afford the fact that should my life be spared till September next, I shall in all probability fill out our colony, and through that means and others increase our subscription to at least ten thousand dollars. I propose also that some efficient agent be appointed to aid me in collecting funds. I have some hope that my brother's church (Troy, N. Y.) will release him for a season. I am also negotiating with a Mr Mills, of Dunbarton, N. H. Whether either of them can be obtained before Fall, or at all, I know not, but I hope one of them, or some other one well qualified, can be secured. A good agent is rarely found.

That we can raise the fifteen thousand dollars contemplated I am confident, and I believe my confidence is well founded. The wise and good uniformly approve our plans, and have aided, and express a determination yet more to aid, in executing them. To fill out the fifteen thousand dollars will doubtless be much easier than to do what, through the grace of God, we have already executed. This amount will provide for one hundred students, whose tuition will pay the salaries recommended. Tuition may be fifteen dollars a year, that is, fifteen hundred dollars in all, and the salaries I recommend with board amount only to eleven hundred and fifty.

That we can have one hundred students in September, 1834, cannot be doubted. There are multitudes of them desiring such privileges, and unless we provide them many of them can never enjoy them. You can build what will be necessary for the commencement of the academic department by the first of December next, and during the succeeding year enlarge so as to employ Brothers Hall and Dascomb as proposed. That teachers may be on the ground when needed, they should be elected as soon as consistent, especially those who commence the school, viz., my brother and Miss Gifford, if you should see fit to appoint them, and they to accept. You perceive in my recent communications that I have latterly enlarged our plans of operation, and it may seem to you unadvisedly, but I trust the following reasons will satisfy you all : The manual labor system requires that the student be carried through his whole course. If the institution be a mere preparatory school for college, the students are always mere apprentices in manual labor, and the benefits of the system are realized but in a small degree. Should we fit them for college only, there is no institution to which we could send them where their manual labor facilities would be continued equal to Oberlin.

Hudson, for want of land, can never render the manual labor of students extensively productive for their support. The Lane Seminary has and can have but little land, and is full and will be full without our students. Moreover, the Principal of the Oneida Institute assured me that a large farm was indispensable to great success in extensive operations, and that the student should be carried through his whole course. Again, the making of our seminary equal to an academy, college, and theological seminary will not at all curtail the usefulness of Hudson and others; for if we will furnish such advantages as I propose, students will fill our seminary who would never enter those now in existence.

The revivals of three years past have brought hundreds of youth into our churches who desire to be educated for the ministry and other useful services, who will not incur debt necessary in such a course as they must pursue at any institutions now in being in our country. This I know from actual conference with youth at the East. Hundreds of promising youth will doubtless be educated for God's service, or not educated, as we shall or shall not provide for them the means of complete education by their own industry and economy. Moreover, it is about as easy to obtain requisite funds, etc., for a complete education, as for one merely elementary. For the amount of the subscription usually corresponds with the character of the institution for which it is raised, and students would not go so far westward merely for an academic course. Let us therefore begin with the academic, and, as Providence permit, grow into the collegiate and theological, which, I doubt not, will be as fast as our students shall advance in their studies. Had we to raise the ordinary permanent fund for president's and professors' salaries, we should fail, but the assurance of all the students we

can accommodate is as good a pledge for their salaries as permanent funds.   What enlargement I have
made in our plans, the development of facts has
made necessary.

———

From J. J. Shipherd.

BOSTON, MASS., Aug. 9, 1833.

To the Trustees of the Oberlin Institute.

DEAR BRETHREN:

I hoped long before this to have received a full answer to my last long and important communication.
I have only heard that you sustained my nomination
of my brother, J. K. Shipherd.   He has declined.
The trustees of the academy he now instructs will
not at all consent to his leaving them.   Being about
to return to Ohio, and under the necessity of finding
some one to fill my brother's place, I have visited
Andover Theological Seminary, and engaged, if you
approve, Mr. Seth H. Waldo, who I believe will succeed as well as my brother.   He will have to leave
the seminary in his Senior year, but I can nowhere
else find the man we want, and the Faculty of the
seminary consent to his leaving.   They, the present
and collegiate classmates of Mr. Waldo, and S. R.
Hall, in whose Teachers' Seminary Mr. W. has
taught, all recommend him.   I shall not therefore
describe him particularly.   He has taught occasionally for twelve years, and with success, both in common schools and academies.   He is about thirty
years of age.   Should he go, he is to have four

hundred dollars salary, and fifty dollars for his expenses to the ground. Being, like all others, in debt for his education, he cannot consistently engage for a less sum. The fifty dollars for his expenses may properly be taken from the outfit money which I am collecting. The four hundred dollars must be raised by tuition. Forty scholars, at one half the tuition which the students of the Oneida Institute pay, will pay the four hundred dollars. The forty we can unquestionably have, if room can be made for them. If not, the smaller number must pay higher tuition. This must ever be our rule. Students must pay such tuition as will raise our teachers' salaries. This rule has worked well at the Oneida Institute for years. It is not safe except in manual labor schools. If you approve the nomination and conditions, please forward as soon as may be an official invitation, with a pledge of the four hundred and fifty dollars, which I am willing to be personally responsible for, and direct to Seth H. Waldo, Andover Theological Seminary, Andover, Mass. As he has seen me only of the Board, please express your readiness to receive him as a brother, and sustain him as a teacher. My invitation to him, which I desire you to ratify, is that he take charge of the Oberlin Institute till it assume a collegiate character, and then if experiment prove that he is qualified, that he fill the professorship of languages. If I mistake not, he will prove the man we shall need at first and permanently. I am happy to find that prejudices against our enterprise are wearing away, and there is increasing evidence that it is the Lord's good work, and will prosper. I have recently developed the plan fully to the Rev. Mr. Woodbridge of this city, and obtained his unqualified approbation of it—from the Infant School to the Theological Seminary. His opinion is probably as valuable at that of any American.

He has travelled extensively in Europe with reference to education, spent about a year at Fellenberg's celebrated school at Hofwyl in Switzerland, was favorably noticed by literary men and societies in Europe, has published a most valuable geography, now edits the American Annals of Education, the first work on that subject in our land. In short he makes, and has for many years made, education the subject of his study and object of his effort. While the distinctive features of our plan are objected to by some, the ablest men and the most experienced teachers that I have met fully and decidedly approve them. We have only to trust in God, and go forward with diligence and zeal, and we may greatly bless the perishing millions of the West. Being so distant from you I have been compelled to do what I should not, without your previous approbation, had I been near, but trust I shall find on my return that we are one in judgment as well as one in heart. If the Lord will I shall see Oberlin between the fifteenth and twentieth of September next. That the Lord may permit us to meet in peace and labor together "with one mind and with one accord," is the prayer of

Your fellow servant and brother,
JOHN J. SHIPHERD.

FROM J. J. SHIPHERD.

UTICA, Aug. 23, 1833.

DEARLY BELOVED PARENTS:

I write you under circumstances of interest which cannot be expressed by letter. I left Ballston, with my dear wife and babe, on Monday morning last, and arrived here Tuesday night—thus far prospered of the Lord on our journey. Wednesday morning brother Fayette and sister Collins arrived from the West, and last evening I had the privilege of binding them together with a cord which death only can sunder. I rejoice that my dear brother is well married. I am happy to call his Elmina sister, and doubt not my loved parents will readily receive her into their hearts as a daughter. Esther and I know her worth, and believe it to be rare, of vastly greater value to brother in his ministry than the wealth and estimables of some city ladies, whom others might have chosen. I hope you will soon enjoy the privilege of judging for yourselves. We part to-morrow morning, they for the East, and we for the West. In parting with them, I seem to be leaving my loved parents, and all my dear eastern friends. I have not before seemed to be separated from you. I have hitherto been like a ship in port, frequently visited, but now I seem like one whose deck is well-nigh cleared, but still bound fast by a cable to its native port, and yet its swelling canvas urging it to a far-off ocean. Yes, loved parents, I feel much of that which swells the bosom of him who casts his last lingering look upon the home of his childhood, clustered around with the endearments of parental, filial, fraternal and other tender associations, and then looks abroad upon a distant land unwelcome and desolate, because the dear ones left behind are not there. Since I began this letter I have had a desperate struggle with my Shipherd heart, but thanks be unto God who giveth me the victory. I previously hoped that in a gospel sense I "should henceforth know no one after the flesh," but "the fondness of a creature's love, how strong it strikes the sense," and how malignant that arch foe who, vanquished once, soon renews his attacks.

But for Him who succors them that are tempted, I might be overcome, and relinquish Oberlin for personal enjoyment among my kindred. But through Christ strengthening me, I can bid you all farewell, and urge on my great and good work till my Master shall bid me rest. . . .

Take, dear parents, to yourselves, and present to our dear sister and niece, and duly to others, the love of your affectionate children—

JOHN AND ESTHER.

FROM J. J. SHIPHERD.

OBERLIN, Dec. 13, 1833.

DEAREST OF PARENTS:

I have before me two precious letters, written by your dear, dear hands, and received at the hands of Brother Reed, and Middleton. They have been before me these two weeks, glowing with parental love, and waking up in my soul filial affection, but I could not answer them till now, without sacrificing my Master's important interests in Oberlin. I say honestly, dear parents, you live in the warmest chamber of my heart, and I feel grieved, but not guilty, that I have not written you before. I have been and am yet pressed out of measure with Oberlin duties. The great Pilot of Zion has committed to my poor hand the helm of a noble ship, which is in the midst of breakers, and laden with Zion's precious treasures. It has seemed to me that in these circumstances I might not let go the helm even to seize the pen in behalf of my beloved parents, or any friend however dear.

Do you ask then if Oberlin has possessed my heart instead of those who gave me birth, and blessings numberless? Oberlin is Christ's, and much as I love father and mother, Christ is dearer than both and all on earth beside. . . . We have lived some two months in a basement room of the Oberlin Institute fifteen feet square—some weeks of the time with another family, and three or four boarders, and Esther without a girl. Now we have great latitude, for we have that room alone—Eliza Branch excepted —and I have one over it for a study and secretary's office in common with the principal. Esther and I have labored unusually hard since our return, but God has given us strength equal to our day. We are all well, colds excepted. Our little ones are in the Institute's primary department, Eliza Branch teacher. Our whole colony have been remarkably blessed with health and prosperity. Eleven families are on the ground, and others waiting to come as soon as houses can be provided.

Some who spent the summer here have gone eastward for their families. Our colonial ground is nearly all disposed of. . . . The Lord is to be praised that we were enabled to open our institute at the appointed time, Dec. 3d, and with thirty scholars. We have now thirty-four boarding scholars, and expect forty for the winter. Applicants are without number, from Lake Erie to the Gulf of Mexico, from Lower Canada to Long Island Sound, from Michigan to the Atlantic. The scholars study and work well. Five minutes after the manual labor bell strikes, the hammer, saws, etc., of the mechanical students wake all around us, and the axe-men in the woods breaking the "ribs of nature" make all crack. Nearly all our visitors—and they are not few—express surprise that so great a work has been wrought here in so short a time. God be praised!

I feel as I said in my sleep the other night, "Oberlin will rise, and the devil cannot hinder it." This my sweet assurance, I hope, rests on God, without whom we can do nothing. . . .

May our Heavenly Father bless you in all things.
Your affectionate son,
JOHN J. SHIPHERD.

Mrs. M. P. Dascomb to Home Friends, Dunbarton, N. H.

OBERLIN, May 24, 1834.

. . . Next morning at five o'clock we took stage
for Elyria, which is ten miles from Oberlin—road
very bad from ruts and mud. We were in constant
danger of overturning. Once when we came to a
ditch in the road the gentlemen got out and took
down a fence, so that we could turn aside into the
adjoining field and ride around the obstacle. At
Elyria we dined, and obtained a two-horse wagon to
transport us, and two gentlemen from New England
going to the Institute as students, to our journey's
end. We found the wagon a very comfortable conveyance, and I was in no fear of being turned out
into the mud, for the driver assured us it could not
turn over. You cannot conceive of a more miserable
road than we had, the last two miles especially, but
still I enjoyed the ride, and our party were all very
cheerful. When passing through the woods I was
so delighted with the black squirrels, the big trees,
and above all the beautiful wild flowers, that at times
I quite forgot to look out for the scraggy limbs that
every now and then gave us a rude brush, till a
warning from Dr. D. that I would get my eyes torn
out, seconded perhaps by an unceremonious lash
from a neighboring bough, would call me to the duty
of self-preservation. Glad were we when an opening
in the forest dawned upon us, and Oberlin was seen.
That, said our driver, is "the city." We rode

through its principal street, now and then coming
in contact with a stump, till we were set down, not
at the coffee house or tea house, but the boarding
house. Mr. and Mrs. Waldo greeted us cordially,
and I have been " very happy from that day to this."
However, I have not got through my story, as from
my last sentence we should have supposed when
children. We were soon introduced to Mr. and Mrs.
Stewart, superintendents of the boarding and manual labor departments. They were formerly missionaries among the Choctaws, and are the very best
of persons. The next day we attended meeting,
which is held for this season in the school-room,
though it is already too small for the congregation.
Mr. Waldo is true when he says: " I never have
seen so interesting an assembly." He preaches
sometimes, also Mr. Shipherd. Till we obtain a
minister we have preaching in the afternoon only,
and the morning is spent in a Bible exercise. All
the congregation are members of the Bible class.
This is to me more interesting than preaching even.
I assure you we have Bible scholars at Oberlin. Our
Sabbath-school is held at half-past eight in the
morning; an excellent superintendent. I shall wish
some time to tell you more particulars of this
school. We have the lesson recited at the Bible
class the previous Sabbath. No question books are
used. Our religious privileges are great here.
Christians are willing to do their duty, and they help
to make meetings interesting. Most of the students
are hopefully pious. They are generally interesting, and very intelligent. Some of them are ap-

parently as cultivated as any I have ever known in New England institutions. I hope before many months to write a long letter to our dear aunt, Mrs. Putnam, giving a more particular account of this colony, institution, etc., but you will wish my first letter to tell of ourselves, and though other things are more important you can learn them from that letter. We have now been here two weeks, health and spirits good, and Oberlin already looks to us like home. Things about us are all going on so briskly, one cannot well feel sleepy. The colonists work with all diligence, and students too, at working hours. You hear great trees falling, see fires blazing, and new houses going up in all directions. There are a few log-houses, which were put up at first, but now they are all building framed houses. A large house for Mr. Shipherd will soon be finished, and this summer another large and very convenient boarding house will be completed. The seminary buildings will not be erected until next year, when they design also to build the professors' houses. We need the boarding house very much at present. We have sixty or more boarders, and of course must submit to some inconveniences, but we do it cheerfully, looking forward to better times. My room is as large as your sitting room, is painted, furnished with two chairs and all our trunks, which make good seats when we have callers. Beside this furniture we have a good table and two libraries belonging to the institution and Mr. Shipherd. These are indeed valuable, and of course pleasant. . . . Do not let me forget the food, or mother will not forgive me. It is plain, but palatable. We shall have more variety when the land is cultivated. We shall have good bread, and milk, much of the time this summer. We always have good wheat and brown bread, and generally good butter. Can have meat twice a day if we choose, but it is not very good, and I generally prefer vegetable food. Our potatoes, which we have for a rarity, are not like yours, but rather heavy. Puddings and nut-cakes are made sometimes, but no pies. Cheese we have now and then, and very good. We have hot water with milk and sugar if we choose, but most prefer cold. I like my drink quite as well as tea and coffee, and better, unless the latter have sugar. Our cold water is not so good as the hills of New Hampshire furnish; can hardly tell what it will be when we are an older country. It is not, however, unpleasant to the taste. To close: we have all that is necessary for us, and so many blessings, we do not stop to trouble ourselves about minor things. In a few months or years we can hope for more of the fruits of the earth. Our wheat fields look finely, though they were a little injured by heavy frosts. Most of the foliage of the woods is dead from the same cause. We are hoping for a new set of leaves. As to our manner of spending time: Dr. D. spends most of his in school duties. And just let me pay him a compliment. I do think him one of the best of teachers. He interests his classes deeply, and enters into the work with all his heart. He has had many calls in this place for medical aid, considering that the colonists have not before been sick; some difficult and dangerous cases among the students, but they are now doing well. I spend three or four hours a day hearing classes recite. Mrs. Waldo also assists in school. The females are very interesting; most of them are from other States, and many from a distance. That department is not yet distinct from the other. I shall write Brother L. soon. He would be happy and very useful here, but I shall not advise him to come till we get a president, and I know not that it will then be best for him to come, if he wishes to study theology, as preparatory and college studies will be pursued at present.

FROM J. J. SHIPHERD TO JOHN KEEP.

CINCINNATI, Dec. 13, 1834.

DEAR BROTHER KEEP:

I have been from home nearly three weeks, but through illness, bad roads, and the unfruitfulness of the field in which I have been, I have obtained but little subscription to our beloved Institute—some two hundred dollars only. I have, however, obtained and communicated information of importance to Oberlin and the cause of Christ. And here God has kindly opened a door to our infant seminary, wide and effectual, through which I sanguinely hope it will send forth a multitude of well qualified laborers into the plenteous harvest of our Lord. I have here found the man for the president of our loved Institute, that is, Rev. Asa Mahan. I desire you to call a meeting of the Board as soon as practicable, and present Brother Mahan as the man of my choice for the following reasons :

1. I was reluctant to come from Columbus to Cincinnati, but in prayer for direction, was constrained to come on. Having arrived here, I cannot see why I should have been sent, except to obtain a president and professor, and through them other benefits for Oberlin. 2. All the "glorious good fellows," as Doctor Beecher used to call them while they were in Lane Seminary, who, as he says, have done right in leaving on account of the abominable laws which the trustees have lately passed—all of them say that Brother Mahan is the man, and that if hc becomes president of our institution, they shall apply to it for liberty there to finish their education. 3. Rev. Joel Parker of New York, former classmate of Brother Mahan, advised him to prepare for such a station, on account of that structure and cultivation of mind peculiarly fitted for that office. 4. Rev. Charles G. Finney said that he had the best mind in Western New York while he was there laboring. 5. He has been of studious habits from early life, although on account of his father's poverty his advantages were limited till his seventeenth year. Then being converted, he entered upon a course of study preparatory to the ministry. From that time, at Hamilton College and at Andover Theological Seminary, and since he has been in the ministry, he has been of studious habits. Consequently, 6. He is a critical scholar in the different sciences, but especially in intellectual and moral philosophy, a department of science commonly assigned to the president.

7. He has, it seems, a peculiar faculty for government, manifest in his family, in presiding over deliberative bodies, and in his influence over the alert minds, with which he comes in contact. 8. He is of good age, being thirty-five. 9. He is inclined and able to labor abundantly. 10. He is a man of inflexible Christian principle who follows the straight line of rectitude, while even great and good men vibrate. 11. He has a well educated and excellent wife who is indeed a helpmeet, and two well managed little daughters. 12. In the midst of a city's temptations, they have maintained a Christian economy and simplicity in their style of living. 13. His interest in our institution is intense, and he would be willing to toil and sacrifice in its behalf to any extent; so would his estimable wife. 14. He has been most successful as an agent, and would doubtless through his favorable acquaintance in New York City and elsewhere secure to us much funds. 15. Arthur Tappan has pledged to the students who have left Lane Seminary, and who recommend Brother Mahan, five thousand dollars and a professorship, for the establishment of an institute like ours, and these brethren say—about twenty in number—that if Brother Mahan becomes our president and Brother Morgan a professor, they will turn all in with us. Finally Brother Mahan is a revival minister of the millennial stamp. I am therefore sure that God will influence all our beloved associates in the Board to concur in this nomination, for there is much rare qualification for the office, and no essential defect of character manifest.

I farther recommend to our Board the Rev. John Morgan, now of Clinton, Oneida Co., N. Y., for the professorship of mathematics and natural philosophy. I do it,—1. Because Brother T. D. Weld recommends him, and Brother Mahan thinks we cannot find his equal for the place. 2. The students before alluded to were at the Lane Seminary under his tuition, and think he greatly excels as a teacher. 3. Dr. Cox of New York, whose pupil he was, I believe, speaks highly of him. 4. I am assured that his moral excellencies are like those which I have ascribed to Brother Mahan. 5. The students who propose to go to Oberlin, and turn in all their influence on his account, and Brother Mahan's, have, Dr. Beecher says, the finest class of minds he ever knew. Not having seen him I cannot speak as fully and confidently as I can of Brother Mahan, but have no doubt that we ought to elect him. I trust the Lord will unite the Board in the election. The election of these men, it strikes me, may, under God, link our dear institution in a chain which may encompass much of earth, binding multitudes in holy allegiance to God.

I design to leave this city on the twenty-third for New York City, in company with Brother Mahan, who has consented to attend me as an associate agent, and I have written Brother Morgan to meet us there. I desire therefore that you should forward your call without any delay to New York, to Rev. Asa Mahan as president, and Rev. John Morgan as professor of mathematics. I desire also that you forward a copy of the call of Brother Mahan to this place, and a copy of Brother Morgan's to Clinton, N. Y. I should not hasten this business thus did I not believe that God approves, and that by complying with my request some thousands of dollars may be secured, and an immense amount of good which would otherwise be lost. Do, dear brother, dispatch this business and write to me and them at New York City as soon as may be. Your son will inform you about fallen Lane Seminary, what I have not room to write.

Your Brother,

JOHN J. SHIPHERD.

FROM J. J. SHIPHERD—PASTORAL LETTER.

NEW YORK, Jan. 27, 1835.

TO ALL THE BELOVED IN CHRIST JESUS, whom I have gathered, not only at Oberlin, but in my heart; "Grace be unto you and peace from God our Father and from our Lord Jesus Christ." I thank my God upon every remembrance of you, always in every prayer of mine for you all, making request with joy for your fellowship in the gospel from the first day until now; being confident of this very thing, that He which hath begun a good work in you will perform it until the day of Jesus Christ. That you may be thus perfected, "I pray that your love may abound yet more and more in knowledge and all judgment; that ye may approve things that are excellent; that ye may be sincere and without offence till the day of Jesus Christ; being filled with the fruits of righteousness which are by Jesus Christ unto the glory and praise of God." And for this, beloved, I not only pray but now write touching a few of the many things which concern your peace, your useful-ness, and the glory of God our Heavenly Father. Trusting that you reciprocate my Christian love and confidence, I speak freely as unto my children, my brethren and my sisters in the Lord.

And first I thank God for the revival of his pre-cious work among you, and say with emphasis, "Quench not the Spirit." Oh, "Grieve not the Spirit of God." That you may not, ponder with much prayer the scriptures on brotherly love and Christian union found in Eph. iv. 1–16; Phil. ii. 1–17; and other kindred scriptures. Also that you may not faint, "Search the scriptures, feed upon and di-gest them till you feel their nourishment in your hearts and their controlling influence in your lives. By much prayer also, drink in of the Spirit largely. Yet, beloved, "Watch unto prayer," lest in an evil hour the world overcome you. If you will do your duty the revival will never cease ; but the fountains which the Spirit has graciously opened in your souls will rise and overflow till they form a sea of glory. If you will do your duty, Oberlin will be a living fountain whose waters will refresh the far-off, thirsty, dying Gentiles and wretched Jews. "Be vigilant," therefore, dearly beloved, "watch and pray," and never sleep, as do others.

In the second place, dear brethren and sisters, per-mit me to exhort you to be "the Lord's peculiar people, zealous of good works." I would not have you needlessly singular, but I would have you actually singular, even among the churches if they continue as they now are. Far better to be unlike them and all on earth, than to be unlike Christ. Instead of taking the blessed Son of God as their pattern, the churches have measured themselves by themselves, and compared themselves with themselves unwisely, till the image of Christ is so lost that God will not instamp their image upon the world. I believe that it is because we are so unlike his Son that he delays to give our likeness to pagan nations. Why should God give a spurious Christianity to the nations yet to receive the gospel? No, beloved, the Church must put off her earthly attire and put on Christ before she can receive to her millennial embrace a regenerated world. It must be so. When the people of God do this they will be peculiar in their diet, dress, and all that appertains to them. The simplicity of Christ will characterize them. This, dearly beloved, you have acknowledged in your "colonial covenant." "Now, therefore, perform the doing of it." That you would, there were pleasing indications when we parted. Oh, how sweet that last meeting that we held in relation to our colonial covenant! And how delightful to see even the aged members of our body crucifying the flesh that Christ might be glorified. My heart's desire and prayer to God has been that they might be steadfast and gain the victory. Let me beseech you all to be thorough in excluding from your diet, dress, and all pertaining to you, everything which in the least hinders your sanctification or the conversion of the world. This subject is magnified in my estimation as one which pertains to salvation, and I pray that it may be in yours. In these respects may you be a "peculiar people." Moreover, brethren, be peculiarly fervent in your charity toward all saints, not merely of your distinctive name, but of Christ's dearer name. Let the door of your church be as wide as the door of heaven, but no wider, and strive to unite the dear people of God under "one fold and one shepherd." To your virtue "add knowledge," for "knowledge is power." And permit me here to request that you enter early upon the system of colonial education, which I recommended last spring, and which the brethren then on the ground resolved to adopt. Reflection and conversation with intelligent persons have confirmed my opinion that the system proposed is one peculiarly worthy of Christ's disciples, not only on account of its intellectual but its moral bearing also. And as property is convertible into moral power, look well to the state of your farms, shops, and all your temporal interests. "Be diligent in business," remembering Pastor Oberlin's plea that good roads be made for Christ's sake.

Peculiar excellence in these respects will commend your religion, and aid in casting up a highway for the Lord. Let me also exhort you, beloved, to be peculiarly zealous and liberal in sustaining the Institute. This is expected of you abroad, and reasonably too. You may through that institution preach by proxy with great power. Let it live then in your prayers, your contributions, your efforts to board its pupils and promote its various interests, and do all this as unto the Lord. The peculiarity which I desire in this case is, that you do all this, not like most communities surrounding literary institutions, for secular gain, but for Christ's sake. Furthermore, lest you become alienated in your minds, keep up an open, frequent intercourse, of a truly Christian character. I have deeply regretted that through the cares of the world we were last season so estranged from each other. Do, beloved, set aside everything which hinders you from knowing each other as members of one body in Christ our Lord. Let religion be your theme, and praise and prayer a portion of your employment in all your social visits. Also strive to keep up a kind of Christian intercourse with your neighbors around Oberlin. Let not those dear brethren who labor in Sabbath-schools and otherwise for the salvation of those about you be weary in well doing, but may others join them till no neighborhood is left. Moreover, let me exhort you, as the Lord's peculiar people, to be zealous in finding out and employing those means by which the world is to be converted. Fear not, brethren, to lead in doing right. There must be a mighty overturning before He whose right it is shall rule over all nations, and the servants of God will have to turn much upside down, as Paul did, before all will be right. There must also be many inventions of moral as well as physical machinery before Satan's throne will be demolished. Who should be forward in these overturnings and inventions if not my dear people at Oberlin? You know, beloved, I would not have you rash or inconsiderate in changing a single custom;

but I would have you study and pray out the mind
of the Spirit and execute it promptly, without asking
how the world or even the Church would like it.
Nothing is more impolitic as well as wicked than to
substitute expediency for duty. This is now a
prevalent sin of the church, which nullifies her
power. It is so prevalent in all the churches that I
fear some of you, beloved, if not all, will yield to its
paralyzing influence. My fears are excited by your
recent expressions of unwillingness to have youth of
color educated in our Institute. Those expressions
were a grief to me, such as I have rarely suffered.
Although I knew that with some of you the doctrine
of expediency was against the immediate abolition
of slavery, because slaves are not qualified for freedom, I supposed you thought it expedient and duty
to elevate and educate them as fast as possible, that
therefore you would concur in receiving those of
promising talent and piety into our institution. So
confident was I that this would be the prevailing
sentiment of Oberlin in the colony and Institute that
about a year ago I informed eastern inquirers that
we received students according to character, irrespective of color; and, beloved, whatever the expediency or prejudice of some may say, does not duty
require this? Most certainly.

For, 1. They are needed as ministers, missionaries,
and teachers for the land of their fathers, and for
their untaught, injured, perishing brethren of our
country. 2. Their education seems highly essential
if not indispensable to the emancipation and salvation of their colored brethren. 3. They will be ele-

vated much more rapidly if taught with whites, hitherto far more favored, than if educated separately. 4. The extremity of their wrongs at the white man's hand requires that the best possible means be employed, and without delay, for their education. 5. They can nowhere enjoy needed education unless admitted to our institution, or others established for whites. 6. God made them of one blood with us; they are our fellows. 7. They are our neighbors, and whatsoever we would they should do unto us, we must do unto them, or become guilty before God. Suppose, beloved, your color were to become black, what would you claim, in this respect, to be your due as a neighbor? 8. Those we propose to receive are the " little ones" of Christ. We must " take heed how we offend one of these ' little ones.' " 9. The objection to associating with them for the purpose of thus doing them good is like the objection of the Pharisees against our Saviour's eating with publicans and sinners. 10. Intermarriage with the whites is not asked, and need not be feared. 11. None of you will be compelled to receive them into your families, unless, like Christ, the love of your neighbor compel you to. 12. Those who desire to receive and educate them have the same right to do it that Christ had to eat with publicans and sinners. 13. Colored youth have been educated at other institutions for whites. 14. They will doubtless be received to all such institutions by and by, and why should beloved Oberlin wait to do justice and show mercy till all others have done it? Why hesitate to lead in the cause of humanity and of God? 15. Colored youth cannot be rejected through fear that God will be dishonored if they are received. 16. However it may be with you, brethren, I know that it was only the pride of my wicked heart that caused me to reject them while I did. 17. If we refuse to deliver our brother now drawn unto death, I cannot hope that God will smile upon us. 18. The men and money which would make our institution most useful cannot be obtained if we reject our colored brother. Eight professorships and ten thousand dollars are subscribed upon condition that Rev. C. G. Finney become Professor of Theology in our Institute, and he will not unless the youth of color are received. Nor will President Mahan nor Professor Morgan serve unless this condition is complied with. And they all are the men we need, irrespective of their anti-slavery sentiments. 19. If you suffer expediency or prejudice to pervert justice in this case you will in another. 20. Such is my conviction of duty in this case that I cannot labor for the enlargement of the Oberlin Collegiate Institute, if our brethren in Jesus Christ must be rejected because they differ from us in color. You know, dear brethren and sisters, that it would be hard for me to leave that institution which I planted in much fasting and prayer and tribulation, sustained for a time by only one brother, and then for months by only two brethren, and for which I have prayed without ceasing, laboring night and day, and watering it with my sweat and my tears. You know it would be hard to part with my dear associates in these labors. And as I have you, as a people, in my heart to live and die with you, you know, beloved, that it would be heart-breaking to leave you for another field of labor; but I have pondered the subject well, with prayer, and believe that if the injured brother of color, and consequently Brothers Finney, Mahan and Morgan, with eight professorships and ten thousand dollars, must be rejected, I must join them; because by so doing I can labor more effectually for a lost world and the glory of God—and, believe me, dear brethren and sisters, for this reason only. The agitation produced by my request forwarded to the trustees, some weeks since, was unexpected. I was sorry that it occurred, but happy that you fasted and prayed it down. I trust that season has prepared the minds of all who devoutly observed it for this communication, which I would have suppressed till my return had I not been under the necessity of communicating the same to the trustees for immediate decision, because our professors and funds are all suspended upon that decision, and myself also. May God of his infinite mercy grant that in this, and all things right, we may be " perfectly joined together in one mind." For two weeks after I left Oberlin I was quite unwell with a cold; but the Lord has since blessed me greatly with health. I have here been some four weeks upon the Graham system of diet, which is nature's system, and my health is essentially improved. Last Sabbath morning I preached in the old Chatham Theatre, now Chatham Chapel, which is immensely large, and more than an hour, and to the Fourth Free Church as long in the afternoon, and yet felt well on Monday morning. I now indulge sanguine hope that through this system of diet and the blessing of God I shall be able to re-engage in pastoral labor. And if on my return in April next, God willing, you, beloved flock, should still concur in desiring me to be your pastor, and concur in doing good to our oppressed brethren of color, I shall bless God for the privilege of wearing out as your servant for Christ's sake.

As ever your affectionate brother,

JOHN J. SHIPHERD.

ASA MAHAN TO N. P. FLETCHER, SECRETARY.

NEW YORK, March 12, 1835.

BROTHER FLETCHER:

Though personally I am unknown to you, I cannot regard myself as a stranger. The residence of your daughter in my family has endeared to us all that are dear to her. Then through Brother Shipherd and others I know you as an endeared brother in Christ. But I have not time nor disposition for compliments now. We are doing a great work, and cannot descend to such objects. My object in writing is to make some statements and suggestions respecting the dear institution to which our energies and prayers are mutually consecrated. To-morrow I expect to start for Cincinnati, after having passed through the middle and western part of this State. Brother Shipherd is expected daily in this city, where he and Brother Finney will commence operations for raising funds, etc.

From all that has been done and promised, our success is certain but for two occurrences which may the Father of all mercies prevent: 1. If we do not "wax fat and kick," and God for this reason abandon us. 2. If those who have control of the destiny of Oberlin stand firm at this crisis. Will the trustees secede from the stand which they have taken, or will they quit themselves like men? If they will, and give the public manifestation of the fact, funds can be raised, all temporalities can be supplied, and Heaven will bless us.

Dear Brother, have you confidence in the Board of Trustees associated with you? If so, write immediately to Brother Shipherd in this city and let him know. Everything, with the favor of God, depends upon this. Through Brother Keep you have no doubt received a notice of his new purposes, and our acceptance of our several appointments. As soon as possible after my arrival in Cincinnati, I intend to start for Oberlin. I hope some log house will be prepared for our reception. There we shall rejoice to stay till better accommodations are provided. Myself, and all associated with me, come upon the field not to live in splendor, but to work for God and a dying world. I hope that we shall be able to say to all our pupils, be ye "followers of us as we are of Christ." Brother Finney is a man of God, full of the Holy Ghost and of faith. His like cannot be found in any other institution in the country. His coadjutors will be men of kindred spirit. Will not the Lord of Hosts be with us, and the God of Jacob be our refuge? He will. Oberlin shall yet become a great luminary in the kingdom of Christ, whose light shall encircle the whole earth. Write me at Cincinnati, as soon as this is received, without fail. Love to all who love the Lord Jesus Christ in sincerity.

Your brother,

A. MAHAN.

FROM DR. AND MRS. DASCOMB, TO HOME FRIENDS.

OBERLIN, April 7, 1835.

DEAR MOTHER:

In a former letter you received some description of Oberlin, but it has changed much since. The number of inhabitants has very much increased during the year that we have lived here, and we are expecting a large accession this spring, as soon as the travelling becomes good. More than twenty of the students who left Lane Seminary are daily expected here to complete their education. Mr. Finney is expected here next week in company with Mr. Shipherd. Some twenty or thirty families will doubtless be in during the summer.

The character which the Institution has assumed, viz., a "new divinity" and "abolition" seminary, will render it popular in New York and Ohio, and the eminent men who have recently been appointed as professors will attract students from all quarters.

Funds will not be wanting, and if these principles and their practical application meet the approbation of God, the Institution will prosper. . . . Do you ask how so many students and colonists can be accommodated? We do not live in "hollow trees," but many of the students will live this season in a temporary shed, which is partially prepared, and is to consist of twenty-five or thirty rooms, separated from each other by rough boards. It is to be shingled with slabs.

The new measures in the Institute will make some change in our situation.

The increase of population will soon furnish business enough for the undivided attention of a physician. On the other hand the plans of the Institute are maturing so rapidly, that the department which is assigned to me will demand the entire energies of one man. Under these circumstances I must either resign my office in the Institute or relinquish the practice of medicine.

I prefer the former for several reasons. 1. I am better qualified for the practice of my profession than for the duties of professor in the Institute. 2d. People have reposed some confidence in me as a physician, but I think it very doubtful whether I should ever gain much reputation, or be able to do much good as a lecturer. 3d. I am not entirely pleased with all the "new measures" respecting the Institute. I have not consulted with the trustees and my friends upon the subject, but I now think I shall resign my office. . . . I can never be sufficiently grateful that I was so kindly received into your family, and allowed to become a son. In every trial, in sorrows and in joys, Marianne is just the companion I need, and everything I could wish. And while she is regarded with daily increasing affection, her dear mother, and brother, and sisters at home will please accept a full share of my love.

J. DASCOMB.

Our folio does not get filled very fast, my dear mother. We intended this should be the letter next mailed by us when we commenced it, but we had a letter from Oakham a few days since, which we thought should be answered immediately, and so, with all our other duties to perform, we have neglected this sheet. I find my school engagements occupy most of my time, yet it is time pleasantly spent. I do not come home at night so fatigued as I used to be when I had a whole school to manage alone. The government of the school, and its general plans, devolve now upon a president, and I have nothing to do but to discharge faithfully my office as teacher of a few classes. I devote most of my time out of school to preparing for recitations.

I must inform you that I am a pupil as well as teacher. I recite daily with Dr. Dascomb's class in botany, being desirous of extending my knowledge of that science. Should Providence give me as much leisure and opportunity as I now have, to cultivate the mind, I intend to improve it.

Last winter I attended the chemical recitations when convenient. You will say I am partial to the professor of chemistry and botany, as I confine my

studies to his department. I shall not refuse to
have other teachers when I take other studies,
though I may express as much regret as some of
the other ladies have at changing teachers. . . .
Mr. Mahan, our President, has been here a few
weeks. We are very much pleased with him. He
has been very successful as a pastor in Cincinnati,
and was urgently invited to become pastor of a
church in New York City at the time he was called
to Oberlin. He is an eloquent preacher, and I think
I never heard more instructive and practical sermons. I trust he will be a blessing to this Institution. . . . I wish our dear friends from " Parker
House" could step in and visit us in our little chamber. It was built purposely for us, and is just such
a neat, quiet little retreat as we love. We removed
from the boarding-house last winter to Deacon
Pease's, and find our situation far preferable to
what it was last summer. Mrs. Pease is a pleasant
woman, and manages her children well. She thinks
much of making her boarders happy. Deacon Pease
is more like Deacon Wilson than any one I know of.
He looks like Uncle Tenney—is ardently pious. It
seems quite proper that the two deacons should be
in the same family, for you must know the good
people have elected your son in Oberlin to that
office. The choice is quite recent. One of the
deacons chosen last summer removed from Oberlin,
and Dr. D. was chosen in his stead. There were but
one or two votes for any other man, which showed
the unanimity of feeling. They choose deacons
only for one year here, otherwise Dr. D. would

have declined on account of his profession, the duties of which will often call him from home.

Mr. Pease's little son inquired the other day what D.D.D. stood for. We saw from his countenance that he was grappling with a brilliant thought, but were unable to guess the enigma. He informed us it was Deacon Doctor Dascomb. Whenever I write a word respecting husband that is complimentary it distresses him as much as it used to A. He has the same low opinion of himself that used to interest me in him in old times. I don't know but the fact of his being no office seeker is the reason that the good people here are fond of electing him. He has been made President of the Lyceum, one of the committee to oversee the Sabbath-school in this place and others connected with it, auditor of accounts for the agent of Oberlin Collegiate Institute, secretary of the Oberlin Temperance Society, and secretary of the County Medical Society, etc. I mention these little things to mother, because I know she will be anxious to know whether we meet with cordial friends in our new home. We have more and better friends than we deserve. You would be delighted with some of our good men and women of the colony, and students of the Institute. . . . As I wrote this I stopped my pen, and raised my eyes to laugh, and as my eyes rested on an object seen from my window, my risibility increased as I thought I would describe it to Hannah. It is the palace of Pres. Mahan. It was not originally erected for him, being the first house erected in Oberlin. It was made of the bodies of the monarchs of our forest in their native state, no hammer or saw being allowed to mar their pristine beauty. The mansion is on Centre Street, being at the north end of a block of buildings in the same style of architecture. In the front of this dwelling is one door, and a few inches from it one window. This whole pile having become somewhat dilapidated by the encroachment of time, or the depredation of village school-boys who have been trained there for a few months past, has been repaired, and a shanty of rough boards added to make more numerous apartments. I have not been in recently to observe modern improvements, but the President says they shall have a fine suite of apartments, a parlor, kitchen, bedroom, etc. His family have not yet arrived, but are daily expected. They have two children. Mrs. Mahan was educated a lady, in affluence. She is said to be a superior woman. Their house will be built in a few months. It will be large. There are but few log houses here. Few of the framed houses are completely finished, but many of them are neat and comfortable. Indeed the log houses are comfortable, and some of them exhibit as much neatness as Mr. Curtis's of D. I had no idea they could be fit for habitations for man. As for our stumps, I have ceased to think of them, except in a dark night, when my unwary steps lead me upon them. We shall soon have good roads, as strenuous efforts are to be made for them. . . .

May the blessing of God rest upon you all, is the daily prayer of.

MARIANNE.

From Arthur Tappan.

New York, May, 1835.

Rev. J. J. Shipherd:

Dear Sir: It is unnecessary for me to say to you that I feel a deep interest in your institution. My actions must have convinced you of this; but very inadequately indeed, for the full extent of my interest in it I should find it difficult to express either in words or actions. I believe with you that it is the work of God and will prosper, though not perhaps quite as rapidly as our desires would have it. But "God's ways are" truly in such undertakings "not as our ways." The storms of opposition, and may be the pecuniary struggles it has to contend with, are perhaps providentially ordered to cause its roots to strike deeper, and to make its ultimate prosperity more certain.

But my object in writing is to say that should you fail of obtaining the aid you anticipate, and that is necessary to carry forward the enterprise with needed celerity, I propose that you shall enable me, or Mr. Wm. Green, Jr., and myself, to raise money on the property belonging to the institution, by mortgaging it to us in trust for the purpose. If you can place security ample and sufficient in our hands, I am ready to say you may draw on me for ten thousand dollars, on the strength of it, in the course of the present year, if it is needed.

Yours in Christian bonds,

ARTHUR TAPPAN.

P. S.—My subscription of five thousand dollars your treasurer may draw for, as it is needed, in drafts at ninety days' sight. This is independent of the above proposition.

Yours,

A. T.

From Lewis Tappan.

New York, May 5, 1835.

Dear Brother Shipherd:

When I paid the first instalment of my subscription, it was my intention, as I mentioned to you, to accompany it with a letter expressing my view as to future payments. Time did not then allow of it, and I write this short letter, retaining a copy, that it may be clearly understood on what footing my subscription stands. The written condition is, that Rev. C. G. Finney should be Professor of Theology in the Oberlin Institution, and the verbal addition was, that antislavery principles should be recognized in the Institution, freely discussed and inculcated; and that the broad ground of moral reform, in all its departments, should characterize the instructions. The subscriptions were to be paid while in the judgment of the subscriber these things were recognized and taught. I wish to be very careful in stating the mutual understanding we had on the subject, because since my subscription was made I have felt and expressed, in your hearing and Brother Finney's, strong doubts whether antislavery principles and practices would be satisfactorily inculcated at Oberlin. Praying God to bless the instructors and students, and make the Institution a great blessing to this land and the world,

I am, dear sir, your obedient servant,

LEWIS TAPPAN.

———

ARTHUR TAPPAN TO J. J. SHIPHERD.

NEW YORK, May 6, 1835.

REV. AND DEAR SIR:

Rev. Mr. Finney left here yesterday for Oberlin. He has the prayers of many here for his safe arrival with you, and we indulge high hopes of his usefulness in the institution to which he has been called at Oberlin. You will doubtless hear that an effort is making on the Reserve by the friends of the Western Reserve College to get him there. I sincerely hope he will not listen for a moment to any such proposition, for nothing short of a thorough change in the men who govern that institution, as well the trustees as the Faculty—with the exception of a small minority—would ensure to the friends of liberal sentiments the glorious results now confidently anticipated from Oberlin. . . . I feel much interested in your institution and shall at all times be obliged to you for any intelligence touching its prosperity.

With great respect and esteem,

I am truly yours,

ARTHUR TAPPAN.

FROM ARTHUR TAPPAN.

NEW YORK, June 15, 1835.

REV. J. J. SHIPHERD:

DEAR SIR: . . . Permit me to suggest that some regard should be had to the style of building, and laying out your college grounds. There is a great defect in this particular in our eastern colleges. Without much, if any, additional expense, good taste may be consulted in the public and private buildings you erect, and the grounds around them. And it will add not a little to the satisfaction of your friends when they visit you, if I may judge from my own feelings.

And is it not true that chasteness in architecture and adjoining grounds has a refining influence on the character, and adds immensely to the enjoyment of life? I feel that it is a religious duty to imitate our Heavenly Benefactor in this as in all his other perfections. With much regard,

Yours,

ARTHUR TAPPAN.

FROM T. S. INGERSOLL—A COLONIST.

To the Board of Trust for the Oberlin Collegiate Institute.

DEAR BRETHREN:

Will you suffer a word from one who loves the cause in which you are engaged? The Lord has made you the almoners of bounty, in a work of most interesting and fearfully responsible character. He has opened wide the hand of his bounty, and poured into his treasury which he has established here in the wilderness, for an express, definite purpose; and that object is no other than the world's conversion to Jesus Christ, in the soonest possible time. And to accomplish this, many and spacious buildings are requisite for the accommodation of those whom God has called to take the charge of others, whom he in his providence has called to prepare to preach the everlasting Gospel; also buildings for the students preparatory to this great work. You, my dear brethren, have taught us to regard this as God's work, God's buildings, God's institution and God's property, and this is right; because you have in a special manner consecrated yourselves to God for this work which he has assigned you. And he has consecrated all the funds, which he has sent here, to a most holy service, and the whole, funds, land, buildings, all, all, have again and again been most solemnly consecrated to God for the above described purpose, by him who was the founder of this institution, and who gathered this colony, and by the colonists whom he gathered, and may I not say by your honorable body also.

Seeing these things are so, what manner of buildings and what manner of work ought your body to direct to be built?

"Be ye not conformed to this world," is the injunction of Him who has called you to be his stewards. Again, those things that are highly esteemed among men—men of this world, impenitent men—are an abomination in the sight of God. My dear brethren, will you build houses for the servants of the Most High God, with his own money, in a manner that will be highly esteemed among men, and because they are so, "an abomination in the sight of Him" for whom they are built? Will you direct or even suffer mechanics to build, even at their own expense, houses here for carrying forward the Lord's work, merely to be esteemed by the men of this world, that you may secure their friendship? Know ye, "that he that would be a friend to the world, is the enemy of God," for, "the friendship of this world is enmity with God." "Ye cannot serve God and mammon." In the house which is built for Brother Mahan, I have found some forty or more dollars' worth of work in the two north rooms which I cannot for my life find any good reason for, except it be to please the taste of a vitiated world. An impenitent master-builder remarked to me the other day, that he thought President Mahan's house might have been built three hundred dollars cheaper, taking size and style, and have it answer the object for which it ought to be built, especially when the public's money was employed for the work. . . .

There is a plain, neat, simple style of building, which commends itself to every man's enlightened good sense, and still will not be highly esteemed by the world, neither is it an abomination in the sight of God.

Will my brethren seek for this style of having the work of the Lord done, which is committed to their hands? If so, from whom will they draw their models? From the word of God, or from the word of Benjamin, or some other human architect?

Supposing all the buildings which are to be erected here with the Lord's money be built in the style of good architectural taste, so that the men of this world would commend us for our good style, and correct taste, and by this we should secure the influence which this world affords—what would be gained? What? I will tell you, my dear brethren. We should gain that which Jesus Christ said on another though somewhat similar occasion, "Woe unto you, when all men shall speak well of you." With much love, and anxious solicitude for the cause of God in Oberlin, I subscribe myself,

Your brother in Christ,
T. S. INGERSOLL.

OBERLIN, March 9, 1836.

FROM J. J. SHIPHERD—PASTORAL LETTER.

To the Church of Christ in Oberlin.

DEARLY BELOVED:

Although the endearing relation which I sustain to you as pastor has existed only about one year, duty requires that it should be dissolved. I thank God, dear brothers and sisters, that this dissolution is not called for because we have fallen out by the way, but for the furtherance of the Gospel. You are in my heart to live and die with you, and your Christian regards to me have been so demonstrated, that I doubt not their sincerity, nor their strength. Yet a strong hand binds us to God our Saviour, and his will is paramount to our pleasure. That it is the will of the great Head of the church, that I should now resign my pastoral office, appears to me plain, in the subsequent facts: 1. I have not been profitable to you in the ministry, I have longed to feed the sheep, and feed the lambs, and reconcile the rebellious to God; but ill health and the draughts of the Institute upon my health and time have rendered it impossible for me to accomplish this work. I can merely pass it off in an ordinary way, which will no more answer for Oberlin than it will do for you to be an ordinary church. 2. The great Head of the Church is opening before me a door of usefulness, wide and effectual, in the work of Christian education, and distinctly calling me into that great and blessed work. So that while I can do but little in the plenteous harvests by personal ministry, I can do much to supply it with effective laborers, and thus preach Christ still, through the Oberlin Institute, and kindred seminaries, which, under God, I may aid in building. 3. In these views, as far as I know, my brethren and sisters concur, so that I need not specify other reasons, nor amplify these, which are as conclusive as they are brief. Permit me, brethren, however, to add a brief expression of my strong desire that you elect as my successor none but a man after God's own heart, thoroughly furnished for the peculiar work of Oberlin. You must not only have a preacher in power, but a pastor in practice, who will be in every home and every heart,

whose soul is imbued with the principle of the Oberlin covenant.

Unless you can get such a man, my advice is that
you settle no one, but rely, under God, upon your
own labors, aided by our dear brethren of the Faculty.
Considering the plenteousness of the harvests, the
fewness of the laborers, and the number of ministers
connected with the Institution, I have sometimes
doubted whether you ought to take, from another
field, such a man as would fill the pastoral office
here. But considering the peculiar and the immense
bearings of this church upon others, and the world,
for their sakes as well as yours, and for the glory of
God abroad as well as here, I advise that you invite the best man you can find on Zion's walls, whose
peculiar circumstances do not forbid his leaving his
present post. I have thought that you and the
trustees might elect jointly a pastor and professor
of pastoral theology, if a man combining the requisite
qualifications could be found. But looking abroad,
in the extensive circle of my ministerial acquaint-
ances, and considering the amount of parochial labors
required in this large and growing church, I do not
believe the man lives who could finish the work of
both offices. Nevertheless if the Colony and the
Institute cannot be bound together thus in one fold
under one shepherd, be sure you settle a man who
will encircle the Colony in one arm and the Institute
in another, holding them as a church in inseparable
Christian union. And now, beloved in Jesus, remember your high calling, your infinite responsibility, and
press toward the mark. You have witnessed a good

profession before the world. Oh, let your practice
correspond. You stand on the pinnacle of Zion's
hill. Oh, reflect the pure cloudless light of the Sun
of righteousness. Remember that, like Thesaloni-
ca, Oberlin must be an example to all that believe,
or reproach Christ and ruin a multitude of souls.
Therefore let the Oberlin covenant, or, in other
words, the Gospel, be stereotyped in your hearts,
and embodied in you, dear brethren and sisters, as
living epistles, known and read of all men. But I
must suppress the overflowing of my heart toward
you, and close by saying, " only let your conversation
be as becometh the Gospel of Christ, that whether
I come and see you or else be absent, I may hear of
your affairs, that ye stand fast in one spirit, with one
mind, striving together for the faith of the Gospel,
and in nothing terrified by your adversaries, which
is to them an evident token of perdition, but to you
of salvation, and that of God. For unto you it is
given in the behalf of Christ, not only to believe on
him, but also to suffer for his sake." That you, beloved, might be perfect as your Father in Heaven is
perfect, is the prayer of your affectionate pastor,

JOHN J. SHIPHERD.

OBERLIN, June 15, 1836.

FROM JOSHUA LEAVITT.

BUFFALO, July 11, 1835.

BROTHER SHIPHERD:

If I am not mistaken your professorship of mathematics has been vacated. While here attending a

temperance convention I have become pleasingly acquainted with Dr. William K. Scott, of Sandy Hill, N. Y., whose character as a teacher of mathematics stands very high, as certified by the late Governor Pitcher, Hon. Henry C. Martindale and other scientific gentlemen. He is afloat now, and I presume could be had for Oberlin. . . . . I can hardly bear to go back to New York without visiting that loved spot, but Mr. Benedict's health is poor, and I must hasten home, as I do not see any special reason to go. Go on, brother; build your houses and select your teachers, and the Lord be with you. I think more and more, from what I hear at the eastward, that John P. Cowles and Brother Barrows ought to be kept before you as candidates for some post, and that they could do you good. Love to Brother Finney and all others. The lectures go well, and we want another series next winter.

Yours truly,

JOSHUA LEAVITT.

FROM LEWIS TAPPAN.

NEW YORK, Aug. 10, 1835.

DEAR BROTHER SHIPHERD:

. . . . I intended to have mentioned to you previously my design to resign the office of president of the association to perpetuate the professorships. I have communicated the same to Mr. I. W. Clark, the secretary. I have so much business of various kinds to attend to that I cannot well act on the above committee. I recommend Brother Wm. Green, Jr., as successor.

The enemy has come out with great wrath and fury. Unusual excitement prevails in the South and in fact throughout the country. Threats of assassination and abduction are loud and frequent. My brother is the special object of the blood-thirsty vengeance of the slavery men. What measures they may take it is impossible to foresee. I suppose the "prudent" abolitionists will accuse us of some injudicious measures that have excited the people throughout the United States, and we shall be told, "The prudent man foreseeth the evil and hideth himself." My house has been named in a hand-bill signed Judge Lynch, as a mark of popular fury. But hitherto the Lord has preserved us, and blessed be his holy name!

The executive committee are firm to a man, determined to go forward, even at the expense of property and life. We feel a calmness and confidence in God that supports us in this trying hour. Out of one hundred and seventy-five thousand publications issued by the American Antislavery Society in July, only one thousand were burnt at Charleston, S. C.—the one hundred and seventy-fifth part! The rest are working their way all over the land. We did not send one to a slave or even a free man of color at the South, though we claim a right to send to the latter. The Lord we trust will overrule "this madness of the people" to the promotion of the blessed cause, and the glory of his name.

With Christian regard to the dear brethren, I am your friend and brother,

Lewis Tappan.

———

Thomas Clarkson to Wm. Dawes, in England.

Playford Hall, Oct. 14, 1839.

To William Dawes:

My Respected Friend :

I am very sorry that in consequence of my having passed several sleepless nights, I was not able to enter so fully as I could have wished, into the object of your mission to this country, when you did me the honor of calling upon me. It is a matter of great pleasure to have had from you an account of the Oberlin establishment. I cannot but take a deep interest in its welfare, seeing how many desirable objects it combines, and how well calculated it is, but particularly at this moment, to meet prejudices, and to oppose the efforts of interested men, who set themselves up, in defiance of the laws of God, to trample under foot human liberty, and to reduce man, to whom the powers of intellect were given, to the situation of the brute. I know not to what a degrading state your unhappy country will be brought, unless a stop be put to slavery. Will you continue long, unless you change your measures, to be reckoned among the civilized nations of the earth? To be familiar with the sound of injustice daily in your ears, and to lend no helping hand, must produce in time a taint or corruption which must injure the moral character. Has not this corruption already begun? Has it not proceeded from blacks to whites?

From a systematic familiarity with oppression have not your rulers begun to oppress you their fellow subjects? You are forbidden to speak, you are forbidden to write, or even to petition on this subject. Where is this the case but in most despotic countries? Surely it could never have been foreseen that this would ever have been the case in the United States. It becomes you, therefore, to do all you can to wipe away this stain from your country. And I rejoice, therefore, to hear that the Oberlin Society has risen up, and that it has had the courage to rise up under such circumstances, amidst the growing darkness and immorality spreading over your once happy land, to meet the evil in question.

I heard with pleasure that the corporation of the City of London received the petition in behalf of the Oberlin establishment with so much courtesy. I cannot doubt of their doing something liberally and handsomely towards promoting the object of it. But after all, it is not so much what they give as the high sanction of their example. This ought to be justly estimated in the United States, and it is to be the more appreciated when it is considered that men of different religious denominations, and of different political parties were assembled to receive the petition. It is highly creditable to this corporation that they should have listened to the petition of American Abolitionists, whom we are unfortunately obliged to consider as aliens in point of country, though they sprang from ourselves. Their motive could only have been a real compassion for the distressed. I trust that God in his providence is opening a way through the Oberlin Society, or that he will open a way, for the relief of the oppressed of our fellow creatures who are the subject of this letter.

Yours truly,
THOMAS CLARKSON.

NOTE.—The vote of the Corporation was eighty-one yeas and eighty-three nays.—*Ed.*

––––––

HON. JOSIAH HARRIS, OF AMHERST, TO HIS WIFE.

COLUMBUS, O., Thanksgiving A. M., 1842.

––––––: I must say to you that you can have no conception of the opposition and prejudice existing against Oberlin College in the Legislature. This year it arises principally from the numerous petitions presented last year for the repeal of its charter and from a book, "Oberlin Unmasked," passing round in the House, and a thousand unfavorable rumors in relation to amalgamation, fanaticism, harboring fugitive slaves, etc., all founded upon rumor, without any evidence of their truth before the Legislature.

Mr. McNulty, of the House, at the commencement of the session, on notice, introduced a bill for the repeal of the Oberlin College charter, which is still pending. It is now in the hands of the Committee on Corporations in that branch of the Legislature. They had not reported yesterday. It is now pretty generally thought that it will pass the House. If so, then will come on the war in the Senate.

I will say to you that I had a little flare-up in the Senate on the subject of a bill to incorporate the Dialectic Association of the Oberlin Collegiate Institute [a college literary society]. The passage of the bill came on when I was the most melancholy in regard to news from home. I said nothing in its favor. The yeas and nays being called for, it was lost.

The next day I got Mr. Walton from Monroe, one of the majority, to move a reconsideration of that vote. I seconded him and gave the Senate a short speech, thanking the gentleman from Monroe, and demanding my right to a reconsideration as a member on the floor of the Senate. The motion carried unanimously. Then I moved it be laid on the table, which was agreed to. All the objection to the bill seemed to be because it had the words, " Oberlin Collegiate Institute." I name the above so that you may know something of the spirit existing in the Senate in relation to Oberlin.

P. M.—Have just returned from the Methodist church and resume. I have conversed with several members about Oberlin. I say to them that the most or all the rumors about the people there are unfounded. They are willing for an examination even by a committee from those most prejudiced against Oberlin College. I say also that they are a component part of my constituency whose rights are invaded without any just cause, as there is not a petition presented to either branch of the Legislature this session for a repeal of their charter. If the subject comes up in the Senate I shall contend against it inch by inch.

I also say that I am no Abolitionist, nor a disciple of Oberlin, but I want to see the rights of all protected on the principle of the old Democratic motto, " Equal and exact justice to all men."

I have opened a correspondence with H. C. Taylor, of Oberlin, who is furnishing me with papers, etc., to enable me to make defence against a repeal. I hope the bill will not pass the House. If it does I shall do the best I can on the subject, whether I am condemned or applauded in my own county.

When I see the rights of people invaded with as much vituperation as they are, right, justice to myself and my country urge me to rise in their defence, though they may think differently from me on most subjects.

NOTE.—" Oberlin Unmasked " was a scurrilous pamphlet published by a dismissed student.—*Ed.*

INDEX.

TITLES in THIS SERIES

geles, 1925), *AROUND THE WORLD BY FAITH, WITH SIX WEEKS IN THE HOLY LAND* (Los Angeles, n. d.), *TWO YEARS MISSION WORK IN EUROPE JUST BEFORE THE WORLD WAR, 1912-14* (Los Angeles, [1926])

6. Boardman, W. E., *THE HIGHER CHRISTIAN LIFE* (Boston, 1858)

7. Girvin, E. A., *PHINEAS F. BRESEE: A PRINCE IN ISRAEL* (Kansas City, Mo., [1916])

8. Brooks, John P., *THE DIVINE CHURCH* (Columbia, Mo., 1891)

9. RUSSELL KELSO CARTER ON "FAITH HEALING." R. Kelso Carter, *THE ATONEMENT FOR SIN AND SICKNESS* (Boston, 1884) *"FAITH HEALING" REVIEWED AFTER TWENTY YEARS* (Boston, 1897)

10. Daniels, W. H., *DR. CULLIS AND HIS WORK* (Boston, [1885])

11. HOLINESS TRACTS DEFENDING THE MINISTRY OF WOMEN. Luther Lee, *"WOMAN'S RIGHT TO PREACH THE GOSPEL; A SERMON, AT THE ORDINATION OF REV. MISS ANTOINETTE L. BROWN, AT SOUTH BUTLER, WAYNE COUNTY, N. Y., SEPT. 15, 1853"* (Syracuse, 1853) *bound with* B. T. Roberts, *ORDAINING WOMEN* (Rochester, 1891) *bound with* Catherine (Mumford) Booth, *"FEMALE MINISTRY; OR, WOMAN'S RIGHT TO PREACH THE GOSPEL . . ."* (London, n. d.) *bound with* Fannie (McDowell) Hunter, *WOMEN PREACHERS* (Dallas, 1905)

12. LATE NINETEENTH CENTURY REVIVALIST TEACHINGS ON THE HOLY SPIRIT. D. L. Moody, *SECRET POWER OR THE SECRET OF SUCCESS IN CHRISTIAN LIFE AND*

WORK (New York, [1881]) *bound with* J. Wilbur Chapman, *RECEIVED YE THE HOLY GHOST?* (New York, [1894]) *bound with* R. A. Torrey, *THE BAPTISM WITH THE HOLY SPIRIT* (New York, 1895 & 1897)

13. SEVEN "JESUS ONLY" TRACTS. Andrew D. Urshan, *THE DOCTRINE OF THE NEW BIRTH, OR, THE PERFECT WAY TO ETERNAL LIFE* (Cochrane, Wis., 1921) *bound with* Andrew Urshan, *THE ALMIGHTY GOD IN THE LORD JESUS CHRIST* (Los Angeles, 1919) *bound with* Frank J. Ewart, *THE REVELATION OF JESUS CHRIST* (St. Louis, n. d.) *bound with* G. T. Haywood, *THE BIRTH OF THE SPIRIT IN THE DAYS OF THE APOSTLES* (Indianapolis, n. d.) *DIVINE NAMES AND TITLES OF JEHOVAH* (Indianapolis, n. d.) *THE FINEST OF THE WHEAT* (Indianapolis, n. d.) *THE VICTIM OF THE FLAMING SWORD* (Indianapolis, n. d.)

14. THREE EARLY PENTECOSTAL TRACTS. D. Wesley Myland, *THE LATTER RAIN COVENANT AND PENTECOSTAL POWER* (Chicago, 1910) *bound with* G. F. Taylor, *THE SPIRIT AND THE BRIDE* (n. p., [1907?]) *bound with* B. F. Laurence, *THE APOSTOLIC FAITH RESTORED* (St. Louis, 1916)

15. Fairchild, James H., *OBERLIN: THE COLONY AND THE COLLEGE, 1833-1883* (Oberlin, 1883)

16. Figgis, John B., *KESWICK FROM WITHIN* (London, [1914])

17. Finney, Charles G., *LECTURES TO PROFESSING CHRISTIANS* (New York, 1837)

18. Fleisch, Paul, *DIE MODERNE GEMEINSCHAFTSBEWEGUNG IN DEUTSCHLAND* (Leipzig, 1912)

19. SIX TRACTS BY W. B. GODBEY. *SPIRITUAL GIFTS AND GRACES* (Cincinnati, [1895]) *THE RETURN OF JESUS* (Cincinnati, [1899?]) *WORK OF THE HOLY SPIRIT* (Louisville, [1902]) *CHURCH—BRIDE—KINGDOM* (Cincinnati, [1905]) *DIVINE HEALING* (Greensboro, [1909]) *TONGUE MOVEMENT, SATANIC* (Zarephath, N. J., 1918)

20. Gordon, Earnest B., *ADONIRAM JUDSON GORDON* (New York, [1896])

21. Hills, A. M., *HOLINESS AND POWER FOR THE CHURCH AND THE MINISTRY* (Cincinnati, [1897])

22. Horner, Ralph C., *FROM THE ALTAR TO THE UPPER ROOM* (Toronto, [1891])

23. McDonald, William and John E. Searles, *THE LIFE OF REV. JOHN S. INSKIP* (Boston, [1885])

24. LaBerge, Agnes N. O., *WHAT GOD HATH WROUGHT* (Chicago, n. d.)

25. Lee, Luther, *AUTOBIOGRAPHY OF THE REV. LUTHER LEE* (New York, 1882)

26. McLean, A. and J. W. Easton, *PENUEL; OR, FACE TO FACE WITH GOD* (New York, 1869)

27. McPherson, Aimee Semple, *THIS IS THAT: PERSONAL EXPERIENCES SERMONS AND WRITINGS* (Los Angeles, [1919])

28. Mahan, Asa, *OUT OF DARKNESS INTO LIGHT* (London, 1877)

29. THE LIFE AND TEACHING OF CARRIE JUDD MONTGOMERY Carrie Judd Montgomery, *"UNDER HIS WINGS": THE STORY OF MY LIFE* (Oakland,

[1936]) Carrie F. Judd, *The Prayer of Faith* (New York, 1880)

30. The Devotional Writings of Phoebe Palmer Phoebe Palmer, *The Way of Holiness* (52nd ed., New York, 1867) *Faith and Its Effects* (27th ed., New York, n. d., orig. pub. 1854)

31. Wheatley, Richard, *The Life and Letters of Mrs. Phoebe Palmer* (New York, 1881)

32. Palmer, Phoebe, ed., *Pioneer Experiences* (New York, 1868)

33. Palmer, Phoebe, *The Promise of the Father* (Boston, 1859)

34. Pardington, G. P., *Twenty-five Wonderful Years, 1889-1914: A Popular Sketch of the Christian and Missionary Alliance* (New York, [1914])

35. Parham, Sarah E., *The Life of Charles F. Parham, Founder of the Apostolic Faith Movement* (Joplin, [1930])

36. The Sermons of Charles F. Parham. Charles F. Parham, *A Voice Crying in the Wilderness* (4th ed., Baxter Springs, Kan., 1944, orig. pub. 1902) *The Everlasting Gospel* (n.p., n.d., orig. pub. 1911)

37. Pierson, Arthur Tappan, *Forward Movements of the Last Half Century* (New York, 1905)

38. *Proceedings of Holiness Conferences, Held at Cincinnati, November 26th, 1877, and at New York, December 17th, 1877* (Philadelphia, 1878)

39. *Record of the Convention for the Promotion of*

Scriptural Holiness Held at Brighton, May 29th, to June 7th, 1875 (Brighton, [1896?])

40. Rees, Seth Cook, *Miracles in the Slums* (Chicago, [1905?])

41. Roberts, B. T., *Why Another Sect* (Rochester, 1879)

42. Shaw, S. B., ed., *Echoes of the General Holiness Assembly* (Chicago, [1901])

43. *The Devotional Writings of Robert Pearsall Smith and Hannah Whitall Smith*. [R]obert [P]earsall [S]mith, *Holiness Through Faith: Light on the Way of Holiness* (New York, [1870]) [H]annah [W]hitall [S]mith, *The Christian's Secret of a Happy Life*, (Boston and Chicago, [1885])

44. [S]mith, [H]annah [W]hitall, *The Unselfishness of God and How I Discovered It* (New York, [1903])

45. Steele, Daniel, *A Substitute for Holiness; or, Antinomianism Revived* (Chicago and Boston, [1899])

46. Tomlinson, A. J., *The Last Great Conflict* (Cleveland, 1913)

47. Upham, Thomas C., *The Life of Faith* (Boston, 1845)

48. Washburn, Josephine M., *History and Reminiscences of the Holiness Church Work in Southern California and Arizona* (South Pasadena, [1912?])